# Fifth Generation Management

**RELATED TITLES FROM DIGITAL PRESS**

| | |
|---|---|
| CIM: The Data Management Strategy | Olin H. Bray |

*Forthcoming*

| | |
|---|---|
| Solving Business Problems: A Guide to Using MRPII Software | Alan D. Luber |

# Fifth Generation Management

## Integrating Enterprises through Human Networking

Charles M. Savage

Digital Press

Printed in the United States of America.

9  8  7  6  5

Order number EY–C186E–DP

dBase I is a trademark of Ashton-Tate Coporation. The Digital logo is a trademark of Digital Equipment Corporation. IBM is a trademark of International Business Machines Corporation. HP is a trademark of Hewlett-Packard Corporation. Netmap is a trademark of Netmap International, Inc. UNIX is a trademark of American Telephone and Telegraph Company. X/Open is a trademark of X/Open Company Ltd. X Window System is a trademark of The Massachusetts Institute of Technology.

The graphic used on the front of the jacket and in Chapters 5–12 is used by permission of Netmap International and is copyrighted by Netmap International, Inc., London, Sydney, and San Francisco. Figure 7.7 is used by permission of Nolan, Norton & Company, Inc.. Figure 9.6, the CIM Enterprise Wheel, developed by the Technical Council of the Computer and Automated Systems Association of the Society of Manufacturing Engineers, copyright 1985 CASA/SME, is used by permission.

The text of this book was processed for typesetting by the author with Interleaf Technical Publishing Software, a trademarked product of Interleaf, Inc.

A BARD PRODUCTIONS BOOK
*Editing:* Alison Tartt, David J. Morris, Helen Hyams
*Proofreading:* Helen Hyams
*Index:* Linda Webster
*Text and Jacket Design:* Gayle Smith
*Composition:* Inprint,Inc.
*Production:* Gayle Smith Advertising Design

Library of Congress Cataloging–in–Publication Data

Savage, Charles M.
    Fifth generation management: integrating enterprises through human
        networking/Charles M. Savage

p.  CM.
    ISBN 1-55558-037-8
    1. Industrial management. 2. Organization 3. Computer
        integrated manufacturing systems. I. Title.
HD31.S322 1990
658.4'02--dc20                                          89-25889
                                                         CIP

# CONTENTS

# PREFACE

The ecology of the world business environment is changing dramatically. Gone are the days of the comfortable protected market niches. And gone are the days of geographic isolation.

Change is everywhere. Europe is putting itself together under the 1992 "single market" banner in ways it has not known since Charlemagne. Japan is opening itself to more foreign products. The Pacific Rim's economic power grows. The Soviet Union and Eastern Europe are repositioning themselves in the family of nations. And Africa, Latin America, Australia, China, India, the Middle East, and other nations are striving for greater involvement in the world economy.

Change in technology is also everywhere. Steam energy is changing to computer power as the main driver of economic life. Telephone connectivity is evolving into combined voice and data links. And isolated companies are initiating multiple strategic alliances with the aid of local and wide-area networking.

Nowhere is change going to be more dramatic than in the way we manage and lead our enterprises in the 1990s. The logic of computers and networking makes obsolete many of the deeply cherished notions of the past.

Yet just as long distance runners sometimes "hit the wall" of their capabilities and endurance, many companies are hitting the organizational wall, or so it seems. They have trouble absorbing more computer-based technology. The reasons for this are often unclear. Could it be that we are putting fifth generation technology in second generation organizations? Could it be that we really are not hitting the wall, but instead are squeezed against a bottleneck? We long to break free of our cramped quarters, confining organizational structures, and shallow notions about management and organization.

Throughout the industrial era it has been possible for the organization to absorb each new wave of mechanical technology. Yet as wave after wave of computer technology beats against our traditional ways of doing things, we find ourselves in the backwaters of confusion and uncertainty. How are we to understand what is going on?

Despite the promise of the new computer technology, flexibility and adaptability remain out of our grasp because of continual turf battles, provincial politics, and rigid control systems. Our confusingly complex organizations have more antibodies than we can cope with. What should we do?

Many are saying the answer is "integration." Put in computers, more computers, and still more computers, then network them together. The literature is full of references to computer integrated manufacturing (CIM) and computer integrated enterprise (CIE). Why is enterprise integration turning out to be more of a challenge than most people expected?

Could it be that integration is much more than just a technological undertaking? People are finding that integration impacts the very structure of our organizations. However, like the immune system of the human body, our organizations resist the imposition of new modes of operation, primarily because they threaten established expectations and balances of power. Many organizations are actually held together by an intricate web of accommodations and IOUs.

Then why bother about integration and networking?

Integration is essential if companies are to become more responsive and agile in dealing with the complexity of ever-changing global markets. Networking is necessary if we hope to work more in parallel across the various functions, such as marketing, sales, engineering, manufacturing, finance, and service. And both integration and networking are preconditions if we wish to manage our multiple strategic alliances with suppliers, partners, and customers.

We certainly do not lack a vision of what we would like to do. However, we are locked in a constellation of assumptions, principles, and values, our inheritance from the industrial era, that hobble our efforts and keep us bottled up in traditional modes of behavior.

Different companies use different metaphors to describe this sense of confinement: stovepipes, silos, turf, tree hugging, functional blinders, and empires. Often engineering and manufacturing do not want to leave their warm and cozy stovepipes and talk with one another. Finance is often encased in its own silo, insensitive to the pressures on the rest of the enterprise. Many departments jealously defend their turf, their hard-won prerogatives. When the winds of change blow, functions usually cling to their trees for protection. Functional blinders cause rework, because one function does not understand another's constraints. Little empires exist all over most companies.

As I have worked with companies over the years, it has become clear that our steep hierarchies, the legacy of the industrial era, are incapable of effectively absorbing and using the computer and networking technology now available. The reason is relatively simple: the space is too confining and people are too bottled in. It is small wonder that many companies are disappointed in their investments in computer integrating systems.

It makes little sense to put vast amounts of money into technology with only a pittance for our people and organizations. Yet this is exactly what we are doing.

In some people's minds, CIM and CIE suggest that we are headed toward "paperless" and "peopleless" factories. These people argue that automation, combined with computers and a few professionals, will make it possible for top executives to sit in their "command and control centers" and direct the future of the firm. After all, the hardware and software will have been connected together in one "automated" and "integrated" whole, from boardroom to shop floor. This vision of CIM is a dead end because it leaves people out of the equation, and people are what give an organization its flexibility and creativity.

I am convinced that if we hope to achieve effective integration, we must make the transition from steep hierarchies to flatter networking organizations: from second generation to fifth generation management. To be sure, there will always be some hierarchy in our enterprises. However, the mode of operation in human networking enterprises is qualitatively different from what we have known in traditional industrial-era hierarchies. Rather than focusing on the computer and manufacturing, we need to develop a new understanding about the requirements of management in the 1990s.

## About this Book

*Fifth Generation Management* has two parts. The first book presents, in dialogue form, what happens when a team of managers in a hypothetical company is forced past the boundaries of its narrow little world. The second book looks at what we have to unlearn, learn, and relearn as we squeeze out of the confinement of steep hierarchies and emerge to the vistas of human networking.

This book has been inspired by the growing discussion of CIM and CIE. It is not about Japanese management practices, although in their own pragmatic way, they are discovering much of what makes human networking possible. Instead, this book looks at management from a Western perspective. It seeks to identify and explain the key conceptual principles that ushered in the two phases of the industrial era and the principles that are now leading us into the knowledge era. And although this book suggests new forms of management and organization, it does not advocate an immediate and radical shift. Each company or enterprise should identify those principles that work for it, then proceed pragmatically toward an integrative environment.

Even though I have been inspired by Ken Olsen's vision, and by the visions of many others within Digital Equipment Corporation, this book is not an official statement of the company's position on enterprise integration. It represents my reflections on where we have come from, where we are now, and where we may be going. It has been enriched by numerous conversations within Digital as well as with others in the industry.

The book builds on years of consulting work in the United States and overseas with top executives from a wide variety of companies. It has also benefited from my active participation in the Computer and Automated Systems Association of the Society of Manufacturing Engineers (CASA/SME).

This book is for those people—senior executives, middle managers, professionals, and workers—who recognize the vital and exciting role they will play in the new era. It is also for those teaching and studying in universities, business, and labor schools who want to prepare for the technology and management roles they will play and who realize that conventional theories concerning "command and control," "span of control," and "one person/one boss" are inadequate for human networking organizations.

The primary focus is on manufacturing enterprises, both discrete and process. This book may also apply to service industries, whether they deal with finance, communication, or the retail and wholesale trades. The industrial-era style and theory of organization have been adapted to the service sector, often too uncritically. Possibly the service sector will shape and define the organization of the future, because it is truly *knowledge intensive* and must use networking effectively to survive.

Finally, there are no quick-fix silver bullets. Market success in the future will depend upon creativity, integrity, and the ability to value differences and learn from one another while working on multiple interacting teams. The intent of fifth generation management—human networking—is to help us put people in touch with one another in elegantly simple, yet flexible and adaptive enterprises. We must dynamically configure and reconfigure our people and resources to address multiple market opportunities.

## Acknowledgments

In many respects the writing of this book has been a collaborative effort, enriched by many colleagues, past and present, too many to list individually. Nevertheless, my sincere appreciation for your support and insight is readily acknowledged.

This particular project was initiated by Jack Conaway, with the support of Dave Copeland and Peter Smith. The horizon has grown to include CIE and the human and organizational aspects of integration. My colleagues on the CIM Human Systems Group, Cris Criswell and Michael Keehan, and Ben Fordham of the Organization Consulting Group offered invaluable support during the project.

I am particularly indebted to Jan Hopland, Warren Shrensker, Larry Gould, Tony Friscia, George Hess, Joe Hurley, Dan Infante, Dan Appleton, Vincent D'Souza, Wayne Snodgrass, Peter Graham, Bonnie Sontag, Dan Borda, Andrew Young, Erik Wintergras, Trudy Sampson, Peter Stroh, John Geesink, Gerhard Friedrich, Olin Bray, David Barlow, Jessica Lipnack, Jeffrey Stamps, Phil Wilson, and Robert Hall. Your extensive comments and encouragement throughout the project have been most significant.

John Galloway, Stew Adams, Leslie Berkes, John Parkinson, and Steve Turley of Netmap International have been gracious with their time and help in this project.

The discussions of work and human time were enriched by work I did with Thomas Blakeley and David Rasmussen at Boston College, and by the support of Rolf Lindholm at the Swedish Employers Confederation and Eric Rhenman of SIAR.

Often those closest to us contribute the most, even without our being aware of it. Without the warmth and stability of a home, the lonely isolation of thought can be unbearable. Carl and Sophia's probing minds challenged me to look more deeply at our patterns of learning and growth. Lena's impatience with the superficial caused me to understand how important it is to be honest and open with one another at home and at work. And my parents, Beatrice and Roy, have been continual sources of support over the years.

Finally, I am indebted to George Horesta and Chase Duffy of Digital Press for shepherding the project along, Ray Bard of Bard Productions for creatively putting my work between two covers, Gayle Smith for the creative artwork, and Jeff Morris, Helen Hyams, and Alison Tartt for the careful editing review.

Charles M. Savage
Wellesley, Massachusetts

To Lena, Carl, and Sophia

Book 1

# Five Days that Changed the Enterprise

# CHAPTER

# 1

# Monday

## The Unexpected Happens

One Monday morning, Frank Giardelli, CEO of Custom Products and Services, Inc., a division of a large manufacturing and service company, arrives at his regularly scheduled staff meeting. Already present are the vice-presidents of the functional departments: Wesley Schroeder, engineering; Vincent Gutierrez, manufacturing; Marjorie Callahan, finance; Carol Soo, sales and marketing; Gregory Kasmirian, service; and Alan Tanaka, human resources. Their casual conversation goes on as he enters the boardroom.

He stands silently in front of them, waiting. The room grows quiet as, one by one, they notice that he is holding the familiar organizational chart. They cannot quite read their names on it, but each knows where his or her name is written.

Now they gaze at him, at the chart in his hands. The tension grows.

"Somebody ask me what's on my mind," says Frank.

"What's on your mind, Frank?" asks Gregory Kasmirian, trying to sound casual.

"I'm glad you asked. This morning I found three major capital requests in my In box." He lays the chart on the table, walks to the flip chart, and picks up a marker.

"Manufacturing wants $175,000 for a shop-floor scheduling system." On the flip chart he writes "175."

"Information Systems wants $80,000 for a relational database management system." Below the first number he writes "80."

"And engineering wants state-of-the-art work stations—half a million dollars' worth, as a matter of fact." He writes "500" and draws a horizontal line beneath the three figures.

Everyone silently mouths the words "seven fifty-five," but Frank turns back to the staff without writing anything further.

"Now, as you know, computer integration and automation are what we're all about. I've asked each of you not to be shy, to let me know what you need if you're going to do your job the way it ought to be done. At least once a week for the past ten years, I've said I don't want this company to take a back seat to anyone technologically, and I've asked you all to help us get to the twenty-first century ahead of the competition.

"And you've done all I've asked. So far, so good."

## Numbers Do Not Add Up

Turning back to the flip chart, Frank draws a question mark beneath the line.

The vice-presidents' attention shifts from the flip chart to his face. He continues.

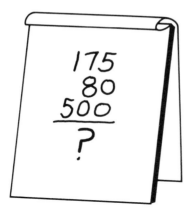

"But this just doesn't add up. Just like most of the automation budget requests over the last five years, it bothers me. And I don't know why.

"First of all, Vincent, I don't understand why that MRP II (Manufacturing Resource Planning) package that cost us a million and a half—not to mention countless hours of training—isn't up to the job. But you're telling me it can't control your discrete hour-to-hour scheduling needs."

Vincent Gutierrez shifts uneasily in his chair.

"Wesley tells me engineering has to have these new work stations so they can move to true solid geometry and a form- and feature-based CAD system. But, Wesley, you're going to want to send your digital files directly to manufacturing, and that'll mean more money for equipment so that manufacturing can read your files.

"MIS's budget is already going through the roof. Four-fifths of it's for maintenance, they tell me. It's eating up our resources trying to jury-rig all our inflexible applications to meet user demands that keep changing. Our information systems experts sing the praises of relational and object-oriented technology, but they haven't given any thought to how we'll tie this new $80,000 system into the flat files we have scattered all over the enterprise. We have legacy databases that we'll have to access for the next forty years because of our product's life cycles and government regulations. And this appropriations request is just a foot in the door, because next MIS will want to move to distributed relational databases, which will cost ten to twenty times as much.

"The more we network, the more translators MIS has to write to get the various application systems interfaced, and then they have to be updated every time we do a software upgrade anywhere on the system. This may end up swallowing the whole MIS department, and the rest of us along with it."

Frank gazes out at his department heads. Several seem to have some thoughts on the problem, but no one speaks. It is as if each is afraid of offending the others.

Frank leans over his chair. "Yes, I know what you're thinking. It's nothing that a little coordination and cooperation wouldn't solve. You're right, of course. If it weren't for office politics, we could straighten this out in a snap.

"You won't say it, Vincent, so I will. You think we should implement 'concurrent engineering,' with products and processes designed in parallel. You've brought this up before. But engineering balks because Wesley doesn't want to harass his already overworked engineers. And you're both right—I'm not taking sides."

## Engineering: King of the Hill

Frank looks at Vincent. "There's more to it than that, of course. Vincent, you've been reading all those business articles about the strategic nature of manufacturing, and you're tired of engineering being King of the Hill. And yet, Wesley, you want to keep the authority for design decisions in your own department. That's only natural. You're both experts in your own areas.

"It's the same with everyone here. You're all experts at your jobs, and you all defend your operations against interference from nonexperts, which means everyone else. But the level of trust between your departments is getting so low it's a wonder our product ever ships.

"It's not as if we don't have a common goal. Several years ago we had management consultants tell us we needed a company philosophy and mission statement. We spent weeks thrashing it out. We were to be 'leaders in our industry on a global basis.' We would provide the 'highest quality and customer satisfaction possible,' as well as 'quick market response while remaining lean and agile.'

"These goals are noble. But what happens is that sales disrupts manufacturing's schedules because the customer wants delivery yesterday. It's amazing how high-sounding ideas can be used to beat up on the other department."

Several people laugh nervously.

## CIM Czar

"Some of my staff have suggested that I appoint a CIM czar—whatever that is—someone who would report to me directly and be responsible for company-wide computer integration. At one point Vincent had a CIM director. It didn't work. Vincent found out right away that integration cuts across all functions, and the CIM director couldn't touch engineering. The walls were higher than anyone had realized. And the CIM director couldn't work with Marjorie's MIS director. They didn't speak the same language. One focused on technical interactive computing and the other on large-batch processing. Even if I appointed a CIM vice-president, the politics in this company would chew him up and spit him out."

Tension fills the room like fog.

Frank continues. "And here I sit, the judge, mediator, and decision maker, supposedly with the wisdom of Solomon. Some of you even want me to be a dictator, so I can push through your pet projects.

"Some vendor was just in to see me with a new color graphics 'Executive Decision Support System.' It was just an overgrown spreadsheet with fancy graphics. I asked him if it could tie into all our different databases. He said he didn't know for sure, but thought it would be easy.

"I'm afraid I was impolite. I laughed."

A few of the vice-presidents laugh hesitantly.

Frank shakes his head. "We keep repeating the same mistakes. Sometimes I think half our middle managers are just overpaid expediters, always chasing mistakes made by other departments.

"So why do we have these problems? Is it you? Are my vice-presidents concerned only with their own skins? Is it that you don't care about the company or your colleagues? I considered that—and there's no way that could be true. I know you all too well. Every one of you is dedicated to this company. Every one of you would go out of your way to help the other guy out of a tight situation. And you've all got good people under you. It's just that you have more than you can do just to stay on top of your own problems.

"Maybe the problem's at the top. Is it my leadership style? For a while I thought that had to be the answer. I wasn't forceful enough, tough enough. I was indecisive. I wasn't paying attention.

"But I've tried everything I know. I've tried collegial and autocratic methods, hands-off and hands-on, Reaganesque and Carteroid. Nothing works."

Frank pauses. He has everyone's full attention. This is not the usual staff meeting. In silence, Frank meets each of their gazes.

"Know what I think the problem is?"

Frank picks up the organization chart from the table. "Here's the problem. This damned piece of paper. It keeps everyone too boxed in. It's too confining."

Slowly and carefully, unsmiling, he tears the chart in half. It is the only sound in the room. No one moves.

## Without a Box, Where Can We Hide?

After a few seconds of unbearable tension, Frank grins broadly. "Now why did I do that?"

Everyone laughs.

"All right. Don't worry, nobody's getting fired. You can relax." A nervous but somewhat relieved rustle goes around the table.

"But only for a minute. Because starting today, you're all going to be earning your salaries, right here in this room. You're going to help me make some major changes in the way this company works—and that will include your day-to-day jobs.

"Now, we've had meetings before where we drew new lines on the chart and shuffled some of the boxes around. Each time we did that, although nobody said so, I came away feeling that I was like a quizmaster on a game show, and that some of you were 'winners' and some 'losers.' It's true, in a way. Although I was simply trying to redeploy our resources where they were most needed, some of you gained responsibilities, and some of you lost. It seemed as though the important thing was not whether the organization was better off—it was whether you gained or lost power. Moreover, you really wanted a clearly defined box so you could build the walls high, and hide if necessary. And from these boxes you could redefine a system of accommodations, granting and asking favors when necessary.

"But this time, we're throwing away the chart and starting with a clean slate. I want you to help me think about this organization in a new way—a way nobody's thought of before.

"Now, I'm definitely not playing quizmaster with you this time. I don't know how it's going to turn out. I want us to rethink this company from the ground up: what we do, what we want to do, what we *should* do. All of you have had ideas about what you'd do if you owned the company, how you'd run it. I'd like to hear them now—big ideas, little ideas, whatever. Let's open our minds, get these ideas out on the table, and give them a fair hearing."

Frank pauses for a long moment, looking into each face.

"Any suggestions? Any thoughts? How do we shove this company into the twenty-first century? Where do we start?"

Vincent speaks, hesitantly. "I think we ought to redefine our business. I mean—well, if the railroads had realized they were in the transportation business, not just the railroad business, they might have competed successfully with trucking and waterways instead of just buying each other and drying up."

"You're right, Vincent," Frank says, nodding. "We should always ask ourselves if we're playing in the right ballpark—and we'll continue to do that. The more critical question is our responsiveness to minor shifts in the marketplace. Timeliness is as critical as cost in meeting market expectations. Second, there is usually a large gap between the strategic business vision, those pretty words on everyone's wall, and the everyday operations of the enterprise. We may feel good that we have finally decided upon our business mission, but that does not help decide which MRP II package we should buy or how to relate it to Just-in-Time manufacturing."

"I've heard that identifying the critical success factors (CSFs) for each department can be useful," says Alan.

## Critical Linkage Factors

"Yes, I know what you mean," says Frank. "If each function understands, say, three to five things it has to do well, it focuses everyone's attention on the critical elements. But it's not enough just to improve your own department's capabilities. The CSFs may keep us bound to our narrowly defined areas of responsibility, our boxes on the organizational chart. As each function looks out for its own self-interest," Frank reminds them, "the self-interest of the enterprise may be hurt. We also need to think in terms of critical linkage factors (CLFs)—the mission-critical business processes that cut across our business and link to other strategic partners.

"For example: what strategic relationships do we need to develop between engineering and manufacturing, marketing and engineering, finance and manufacturing, and so forth? And what strategic alliances do we need with our suppliers and customers? Without mastery of these strategic critical linkage factors, we can never be market-responsive."

## Market Responsiveness

"Let me ask all of you a question. Just how responsive are we to the market? On a scale of ten to one, ten being totally flexible and responsive, tell me how responsive you think we are right now."

The vice-presidents look at each other. Wesley Schroeder says, "Speaking for engineering, I'd say we rate an eight. We generate a lot of engineering change orders (ECOs) to respond to market changes, and we're ready to generate more any time marketing or manufacturing asks for them."

Vincent groans. "Yeah, Wesley, but your changes play hell with our process sheets and setup routines. And if that isn't enough, sales promises short delivery times because we're supposed to be customer responsive, but this is always jerking the scheduling system. I'd say four."

"And don't forget inventory costs," adds Marjorie Callahan, expressing finance's frustration with the constant changes.

"We're always behind schedule," continues Vincent. "You may call it internal flexibility, but I think in some ways it's lack of discipline."

Carol Soo says, "Maybe we are flexible, but while you guys are messing around changing the product, marketing doesn't get word in time to work up a good ad campaign. I think we're a three or four."

The vice-presidents continue to debate their responsiveness index. They cannot agree on one number. It is somewhere between four and seven.

Frank interrupts. "Now we're back to how our departments don't interact well. That tells us something, doesn't it? Let's try something else." He picks up a marker and stands beside the flip chart. "Let's see if we can figure out how this organization really works."

## Segmenting the Ring

He sketches a large circle and another, smaller circle inside it.

"Let's say that this ring represents our company's management. Now, instead of the usual pyramid, let's fit our managers into segments of the ring. Wait, I'll divide it up proportionally so we can tell which department is which." He tears off the sheet and redraws the diagram as six separate, unequal segments.

"This is about how our management people divide up, I think. Wesley, how many key people do you have in engineering? Seven?"

"Uh . . . right," says Wesley. Frank marks off seven divisions in the engineering segment. Asking each vice-president in turn, he divides the other departments. They have no trouble listing their key people.

"Now let's do the same with our computer systems." On another flip chart Frank draws another ring. He continues, "Notice that the individual segments of the ring can represent either people or applications.

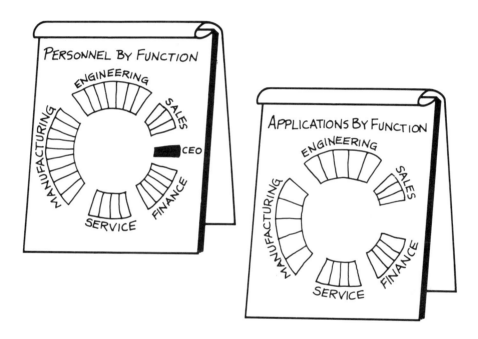

"Carol, what computer applications do you use in marketing and sales?"

Carol is embarrassed to find that she cannot name more than three out of the many applications her sales and marketing department uses: order entry, price book, and the key customer list. In engineering, Wesley's applications include new product development, computer-aided design, parts list, bill of materials, configuration management, and one other he cannot remember. Vincent's manufacturing department has an MRP II application, planning and scheduling system, cell control library, factory simulation package, and data collection. Finance maintains the payroll, employent history file, accounting, and sales consolidation. The others think hard to remember their key applications.

Frank looks at them and smiles. "Okay, let's call it a day. We'll meet again tomorrow morning. Bring the names of all your people and the applications you use, and we'll continue filling in these circles.

"If it's any consolation to you, I don't know everybody's name, either." With a chuckle, he walks out of the room, leaving behind six dazed vice-presidents.

# 2

# Tuesday

## Sorting Out People and Applications

The next morning they arrive armed with sheets of paper, still uneasy, but curious about what Frank is up to. After Frank greets them with what they consider untoward cheerfulness, they quickly complete the job of filling in the names of their managers. The applications, however, continue to give them trouble.

"Frank, I honestly don't know all the computer applications my engineers use," says Wesley, waving a sheet of paper. "They're the ruggedest bunch of individualists you ever saw. A lot of them buy their own stuff or pick up shareware off their bulletin boards. Some even write their own programs and reconfigure their computers. Most use a few programs—the ones on this list—at least part of the time, but the others are used by only one or two. I can get the names, but it'll take a little time."

"That's all right," replies Frank. "We'll use what you brought. It's a good illustration of our problem, anyway." They spend the next half-hour filling in the applications diagram.

They soon realize how little they understand about how their departments use the various applications available to them. They bemoan the fact that they do not even have a complete and up-to-date list of all the major applications and how they are interfaced.

"Now let's talk about two areas: new product development and order entry. These are two of our most important business processes. Wesley, I'd like you to help me out on this one. Take this blue marker and draw lines showing which people communicate with each other when you're designing a new product. Take your time."

Hesitantly, Wesley begins drawing blue lines across the personnel ring. He stops, studies the diagram, and draws more.

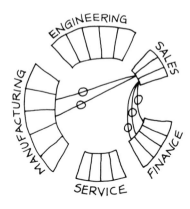

*Interfacing Order Entry Applications*

O = Translator

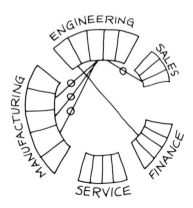

*Interfacing New Product Development Applications*

O = Translator

"Now link up the order entry applications—at least the ones you're aware of—the same way. Show where translators are used between interfaced applications. Then it's Carol's turn for show and tell in green."

When Carol has finished sketching, she remarks, "Look at the lines on this applications ring! If you update just one application, you have to change three, four—no, five translators! And that's just sales. No wonder the MIS maintenance budget is so high! Not to mention the time we waste on each changeover."

At this point they all add their systems to the same figure, quickly discovering that it is covered with interfaces and translators.

George exclaims, "What a spaghetti stew!"

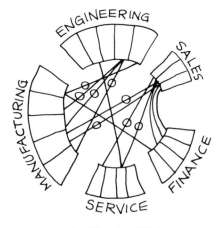

INTERFACING MULTIPLE APPLICATIONS

O = TRANSLATOR

"Well, look at the number of stand-alone applications," says Vincent, who is adding his department to the diagram. "They're not much good for communication, but at least they don't add to the maintenance budget."

"No, they cost us in other ways," says Greg. "I'd rather spend the money for the linkages, even with update costs. Look at the duplication of effort: Engineering and manufacturing are keeping separate bills of materials."

"Exactly," says Frank. "I count four bills of materials and five separate ways of listing parts, none of which can be used by another department without a consistent set of core definitions. That's a waste."

"So we're stuck," says Vincent. "Either we pay to maintain linkages, or we don't communicate."

## Expediting Is Expensive

Frank is silent for a minute. Then he asks, "Will each of you please circle in red all of your people who spend more than 30 percent of their time expediting orders?" They do so—and are stunned to see the number of red circles on the diagram. Obviously they ram through far too many orders.

EXPEDITORS BY FUNCTION

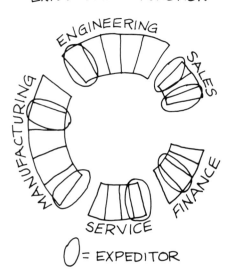

$O$ = EXPEDITOR

As the morning wears on, they begin to see that new product development typically involves handoffs from a key person in one department to a key person in the next, with little interaction between managers and professionals across functions. They discover that many engineering change orders are generated because engineering doesn't understand the practical limitations under which manufacturing operates or the potential service problems in maintaining the products in the field. Because of these conditions, problem fixes must be expedited.

Although each vice-president believes that his or her department has a great deal of flexibility, it soon becomes apparent that the company's responsiveness index is lower than they originally thought.

"Four," says Vincent.

"Three or four," says Alan. Everyone agrees.

"Any ideas why?" asks Frank.

Marjorie speaks. "Well, it looks as if nobody knows what's going on—outside his or her department, that is. Sometimes even inside. Nobody's got the big picture."

## Multiple Dialects

"I think you're right," says Vincent. "And it's too bad. I've got some eager people in engineering. If they had some idea of how your departments operated, they'd fall all over themselves to help the whole outfit work at top efficiency, just to see if they could do it. But they don't speak manufacturing. Or service, or finance. Neither do their machines."

Greg smiles. "Suppose Berlitz could help?"

Everyone laughs. "No," says Frank. "But you're on the right track. There are definitely some language barrier problems here. Can't cross the border unless you speak Manufacturese. Or Marketese."

Frank continues, "Sometimes I wonder if we *want* to learn to speak the same language. If there are all these dialects, top management can't possibly understand what is going on in the functions, making it easier to cover up mistakes. I have watched other companies try to introduce a common data dictionary. Often the effort grinds to a halt because the functions are fearful that if others can understand what is going on, they can no longer manage their own news."

Marjorie peers at Frank. "So that's what you were doing? Tearing up the borders?"

"You're right on the mark," says Frank, grinning. "Our organizational chart has become a blueprint for the walls separating functions, rather than a guide to the channels of communication. The walls have bred distrust and shortsightedness. It's easy to understand why our flexibility index should be so low."

Wesley lights up. "Now I realize that the organizational chart symbolizes a mindset that can block communication instead of supporting it. There have been too many filters and baffles in our company. With this classic structure, it's hard for one function to learn from and with the others. If there is all action and no learning, the seedbeds of creativity and insight dry up."

"I think what we have to do is start learning to speak each other's languages," Frank replies. "But the key word is 'learning.' We—and all our people—have a lot to learn from each other on a continual basis.

"Let's meet again tomorrow with this thought in mind: What can we do to get our departments to start learning from one another, stimulating each other's creative juices, anticipating each other's needs? And let's think of ways to help our company's vision grow from within, rather than handing it down from on high.

"Okay, let's go to work."

# CHAPTER

# 3

# Wednesday

## Battle of the Boxes

Spirits are high on Wednesday morning. The department heads have been thinking independently of solutions to the company's communication problems. Several think they have the answer. Wesley is the first to offer a suggestion. He walks to the flip chart and on a new sheet of paper begins sketching part of the old organizational chart, drawing a new box connecting manufacturing and engineering.

"I can assign one of my design engineers to a new liaison position," he says, "and Vincent can do the same with one of his people. The first thing these two will do is to study the translator problem. Then—"

Frank interrupts. "I'm sorry, Wesley, but I tore up that organization chart on purpose. We're not going back to that. We need to start from scratch. Remember, your box doesn't exist anymore. Nor any of yours," he says, addressing the group. "But otherwise you're headed in the right direction." He tears off the sheet Wesley has drawn on and throws it away.

Wesley, puzzled, falls silent.

Gradually the vice-presidents fall into dispirited, disjointed arguments over the merits of MRP II, CIM, Just-in-Time, Total Quality, and other management concepts; but mostly they cover old ground, and for a while no new insights occur to them. Most of the disagreement has to do with the lack of effective coordination between functions, the small details that are overlooked daily.

## An Issue of Ownership?

Suddenly Vincent looks up and says, "I think I know why we're thrashing around so violently. Frank has said we can't solve our problems by moving boxes and this is making us feel profoundly uneasy. Somehow, we still have to determine who *owns* what! If we can't tell who owns what area, it's hard to know how to hold someone responsible."

"That's it," shouts Marjorie.

Silence.

Marjorie continues, "Our model presupposes mutually exclusive ownership of an area of responsibility, but many market opportunities can't be easily fit into predefined narrow little boxes. Yet our reward and measurement systems have been fine-tuned to reward or punish people for what they do in their boxes, not what they do in the spaces between or outside the boxes. In fact, most cross-functional work remains hidden from the compensation and benefits systems. It's little wonder we're having trouble thinking of ways we can work together in parallel. I'm convinced we're hung up on the ownership issue. We're too preoccupied with who owns what to know how to work together."

"Let me see if I understand what you mean," says Vincent. "We're learning through our work in 'design for assembly' that engineering and manufacturing have to share much more information up front if we're going to design, manufacture, and assemble our products. Our areas overlap. We interrelate, not by going up and down the chain of command, but by sharing knowledge and understanding with one another. We can't be worried about who owns what when we need to rely on who knows what."

## Design Product and Process Concurrently

"This is beginning to make more sense. Putting design and manufacturing engineers together is a good idea after all," responds Wesley. "I know of several companies that are doing this, designing the *product* and the *process* concurrently, in an iterative manner. Rather than trying to capture everything in the rules, they're agreeing on a core set of rules, then relying on the capabilities of the engineers, working cross-functionally, to add the fine touches.

"Some remarkable things are beginning to happen. Instead of the recriminations that are usually hurled back and forth across the no-man's-land between engineering and manufacturing, a new sense of dynamic creativity is developing. They're finding ways to design and manufacture their products, cutting cycle time and improving inventory turns and quality."

"Well, then," says Vincent, "is there any reason we can't get into simultaneous engineering? That is, if you're agreeable, Wesley."

Wesley and Vincent look at one another and nod their heads in agreement.

Vincent breathes a sigh of relief and quips, "Perhaps the engineering community will no longer insist on being king of the hill."

"Sounds good to me," says Frank. "Just figure out a way to do it without drawing one of those infernal box-and-line masterpieces. The idea is perfectly good. It's just that isolating ourselves in our compartments isn't going to get it done. We'll just get back to the old 'Whose fault is this?' syndrome."

## Working in Parallel

"As long as we're discussing the idea of working in parallel," says Carol, "let's think about marketing. My group is tired of being disconnected from the whole process. In spite of our recommendations, engineering has always done as it pleases. Can marketing be included in these iterative efforts?"

"Whoa," says Wesley. "All we're talking about is combining design and manufacturing engineering. Before we get in over our heads, let's see if we can make simultaneous engineering work. We gotta crawl before we can walk."

"I'm serious," Carol retorts. "You guys always take the product and ride off into the sunset before we even get a look at it. We find out what you geniuses have done the day before we have to advertise it. When we make marketing decisions, we don't know how to distribute it or what to say about it. If we were in on it from the start, we'd know about all the nifty features you designed into it, and who it's best suited for. The disconnects really add unnecessary complexity to our work."

"But—"

"Count me in, too," says Gregory. "Service has to deal with the customer after the sale. And you engineers don't make it easy on us. I could tell you a few things about serviceability and warranty complaints. You need to sit down with some of my people for an hour or two. You'd get an earful. Our concerns also have to be designed into the products and processes."

"Look, Gregory, we've been over this before," says Wesley. "It's not a design problem. Our buyers don't understand how to operate the products. If marketing could turn out a decent instruction manual, you wouldn't have these complaints."

"Oh, it's marketing again," says Carol. "How can we contract out for a manual when we don't even know what the thing does?"

Fortunately, the lunch break gives everyone a chance to cool down and think more objectively about the morning's discussion. Following lunch, Marjorie, who has been relatively quiet all morning, observes, "Our simplistic input-output model of the organization, which assumes that we feed raw materials and ideas in one end and out comes well-developed products, is really full of mazelike complexity."

## Lost in Complexity

She continues, "Perhaps if we learned to work in parallel from the first—more complexity, if you want to look at it that way—then the process of designing, building, and supporting a product will end up being much simpler. Kind of a paradox, isn't it?"

"I think I see what you're getting at," says Frank.

"I'm not sure I do," says Wesley.

"It's like this," says Marjorie. Picking up a marker, she draws a simple graph on the flip chart.

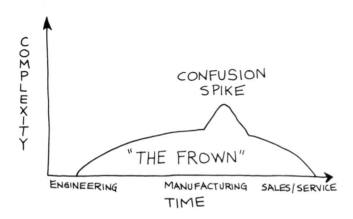

"If we make the *x* axis time and the *y* axis complexity, here's what we've been doing. Each product we produce starts out simply—just an idea in some engineer's mind. As we start developing it, it gets more and more complex. Engineering change orders, specification changes, marketing considerations—everything crowds in and complicates the process long after the original design is finalized, creating confusion spikes. We waste a lot of time checking up on other departments' work. This time doesn't show up in project costs; it just gets hidden in overhead. Then we finally get the product on the market and, except for service, we lose interest in it—less complexity. Finally we take it off the market and we're back to zero. Most of the complexity is here in the middle of the process. And finance can't provide an accurate accounting of the cost. The curve looks like a *frown*."

Marjorie continues, "Our simplistic organizational chart, with its narrow job and departmental definitions, adds to the complexity of our activities because of all the built-in blocks and dead ends. Moreover, from an information management point of view, we have been relying on antiquated systems to transmit significant knowledge between functions. The spaghetti-like interfacing between applications is a big contributor to this uncontrolled complexity. But if we were all involved in the initial design work, each specialist putting in his or her own design considerations, here's what it might look like."

## Managing Complexity

Marjorie maintains the floor. "Many of the confusion spikes have been coming to light as we move toward both Just-in-Time and Total Quality efforts. In addition, because of the distrust between functions, many activities just exist to check on another department's work. These activities add no value to the product, just costs that are usually buried in overhead.

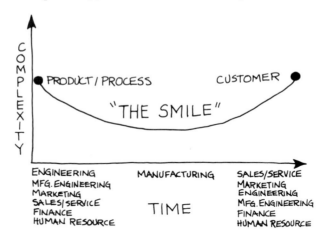

"As the functions—marketing, engineering, manufacturing engineering, and sales/service—work in parallel in task teams, most of the complications can be dealt with up front. This makes manufacturing simpler, because manufacturing constraints are understood at the design stage. As a consequence, the curve droops in the middle. Then it rises again at the right because we can deal with more complex market opportunities, like a *smile*. Typically customers are not buying isolated items; they're buying products and services that fit into a complex web of other interrelationships. As we work with customers and understand their multiple and varied requirements, we should be able to use this learning in our design efforts.[1] The market differentiator for many companies in the future will be their ability to master complexity and to feel at home with multiple interrelationships."

"I like that, Marjorie," says Vincent. "And I think we may already have stumbled across a way to get there. Remember when Wesley and I started talking about simultaneous engineering? Everybody jumped in and wanted a piece of the action."

## Customer Expectations

"Let's say that we decide to market a new product line. The first consideration is, of course, satisfying a customer need." Vincent sketches an uneven oval and labels it "customer expectations."

"Now—with concurrent or parallel engineering alone, here's how we'll start designing this new product. Engineering and manufacturing will collaborate to make sure the product not only satisfies customer expectations but also is easy to manufacture."

"But let's carry this principle further," suggests Wesley. "Let's include marketing's input from the start. That will get Carol into the loop and give us a better handle on advertising and distribution. And we'll include service, so we'll have a product that breaks down less and is easier to repair. We also need Gregory's experience and insights up front."

"You're right, Wesley," responds Vincent. "Without everyone in the loop, it's easy to misinterpret customer expectations. Often customers are not exactly sure what they really want. Competitive products add to the confusion. In addition, customers are waking up to the life-cycle costs of products."

Vincent draws the figure.

"Know what that reminds me of?" asks Marjorie, who is an accomplished pianist. "Customer expectations are much like the themes in a piece of music. The themes are understood through careful listening. Moreover, they're developed and modified over time, as are customer expectations."

## Customer Expectations as Themes

Marjorie continues, "In order to pick up the theme or themes, a musician needs to be in tune with the music as well as having a sense of rhythm. Some pieces of music are easy to grasp while others take skill and knowledge. Difficult themes are often the most engaging and satisfying because of their subtleties. Analogously, the themes of the marketplace have their own rhythm and timing. If a company can pick up the subtleties of the themes and develop appropriate responses with proper timing, then it's likely to achieve success."

Marjorie adds, "We need to reinforce the idea of building teams of professionals from the four functions, teams that will work together to discern the themes and develop appropriate responses."

Wesley catches on to Marjorie's reasoning and reflects, "In the past, because of our functional fragmentation, too many good ideas got buried in the bureaucracy or dropped through the cracks of petty politics."

Vincent agrees. "We ought to add more than just marketing and service to our diagram. Certainly other functions, such as finance, information systems, sales, and materials management, can and should be included when it's appropriate."

Alan asks, "Aren't customer expectations like the sheet music? We all have different parts to play, and if we play well together and are sensitive to customer expectations, we'll make real music."

"Right," says Frank. "Otherwise, it's like an orchestra warming up, with everyone tuning his own instrument and nobody paying attention to anyone else."

Marjorie jumps back in. "Let me caution you, gentlemen. The orchestra analogy is only of limited value. In business, the customer themes aren't orchestrated on sheet music. They're often ambiguous, contradictory, and ill defined. In fact, they remind me of some of the images I've been seeing in the growing literature about chaos."

"I see your point, Marjorie. Does that mean we should go back to the old line organization?" asks Wesley.

"Absolutely not! We have no chance of listening well to the faint themes of the customers if we're so busy worrying about our lines of command and our boxes," responds Marjorie. "We should enlarge the circle of involvement."

## Cross-Functional Task Teams

Vincent and Alan agree, and speak almost in a chorus: "Let's take it all the way and add finance, information systems, sales, and materials management to the orchestra."

Vincent is up at the flip chart sketching all eight functions in an outer circle surrounding the "customer expectations" oval. "We could call this whole thing a cross-functional task team."

Carol suddenly says, "There's not just one theme in each market engagement, but multiple themes. Perhaps each theme should have its own team? The selection of themes and the composition of the teams is a challenging judgment call."

"What about strategic planning?" asks Gregory. "Does this put us in closer touch with the market?"

Marjorie laughs, "Sometimes it's done at such a high level of abstraction that it amounts to one guesstimation heaped upon other guesstimations! Most functions don't really believe in the numbers generated; even if they use them they manage by variance. At the same time, there's value in our planning process because it forces us to sort out our thinking together. This helps us to clarify the context in which we work and allocate the necessary resources."

Carol suddenly lets out a loud "Aha!"

They all look at Carol's bright face and ask, "What is it?"

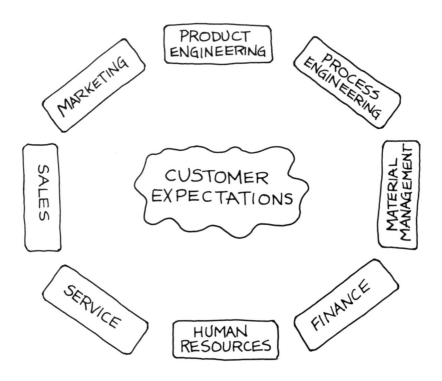

"You notice," responds Carol, "the way the functions have circled the customer expectations?"

Everyone nods their heads, but they still do not see what has caught Carol's attention.

## Customer Expectations: Multiple Amoebas

"Typically problems don't come in nice round or square patterns," Carol continues. "We're not dealing with just one customer, but with patterns of customer expectations. These expectations are conditioned not only by customer wants and needs, but by government regulations, competitive pressures, emerging technologies, and resource constraints. If I were to draw these customer expectations, they would probably look more like multiple amoebas, perhaps something like this."

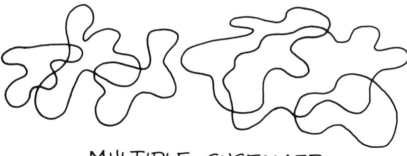

## MULTIPLE CUSTOMER
### EXPECTATIONS

"What do you mean, Carol?" asks Frank.

"I'll show you." She goes to the flip chart and uncovers a fresh sheet of paper. "We're used to addressing market opportunities like this. Frank, please excuse me, but I really need to draw an organizational chart." Frank laughs.

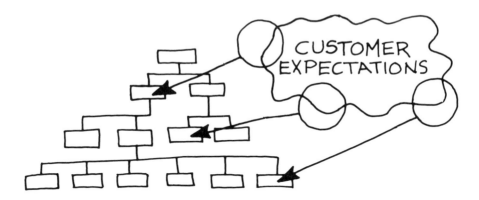

Carol takes the marker to the flip chart. "I'm drawing just one amoeba-like lumpy shape on purpose. Don't laugh, Vincent. Most market opportunities are shapeless, anyway, because they're distorted by outside pressures.

"But the point is that we always deal with the complex market opportunity, or actually several at once, by splitting them up among functions. Each function tears off its chunk and goes off to work on it by itself.

"Then we're supposed to meet again and paste together a solution—a new product. But we end up missing pieces of the puzzle, because parts of the opportunity are overlooked and aren't assigned to anybody, and because people are limited to one small part of the problem, like a horse with blinders. The result is that issues fall between the cracks. It's a wonder that we've done as well as we have over the years." Carol pauses, then continues.

## Circling Customer Expectations

"Now I would like to tell you why I shouted 'Aha!' a few minutes ago. When Vincent added the functions around the customer expectations amoeba, I realized that this reverses the process. Instead of breaking the problem apart, as we traditionally do, we need instead to circle the problem with resources from the various functions like this." Carol moves to the flip chart once more and draws another figure.

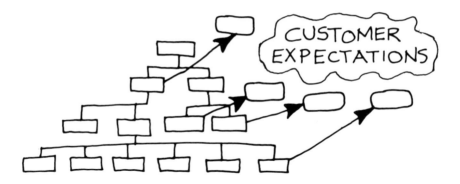

Marjorie winks at Carol. "Do you realize what you've drawn? You've just suggested a reversal of two hundred years of history. Haven't we been taught to take a large problem apart and work on it section by section, letting each specialist focus on his or her areas of expertise? Now you're suggesting that the specialists work together as a team, sharing their knowledge and insights not only to solve the problem, but to come up with new and innovative offerings. As we start to do this, several things will begin to happen. First, we'll learn from one another. Second, we'll be able to respond more adequately to the market challenge. And third, our responses are likely to be more innovative and creative."

Alan comes alive. "If I were to put terms on it, I'd say the old approach is analytical, and the new one is holistic. Instead of mutually exclusive boxes, people's areas of responsibilities overlap like Venn diagrams. This way, the whole amoeba is covered."

They all study the diagram in silence for a moment.

"If it keeps all these rugged individualists in touch with each other," says Vincent, "then I'm for it."

"It will," replies Marjorie. "Marketing people will share their insights with engineering, manufacturing will learn from service, and people will come out knowing a lot more than when they went in. We'll design and assemble a better product. It can't help but make everybody more creative."

## Customer Visits

Wesley shakes his head, but not in disagreement. "Carol, your last diagram just hit me. I realize how seldom I insist that our engineers go to customer sites. They're usually too busy to take time with customers, much less understand the constraints under which manufacturing lives. If, however, I assign my engineers to different teams, it's likely that their work will be much closer to the mark the first time."

As Carol listens to Wesley, her face lights up again. "Wesley, I just realized another factor at play here. I've always been struck not only by how your engineers don't have time for others, but by how little they share their knowledge between project groups. If we learn to work more effectively as multiple cross-functional teams, then we'll be able to deal more effectively with the market's complexity."

Carol continues, "Instead of having to simplify everything so we can assign it to one function or another, we'll be able to deal with the rich complexity of our competitive environment.

"Most companies, ours included, manage multiple products," she explains. "Each product or service is initiated in a fairly simple manner in response to a generally felt market need. The projects tend to get more complex over time, primarily because of all the factors that were not thought of during the earlier stages of the life cycle. Marketing does not specify customer expectations clearly enough. Engineering does not listen carefully, nor does it appreciate manufacturing's ability to hold tolerances on certain designs. Finance tries costing based on vague similarities to past experiences."

Marjorie begins to see where Carol is going. "Are you suggesting that if we work as cross-functional teams, we'll be able to deal with the complexities on both sides of the inverted curve, the smile?"

"Exactly," answers Carol. "The more work we can do up front to size up the pattern of customer expectations, the better targeted we'll be in the market. In addition, we need much better control over our manufacturing processes, so we can hold our processes within specifications. This is why I'm so pleased, Vincent, that you're spending so much time and effort on Total Quality Management. And with our teams, we'll not only be able to deal with the development phase, but we'll also enhance the quality of our interaction with the market when the products are ready. We'll be able to integrate our products into a customer's environment in a way that gives us a competitive edge."

## Complexity: Enemy or Friend?

"I'm still confused," notes Alan. "Is complexity the enemy or a friend? Excuse me for being dense. Could you go over the distinction you made earlier, Carol?"

Carol looks at Alan and pauses. "Alan, you're right. It is confusing. We're using complexity in two ways. In the first figure, things got more complex because of shortsightedness in the system, causing the confusion spikes. In the second, by learning to work together, we're able to deal with much more complex issues and opportunities. Imagine customer expectation bubbles at the end of the inverted curve with teams which are circling these amoeba-like customer opportunities. As we learn together about customer expectations, we'll be able to transfer this learning to the front end, so our products and services will be better targeted and more timely in their introduction."

Carol continues, "We'll only be able to do this by learning to learn together on the teams and between teams. Our ability to learn as an organization will become our lifeblood, giving us new knowledge, insights, and vision. Alan, as director of human resources, you not only need to help us develop a learning culture, but you must also help adjust our reward and measurement systems. Today they work against good cross-functional collaboration."

Energy is flowing in the room. Everyone seems to need to talk out the implications of Carol's discussion. Little discussions break out all over the room. This goes on for twenty minutes. Then Frank gets everyone's attention.

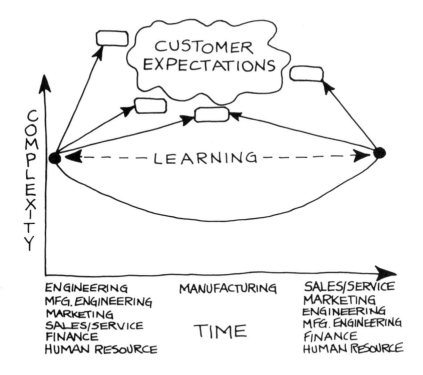

ENGINEERING    MANUFACTURING    SALES/SERVICE
MFG. ENGINEERING                 MARKETING
MARKETING                        ENGINEERING
SALES/SERVICE                    MFG. ENGINEERING
FINANCE           TIME           FINANCE
HUMAN RESOURCE                   HUMAN RESOURCE

Frank sums up the work of the afternoon, as it is getting close to 6:30 P.M. "We have started out by reviewing our responsiveness index. This turned out to be much lower than we had expected, because of the fragmentation, inflexibility, and distrust within the organization. We then hit a most productive vein in our discussion, as we explored the concept of simultaneous or concurrent engineering and the use of cross-functional teams. As objections were raised to including only engineering and manufacturing, we broadened the concept to include marketing, service, and the other functions. We also began to understand the role of themes in our interplay with the market and the shift we need to take from parsing out a problem to treating it as a whole entity. I want to thank you all for a most creative session."

The group decides they should meet tomorrow for another full day, if needed. Frank is pleased because now they are showing a new spirit.

# 4

# Thursday

## Who's in Charge Now?

The next morning, everyone is in high spirits, full of energy and ideas. The sting of the torn organizational chart is subsiding. Only Carol seems less than ebullient. She is quiet until Frank opens the meeting.

"How," she asks, "are these cross-functional teams supposed to be monitored and controlled? All this talk about cooperation and creativity sounds inspiring and uplifting, but who's in charge? Do these teams just go rambling off without guidance or limitations?"

The reaction to these questions surprises Carol. Marjorie and Wesley both point out that the questions are inappropriate. "They're reminiscent of the old organization, the one we're outgrowing. The teams need to be self-directed. They should have their own autonomy and control their own work."

Carol persists, "The company cannot tolerate autonomous teams, even if they're cross-functional, because they'll go off in all sorts of directions.

Where will they take the company? Will they commit us to undertakings for which we're not ready?"

Carol determinedly points out, "I've lived through one management fad after another: work simplification; the human relations movement; group dynamics; transactional analysis; Theories X, Y, and Z; Quality of Work Life; and the participation movement. More current theories include Design for Assembly, Total Quality, Just-in-Time, and Quality Function Deployment. Now I've just read about two new buzzwords: Total Employee Involvement (TEI) and Management Value Added (MVA). I'm sure there will be conferences, articles, and perhaps a journal touting these ideas. But my skepticism has conditioned me to look below the hype for the substance.

"I know autonomous teams, however well meant, will tend to pull in different directions, unless . . ." Carol pauses. "They'll be a disruptive force unless their efforts are somehow shaped by an agreed-upon context."

Wesley begins to sense that there is some truth in her lonely voice. She is a reality check. Enthusiasm alone cannot redefine the corporation. The others begin to see that somehow the context must be articulated. Wesley turns to Carol and asks, "Don't the multiple teams, working on different themes, have to understand how their work fits in with the enterprise's vision? In fact, isn't it important for the teams to temper this vision with a good deal of their own realism, gained from close interaction with the market and computer technology?"

## Vision Defines the Context

Marjorie begins to understand Carol's point. "The corporate vision is a living force in our lives. It's not just a projection of where the corporation wants to be in three to five years in terms of market share, return on assets, and customer satisfaction. An effective vision will have a living presence, influencing the many large and small decisions made each day. Although it's future-directed, it is very much here in the present as a real force."

The group struggles to understand more about the role of their corporate vision.

"Can't we agree that it's a composite of a number of elements, including our strategic plan and corporate goals, together with the company philosophy and mission statements?" asks Marjorie. "Today they're an inconsistent hodge-podge."

Marjorie continues, "The vision should also include the values that hold things together. As we look at the need to integrate functions internally and our resources externally, I'm beginning to realize that the vision will include what Frank has called 'critical linkage factors.' CLFs are the strategic and tactical linkages that must be maintained internally and externally in order to leverage our market position."

"Why," asks Gregory, "is this vision organic? And where does it come from—us?"

The members of the group are surprised by their humility. Frank points out, "We're not the all-knowing forces within the corporation. We really depend on many others to help develop our visions. Perhaps the teams can play a larger role in helping discern and develop the market themes."

## Continually Refreshing the Vision

A consensus soon develops, something that flabbergasts everyone. Vincent captures their thoughts: "As the teams do their work, they will have to help condition and grow the visions of the enterprise. Remember how Johnson & Johnson has periodic credo challenges, where employees can challenge the company's credo or mission statement. Perhaps we should hold a quarterly meeting where the teams will be expected to challenge the current enterprise vision."

"A vision challenge will serve several purposes," Vincent continues. "First, the teams will have to think through the ideas they're challenging. This will have the effect of helping to internalize the vision. Second, as they challenge the vision, explaining their positions, they will be affecting the other teams. Third, this periodic meeting will ensure that the vision remains current. And fourth, the challenges will inject realism into the vision. Too often, it's easy to get carried away by market success or failure. Things can look either too bright or too bleak."

"You mean," concludes Marjorie, "that the vision serves to set a context, provide the values, and supply the direction for the hundreds and thousands of large and small decisions made every day within the enterprise. As a cohesive force, it has a large role to play in interrelating multiple activities. It gives direction and purpose to the cross-functional task teams." She sketches a figure on the flip chart to illustrate her statement.

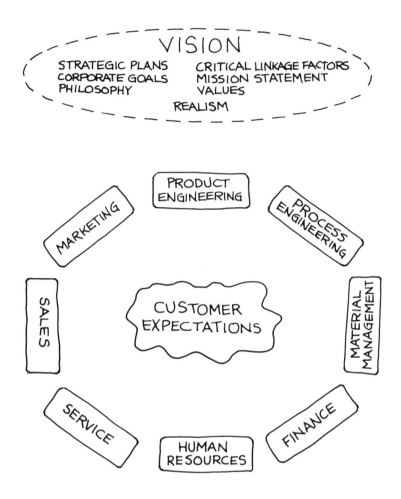

Gregory remembers the prior discussion about the responsiveness index. "I just thought of the problem of intertwining all the application packages using fixed translators. Will visions alone hold us together? Certainly they're key, but I suggest that they're only a part of a larger whole."

"You have something, Gregory," responds Marjorie. "It will be difficult for the various functions to work together if we haven't sorted out our individual dialects, the unique terminology each function uses. Moreover, we'll be handicapped if we don't sort out key common data elements—for example, if the teams have to use multiple bills of materials or multiple parts lists."

## Knowledge as a Resource

Gregory's face lights up. "The teams will need access to a common knowledge base, a common capability, and a common way of describing key elements. They'll need to know-how, know-who, know-when, know-what, know-where, and know-why."

Gregory continues, "The *know-how* is the skill base, developed over the years. It includes the trade secrets, engineering standards, and expertise of the enterprise. The *know-who* identifies the people with information, both internally and externally, the informal network that gets the work done. The *know-when* involves our sense of timing and rhythm in developing new products, managing lead times, closing out old products, and pacing the market."

"And," adds Marjorie, "the *know-what* is the mastery of a consistent set of meanings. It may include the data elements (entities) in a database, in applications, group technology, classification and coding, test specifications, or standards. Consistency of meaning makes it possible to see significant patterns more easily, predict trends, and develop customized solutions. The *know-where* is the ability to identify appropriate market niches. And the *know-why* involves our knowledge of the context and how it relates to our particular efforts."

"You know," notes Frank, "I'm gaining a new appreciation for the work engineering and manufacturing have already done on group technology and a classification and coding system. I see now that engineering's desire to use form- and feature-based solids modeling will make it much easier to remove the slash in CAD/CAM. And I sense that work on relational and object-oriented database technology will begin to give us more flexibility than we're presently getting from our flat and hierarchical files. They all represent a systematic sorting out and organization of our collective knowledge."

"Our key assets are the knowledge bases that individuals have developed in their heads," Marjorie points out. "And this knowledge, developed in the past, is a constant and continued resource in the present for our professionals."

"I wonder," says Vincent, "how much of the knowledge needed to run our company can be captured in our databases and applications?"

## Linking the Knowledge Bases in People's Heads

After discussing this among themselves, they agree that perhaps as much as 30 percent of this knowledge can be embedded in computer-based systems. A larger percentage of the knowledge, perhaps 70 percent, will never be captured within common databases, but will remain in the heads of the company's managers, professionals, and employees.

"Now I'm beginning to see why it's such a challenge to bring this knowledge together in the task teams," remarks Carol.

Frank sketches a circle on the flip chart to represent the organization's knowledge base.

They look long and hard at the figure. Several questions come to mind. Carol articulates one of them. "Must the participants in the effort, who come from the different functions, be physically co-located?"

Vincent reflects, "It shouldn't be necessary if the enterprise has a well-developed local and wide-area network and a way of moving information, even graphic information, easily about the network. Of course, face-to-face meetings during team formation, at critical points, and for important milestones are crucial. This will help achieve that dynamic creativity that comes with and from personal interaction."

## Teams: How?

"How many persons will participate on the teams?" asks Carol.

"As far as size, I can see a minimum of three or four people, but larger teams could easily have eight or ten or more. We ought to keep the core of each team small and access the other members over the net as much as possible. The core group could be dedicated to the job for a specific term, with the other members on call as needed. Probably most people would be members on call for several teams, depending on their knowledge and the teams' needs."

"How will the teams keep their tasks in focus?" asks Carol.

"They'll be responsible for developing detailed project plans, perhaps using a project management software package," responds Marjorie. "This will help the teams think through the many interrelated steps in the processes. They'll also be responsible for developing working budgets, in terms of both time and cost. Furthermore, they will be expected to monitor their own progress accordingly and negotiate changes in scope with top management."

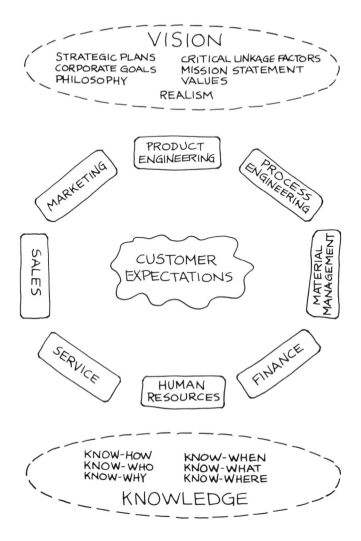

"How will the teams be directed?" Carol continues.

"The teams will have project leaders assigned or selected by the team," suggests Marjorie. "The teams should be self-directing and self-focusing as they develop an understanding of what needs to be done, and they should be able to respond to the contingencies of the market as they arise. This will be done in the context of a clear charter (vision) covering the teams' objectives."

Carol continues, "What will be expected of the teams?"

This time Wesley captures the consensus of their discussion. "The teams will need a good deal of discipline. They'll be held together by well-understood norms instead of by bureaucratic policies and procedures. They'll be expected to work on assigned tasks while at the same time making sure that these tasks are undertaken in a way that supports the enterprise's vision."

Wesley continues, "The teams will also be expected to help this enterprise vision grow, based on their experience and the insights gained from their efforts. Moreover, they will be expected to add to the knowledge base in a systematic manner. This might take the form of creating organized test specifications or of adding well-defined data elements to the enterprise data architecture. The list is almost endless."

"How will participants on the teams be evaluated and rewarded?" asks Carol, persisting with her questions.

Vincent, looking pensive, turns to Alan and asks, "Alan, yesterday we were talking about how to reward the kind of team action we need to make this idea work. Have you had a chance to think about that?"

## Team Self-Evaluations

"Yes, and I've also been listening carefully to what's been said today. One thing that stands out in my mind is that the team concept puts everybody on pretty much the same level, or maybe two levels—core and support. The team leader is not a supervisor as much as a coordinator, so it's not his or her job to evaluate or measure individual performance. Therefore, I'd suggest that each team evaluate its own people. That is, all the members would rate themselves and their colleagues, say, halfway through and at the end of the project. These ratings would be one of several factors determining raises and promotions."

"Interesting," says Carol. "What criteria would this peer evaluation use?"

"Contribution to the team effort would be the main criterion." Alan ticks off several points on his fingers. "The insightfulness of an individual's contributions, ability to teach and learn from one another, ability to add to the enterprise's knowledge base and vision, ability to build trust, ability to challenge and be challenged until the truth is discovered, ability to incorporate and use existing design and process capabilities effectively, ability to help the enterprise advance technologically, and awareness of the competitive environment."

"That is quite a list," comments Carol. "I thought you were only concerned about human resource issues. I'm beginning to see a pattern. First, we use more cross-functional multilevel teams, and second, we change the way people are reviewed. Intriguing! But aren't people influenced by the way the measurements are kept?"

## Accounting Procedures

Carol has her next question ready. "What will happen to the traditional accounting procedures?"

This topic spurs a lot of emotion.

Alan, who has been rather quiet up to this point, sees his opportunity to get some frustrations off his chest. Turning to Marjorie, he says, "Would it be possible for your department to rethink the age-old procedure of burdening direct labor?"

Alan continues, "I've noticed that the line between direct and indirect labor is blurring. If we start to do more work in small teams, we need to begin to treat all our efforts as definable projects against which charges and costs can be maintained. Wouldn't this make it possible to obtain truer costs and help us determine which efforts are contributing to the bottom line?"

Marjorie is less defensive than the others expect. She picks up on Alan's comments and suggests, "The changes you've mentioned will also help to redefine the traditional capital investment rules. The teams will have a much better feel for the significance of the investment request, more so than for the traditional functional requests. Certainly, part of the justification process will be to show how the team or teams expect to use the investment to support their project effort. This will, in essence, build more visibility and accountability into the capital budgeting process. Frankly, I've always felt we needed this capability. And we'll need to move to activity-based accounting to better track the work of the teams."

## Team Composition

Carol brings the discussion back to teams, asking, "How will the teams be composed or put together?"

Vincent, who has taken a keen interest in the task team approach, continues to share his thoughts. "Some of the teams will need to be assigned. Others may represent a coming together of people with mutual interests who define a task area and gain approval to initiate a project."

"You mean," responds Marjorie, "that as the enterprise shifts to a style of working that identifies key themes, there will be a good deal of self-selecting of teams? This suggests that people will be expected to take initiatives in a network environment rather than waiting to be asked to do something."

"Yes," responds Vincent. "At the same time, the existence of a well-worked-out and flexible project management approach will make it possible to deploy and redeploy resources as needed. Moreover, it's likely that gaps in capabilities will quickly show up. I'm beginning to realize that this is a key benefit of a peer-to-peer networking environment. Instead of losing things in the cracks between departments, people will have a way of easily highlighting what needs to be done, setting priorities, and mustering the necessary resources."

"Wait a minute! Wait a minute!" interrupts Wesley. "You all know that our culture does not make it easy to build teams. We fight too much with one another."

Alan almost falls out of his chair. "I never thought I would hear those words. I've been so frustrated for so long over our inability to build teams. Do you mean that I'm finally going to have a chance to get our organization out of the last century?"

Everyone looks at Alan and nods. Wesley summarizes the group's thinking. "Yes, Alan, you have your work cut out, and we will support you. We not only need to learn more about team building, but we must find an easy, straightforward way to do team problem solving. I know you've had considerable experience with group dynamics, but frankly I don't think we're looking for a mushy approach."

"I think I know what you mean," responds Alan. "Although feelings are important, we need a team approach that is more cognitive. I've noticed that in the past when we have tried working in groups, two things occur. Either the team members treat the conference table as a place to negotiate, or they become a mutual therapy group. Wesley, you want to avoid both extremes, don't you?"

Wesley smiles and responds, "Yes! What I'm looking for is a situation where the team members have an openness and trust, so they're free to think out loud together. I've seen teams click. They're able to take a topic and discover things as a team that are out of their reach as an aggregate of individuals."

## Jazz Combos

"Do you mean," asks Alan, "that we need an approach to teams that draws on both the knowledge and visions of its members? It reminds me of the way a good basketball team or jazz combo works."

"Yes, that's it," responds Wesley. "In many ways this is the way groups of engineers work already, but now we must broaden the circle to include the other functions on the teams. I can see right now that the arrogance of many of my engineers has to be overcome. With a little reflection, I can see that my department has been a large part of our problem."

Vincent hardly believes his ears. "You mean, Wesley, that your people will begin to do more listening?"

"Our ability to listen, cross-functionally, will determine our success or failure," suggests Alan. "In the past, we've failed to take the time to listen carefully to one another. We've been too busy chasing engineering change orders (ECOs) to have time to listen. But if we had listened earlier on, probably we could do without two-thirds of the ECOs."

"If we start to listen more and work more cross-functionally," remarks Marjorie, "then we shouldn't think of our people as locked in their little boxes on the organizational chart. Instead, my guess is that we should think of our people as resources on call."

"That's a scary idea," remarks Gregory. "Those little boxes can be warm and comfortable to many. They offer protection. They're a place to hide. Now you're suggesting that people think of themselves as resources instead of personal property. Won't the incompetent worry that they'll be discovered?"

"And what about us? Frankly, we've often refused to allow our resources to be used by other departments because then we can't get our jobs done," Marjorie continues. "We've often measured our importance by the number of resources at our beck and call. Gregory is right; when we see our people as cross-functional resources, we'll be forced to change our own attitudes toward them."

"In the past, theory has supposed that everyone is a fixed resource, with a clearly defined job description," comments Alan. "Now we must begin to think of people as virtual resources who can play on multiple jazz combos."

## Virtual Resources

"Alan, what do you mean by the words *virtual resources*?" asks Carol.

Alan responds, "I've been reading lately about virtual memory in computer systems. It's been around for awhile in mainframes and minicomputers, but it's just now spreading to personal computers. Often an application requires more random access memory than is available in the computer. So instead of putting the whole application into RAM, the operating system swaps portions of the program into and out of it as needed. In other words, the extra memory isn't permanent, but it's available."

Marjorie's face lights up. "You mean, Alan, that our people should be available to be pulled together as the need arises to work on specific projects?"

"Exactly. Instead of seeing the boxes on the organizational chart as defining the limits of interest," answers Alan, "we need to think of our people as adaptive and capable of working together with others to find new and unique solutions to our business and technical challenges."

## Centers of Excellence

Carol responds with another question, "What will the function of the departments be?"

"Are we sure we know what we're getting into with this line of reasoning?" comments Gregory. "In the past, we've measured our importance by the number of direct reports and budget expenditures we can authorize. We're also very conscious of our position on the organizational chart, one level below the top. Are our roles shifting?"

"If Alan is right," notes Marjorie, "our roles are certainly shifting. Our functions are going to become *centers of excellence*. We'll be creating virtual resources that can be drawn upon to form the necessary project or task teams. This means we're going to have to get better at picking the best talent available, because we'll be judged by the quality of the people we have in our functions. In the past I've seen how executives have sometimes picked mediocre talent so they will not be threatened in their positions."

Vincent interrupts, "I see now how expensive a senior executive's insecurity can be. It shuts the door to top talent."

Vincent pauses, then resumes, "I'm also beginning to realize that our key management roles will be to orchestrate the teams, their project efforts, and the interplay between them. We'll need to help articulate the context in which these teams carry out their projects. And ultimately we'll be responsible for the quality and clarity of the enterprise's vision and knowledge."

"Perhaps," suggests Gregory, "there should be three senior vice-presidents—one with responsibility for the enterprise vision, one for day-to-day operations, and the third for the collected knowledge. These senior vice-presidents can rotate annually. If they know that they'll have to take care of another aspect, they'll act with care, so that the three elements will be complementary."

"There may be some merit to this proposal," says Marjorie. "But wait. It may only add another layer to the organization and increase instability, because the vice-presidents will want to change directions in their particular area annually. Actually, it is a silly idea. Instead, it should be our collective responsibility to work together to ensure the quality and integrity of the vision and knowledge. Moreover, we also have a responsibility to support and interact with the teams, making sure they have the resources needed to get the job done."

"There are several other questions we must tackle," Marjorie adds. "How will accountability, focus, and coordination between teams be maintained? Will fragmentation really be overcome in this new approach? And what impact will this new model have on our managers, professionals, and employees?"

As the day is growing long, Frank suggests they take up these questions tomorrow. "I want to commend you on the quality of your effort, insights, and creativity."

# Friday

## Accountability, Focus, and Coordination

On Friday they meet with a feeling of optimism. They've worked together better than ever before, and it appears as though the cross-functional task team idea might soon bring an end to the functional fragmentation that has long plagued their company.

Carol begins, "The use of cross-functional teams will certainly help overcome the fragmentation we've all been experiencing. Instead of working sequentially, we can move toward a parallel operation where the product and process can be designed with an eye to its marketability and serviceability."

"This will have an interesting impact," adds Alan. "Everyone involved will constantly be challenged to deepen and broaden his or her knowledge and skills. Individual growth will be a valuable component of this overall approach. Instead of being put into narrowly defined task slots, people will be expected to use their knowledge, skills, and experience to help master a given task. The excitement of discovery is likely to be a strong motivator in the overall process, and the recognition and challenge that comes from one's colleagues will also be rewarding."

True to character, Carol asks, "How do we maintain accountability, focus, and coordination?"

Gregory notes, "The use of teams, steering committees, ad hoc committees, and task forces isn't a new idea. Our company has long used these groupings. Why haven't they worked more effectively?"

"Could it be," notes Alan, "that in the past, participants on the various group efforts have felt that they had two jobs to perform, their assigned job as shown on the organizational chart and the add-on task? For the most part, they're measured and rewarded by their performance in their assigned tasks rather than on participation in group efforts; therefore, they often resent time away from their primary areas of responsibility."

## Team Visibility

"In addition," adds Vincent, "there has been no convenient way of 'seeing' who is participating on which team. Group work has been, for the most part, an invisible activity because it never shows up on the organization chart and traditional reward systems don't factor it in."

Frank has been actively listening. He can't constrain himself. "These group efforts have often lacked discipline in capturing what they've learned, both positive and negative, and making this knowledge available to the larger company. They've undertaken narrowly focused assignments and have often been unable to impact the larger processes such as material flow, accounting, and distribution systems. In fact, often participation on task teams is as much a defensive matter to protect the functions' prerogatives as it is a way to bring lasting changes."

Frank continues, "If the use of task teams is to become a way of life, they must be given high visibility. They need discipline and accountability so that we can help our visions grow. We must have teamwork of teams. We have to network our teams so they can support one another in supplying knowledge and vision. The visioning will act as a beacon, giving focus and direction to the team efforts because the context will be understood. This will help to increase accountability. Moreover, access to the collective knowledge of the company will provide consistency to the efforts."

"But wait a minute," demands Vincent. "We're not going to do everything with cross-functional teams; there is still work that requires dedicated resources. For example, factory operations and order processing must be part of the daily routine for some employees."

"This is very true," agrees Frank. "However, what I need at this point is a way to see relationships both within and between departments. Moreover, I need a way to maintain clear lines of responsibility, even if I don't use the traditional organizational chart, the one I tore in half on Monday."

"This circular thing intrigues me." He walks to the flip chart and turns back the pages to the circular diagram showing lines of communication. "We've already shown here how people communicate between functions when the work is getting done. Maybe we could break the functions down into circles, too."

Outside the larger ring, he begins sketching smaller rings of positions, showing the individuals in each department.[1]

"Okay, I'm showing the department head at the three o'clock position, the same place the CEO is on the big ring. The lines show the official reporting relationships within the company and within each department. I am penciling in your initials, showing where each of you fits on the larger ring and how each of your departmental reporting relationships looks today."

"That's what the old hierarchical chart showed," exclaims Carol.

"Yeah, but it's different," says Frank. "Notice how on this circular chart it's easier to show informal lines of communication between departments.

"Suppose we were to give all our employees questionnaires and ask them to indicate with whom they communicate when they're working on a particular task. We could then show this interaction on the chart. We would soon recognize that this resembles the informal organization rather than the official hierarchy as we have known it. The patterns of interaction reveal the knowledge structure of the organization, who knows what and whom.

"I just happen to have some questionnaire results. Here's the pattern we get for new product development." Reading from a sheet of paper, he draws lines in the smaller circles representing sales, engineering, and manufacturing.

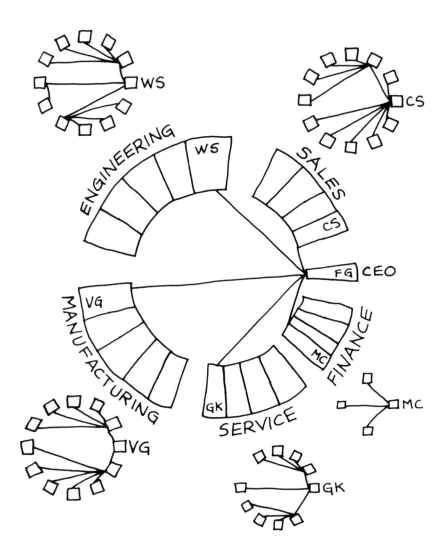

"In this case, we've got a key engineer—here in engineering, naturally—whom everybody seems to communicate with."

Wesley looks puzzled but says nothing.

"Notice also that neither the CEO nor most of the department heads are involved. The link with finance is tenuous, and service is out of the loop entirely."

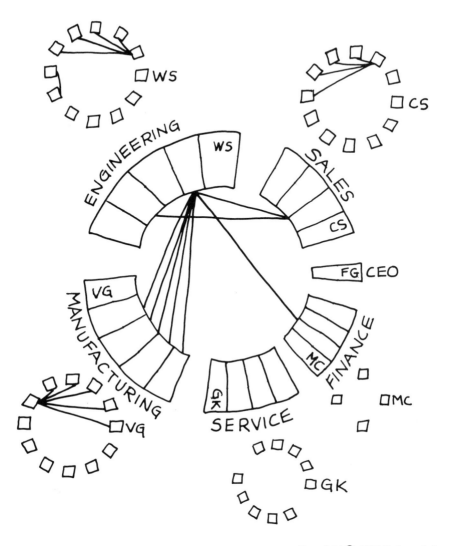

"That's exactly what I was saying," says Gregory. "We're not consulted on design for serviceability, but we get saddled with all the service hassles and warranty costs!"

"Wait a minute," says Marjorie. "This isn't our own company, is it?"

"Caught in the act!" says Frank. "No, these are results from another company, but we seem to have hit a nerve, haven't we? Our own situation would probably look a lot like this."

"We never completed the applications ring," says Vincent. "Seems to me that we could use it the same way to show how our computers and programs are interfaced. Marjorie, is that information available?"

## Information Management

"I asked our MIS manager yesterday. He was embarrassed to tell me he didn't know. But he agreed that it's costing us too much to keep the applications aligned. There are so many hooks and translators that every time one application is upgraded, several people spend months updating interfaces."

Frank looks around the room and says, "I'm beginning to understand that our challenges are both human and technical, in a way I hadn't expected. How can we ever expect to move toward a virtual organization when we don't have a good handle on our information management?"

Frank continues, "Wesley, what is the prime output of your engineers?"

"That's simple," responds Wesley. "They produce workable prototypes that are then given to manufacturing together with the release documentation."

"Does this mean," asks Frank, "that the engineers think primarily in terms of a physical product? How readily usable is the information they provide with the prototype?"

"Do you want to know the truth?" asks Vincent.

Frank nods his head.

"You would be surprised how difficult it is to take the engineering documentation and turn it into effective process plans. There's missing data. The test specifications usually aren't included with the drawings. Often the parts and boards can't be produced as they were drawn. We must return to engineering with a long list of requested changes," complains Vincent.

"And Vincent just sees part of the problem," adds Gregory. "In the service department we suffer from lack of timely documentation. We often don't know what revision level to work on."

Frank jumps back into the discussion. "I suspect there are other problems. Vincent, I've also heard you complain about how difficult it is to take CAD data and use it to drive your equipment. Are we suffering from an unsorted and spaghetti-like maze of interconnections between applications?"

Several of the vice-presidents nod their heads.

"I'm beginning to realize the need to change our expectation patterns," says Frank. "Wesley, what if we said your engineers are expected to provide *useful digital data* to the other functions rather than just prototypes? What if in developing your CAD drawing, you could strip out the bills of material to send to purchasing, strip out the geometry to be used directly in our numerically controlled equipment, and strip out the test specifications to feed to the testers?"

Wesley winces. "The other departments aren't ready. They wouldn't know what to do with the data if we provided it all."

Tempers rise.

The only one who remains calm is Frank. He says, "I've read and heard much about the 'factories of the future' and how they're going to change everything. But I seldom if ever read anything about what to do with a company's existing systems that have been pieced and patched together with rubber bands and bailing wire. If we want to use our people as virtual resources, we're going to have to do a lot of sorting out of our existing systems. This is going to be hard work. Perhaps we should begin, as I suggested at our first meeting, by looking more closely at the existing patterns of interaction between people and application systems. We can then discover the patterns we have to deal with."

Cooler heads begin to prevail. The vice-presidents realize that they need to see how they actually operate, in terms of both interactions between people and applications interfacing. This is the only way they will find out where communication has broken down.

## Peer-to-Peer Interaction

Marjorie speaks up. "We're not going to solve our many problems by continuing to work as we have been. I've just noticed something powerful in your circular model, Alan. Even though the official hierarchy remains intact, the circular model really highlights the peer-to-peer nature of relationships. It's not power but knowledge that's the key element."

The group listens closely to Marjorie as she continues. "Our task as leaders is to facilitate the interaction between key people in each of the functions. We have to spend time with our people and get to know their abilities. Have you realized how little time we typically spend in deeper conversations with our people, listening to their experiences and aspirations?"

"Remember the hierarchical chart you tore up, Frank?" asks Marjorie. "I now realize that we've typically defined the job requirements of the boxes, and if we find a person who has enough qualifications, we plug him or her into the slot. We've really been focusing on the function, not the person. What if we reverse this process? If we create centers of excellence in marketing, engineering, manufacturing, finance, service, and human resources and staff them with able people, our challenge becomes one of pooling the right resources to get the task done. We'll have to rely on the teams to do their own fine-tuning of their efforts."

"Thanks, Marjorie," responds Alan. "I see how we can use the circular model and pull people together to work on the many 'sorting out' problems we're presently facing. We can experiment with a new style of working that can then be used on a daily basis with almost all our operations to support new product development, the introduction of a new generation of process technology, or the building of a customized marketing response."

## Empower, Not Power

Vincent nearly shouts, "So often in the past I've been preoccupied with my *power*. Instead, what I really need to do is *empower* my people. The hundreds of little decisions they make each day are what improves the enterprise and determines our profitability."

Alan redraws his diagram, this time adding multiple cross-functional multilevel task teams around the circle.

"Notice," says Alan, standing at the flip chart, "that each of the little squares can be identified by name, so it's easy to see who is participating on each of the task teams whether they are working with clients or on project tasks. This chart gives visibility to the invisible. Usually task teams are created but remain invisible to the rest of the organization, unless they have very high-level participants. Moreover, these teams are often unaware of the other teams. In spite of the multiple teams, it seems everyone still looks to the CEO to solve all the major problems."

Wesley looks pensive. "I now realize why a company so often has difficulty acting decisively in the marketplace. Often, too many expectations are placed on the CEO. The CEO is expected to be infinitely wise, with nerves of steel and an ability to mobilize the company on a moment's notice. This is extremely difficult if the organization itself isn't made up of strong people who can work well together."

Everyone looks at Frank as Wesley continues to speak. "Moreover, when the organization works in a sequential manner, using a series of handoffs, it is easy for things to fall between the cracks. Much of the energy of the organization is absorbed in the border skirmishes between functions. Rather than empowering and encouraging one another, the functions tend to sap one another's strength. This often leads to clumsy and poorly timed market responses."

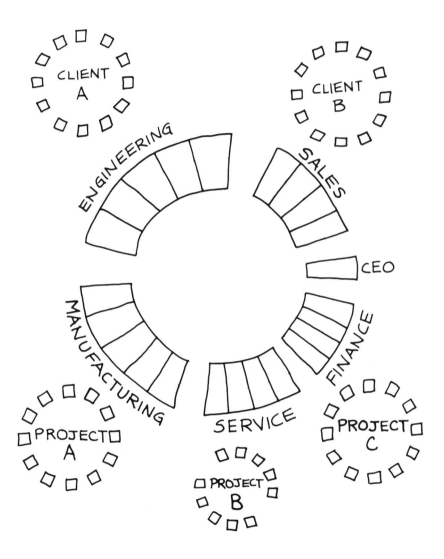

Frank smiles. "People expect too much of the CEO. He or she is expected to be able to leap tall buildings in a single bound. But that's an illusion. It takes a building full of people to throw the CEO that high. Strong people.

"But a building full of strong people may spend all their time fighting with each other unless their energy is properly harnessed, which is what we've been attempting to work out this week.

"Until now I've never known who in this company was working on what at any given time—except theoretically, of course, on the organizational chart. Now, finally, I can envision calling up a listing of task teams on my computer screen and seeing who is on which team, what they're working on, their project plans, budgets, status, and so on. It opens up a whole new world for me.

"Of course, I'll have to resist the temptation to micro-manage by calling people and telling them what to do. That would squelch the team idea. Instead, I'll lead by asking questions. Professionals love questions. I'll try to ask only high-quality questions, because professionals hate commands. They like to rise to the occasion and show how much they know rather than showing how obedient they can be."

He looks intently at Wes. Everyone laughs.

Frank continues. "My job will also be to work with Marjorie and Alan in making adjustments in our accounting and reward policies so we'll be more supportive of task teams."

## Vision and Knowledge: Context and Resources

"We'll all work toward sharpening our enterprise vision and making sure the teams contribute to our pool of knowledge." He adds haloes of "knowledge" and "vision" to the chart.

"We'll do this by articulating and challenging that vision, making knowledge readily available to anyone, near or far, who needs it, and by encouraging open and honest dialogue by rewarding creative participation.

"Team coordination will come from our work as a management team, supporting and nurturing the task teams. We'll challenge them to sharpen their own focus and to help us with the enterprise vision as we deal with the multiple themes of customer expectations.

"As the cross-functional teams work together, they'll begin to *pull in* the appropriate technology needed to get their jobs done. This will be a

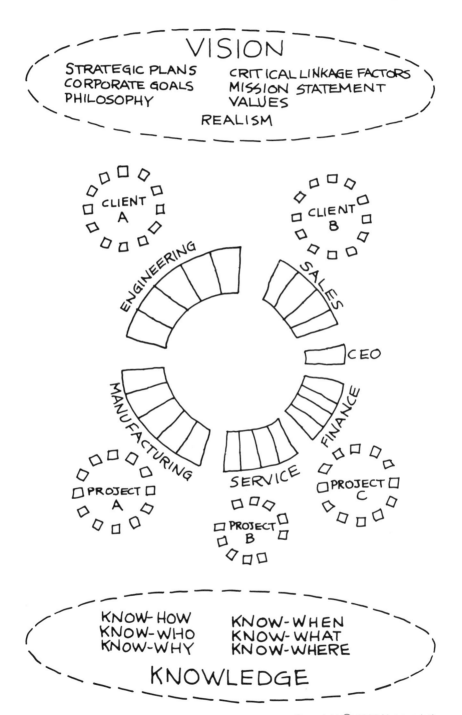

tremendous relief. As things work now, one department champions one solution while another chooses something else. They magnify the vendor's claims out of all rational bounds. I wish I had kept a list of the promises made with the capital requests I've received over the last five years. Had they all proved true, we'd be on the Fortune 100 list rather than the Fortune 500 list."

Vincent is a little skeptical. "I fear our people will drown in the 'groupness' of the teams. What will happen to individual initiative?"

Alan smiles, realizing that manufacturing operations in most organizations are made up of fire fighters. "Is your definition of individual creativity one that allows heroes to emerge to put out the fires of inefficient operations?"

Vincent looks the other way, recognizing the truth in Alan's question.

Wesley interjects, "The task teams will encourage both individual and group creativity. They represent a statement of trust in our people, a statement of respect, and a statement of challenge. If they don't, in turn, trust, respect, and challenge one another, they'll never get their work done on time and within budget. This environment can't help but breed creativity, tempered by realism and a strong sense of direction."

"I like those thoughts after all," admits Vincent. "We'll be able to leverage our assets much more effectively. It pains me to see us not using our people's knowledge. It pains me to see us so slow in ramping up production. It pains me to see us failing to leverage the capital investments we've already made. And it pains me to see us with such timid visions."

Vincent responds, "It would hardly be worth the effort. The old hierarchical organization has hidden so much from view. It creates unintended expectations of importance. It clouds the real issues so they're never clearly seen. And it has an open bottom where all sorts of learning has fallen out, never to be captured in a useful form."

As Vincent is talking, Alan points to the "vision" and "knowledge" elements on the model. "Without these elements it would be hard to keep the task teams' efforts in focus. They make it possible for the functions to work in parallel in task-focusing teams on the "smile" curve which we discussed on Wednesday."

Frank turns to the others and asks, "Do you feel you can manage this organization?"

A mixed chorus of "Yeses" goes around the room.

"Next year at this time, remind me to ask you again to rate our responsiveness index. I think that'll be interesting.

"One last thing." From his briefcase Frank pulls a sheet of paper with a long strip of clear tape down the middle. It's the torn organizational chart, now resurrected.

"After we adjourned on Monday, I fished this out of the trash. I wasn't sure what we would end up doing with it—or without it.

"But we've come a long way since Monday. And now it's time to give it a proper sendoff. We don't need the box-and-lines chart any longer. It was too confining. We've preserved the nominal hierarchy, but cast it in a circular form where it is easier to focus on the interaction of knowledgeable people. We no longer have to work sequentially, but can work in parallel with one another on multiple task teams."

Frank turns to Wesley. "Wesley: lighter, please."

He ignites a corner of the sheet and drops it, flaming, into the trash can. As they watch, the old organizational chart is consumed in a volcano of energy, knowledge, and vision.

**Book 2**

# Integrating
# Enterprises through
# Human Networking

# CHAPTER
# 6

# Introduction: The Past and Future

The case study of Custom Products and Services in Book 1 shows some of the challenges before us. Frank Giardelli realizes he cannot continue to stuff computers into his existing organization and expect to leverage value out of these investments. As he looks at the last five years, he knows he cannot get ahead without redefining the organizational context.

Giardelli and the vice-presidents understand that their biggest challenge is to manage complexity rather than just cost and time. The swirling multiple interrelationships, both internal and external, are often more chaotic than orderly. Only if the creative abilities of the people—employees, professionals, and managers—in the firm are unleashed can they expect to respond effectively to the multiple challenges of the market. Finely tuned bureaucracies with carefully defined policies, procedures, and job descriptions are no match for the next decade. They are too confining and rigid and are always out of alignment with the market. They cannot maintain a creative dialogue with their suppliers and customers.

In their place Giardelli and the others realize that they must establish visions, values, and norms that can define the context and provide both resiliency and direction.

Giardelli knows it is not enough to just look up and envision the "dream organization" of the future, because the legacy of their past assumptions, attitudes, and decisions will turn their dreams into nightmares. To get ahead, they must look at the future and the past at the same time.

In Book 2 we explore the management challenges of the next decade, but we also take a long hard look at the past, the ideas and assumptions of the early and late industrial eras. This past is still very much a part of our thinking, conditioning our technical and business reflexes. We can only master our desired future if we can sort out our past. Yet the ideas and assumptions of this past which flows with us are largely bankrupt.

## Bankruptcy of the Industrial Era

The constellation of traditional assumptions, principles, and values of the industrial era is bankrupt. This bankruptcy will not be overcome simply with an infusion of new computer-based technology.

Agricultural-era principles could not cope with the onset of machinery-based technology. New forms of management and work were developed to leverage the power of the steam engine and all its derivatives. The industrial era used new principles to divide work, reward people, and control activities.

Steep hierarchies, the creation of the late industrial era, are under extreme pressure. They cannot provide the flexibility and responsiveness needed in our increasingly competitive global markets. Instead, there is a need for more effective integration within companies and between themselves and their suppliers, partners, and customers.

Flatter network enterprises are beginning to emerge in their place. This networking has two dimensions: (1) the technical infrastructure which links computer systems and people, and (2) the human process of networking with other people.

We are fascinated by the wonders of local and wide-area networking technology. This technology is allowing us to interface applications, processes, databases, and people in new ways. Networking technology is absolutely essential if we hope to build agile enterprises, but it is not enough by itself.

Human networking is at the core of the integrative process. It is an ongoing process of reaching out to one another to form multiple cross-functional work teams. We do not only need teams, but "teamwork of teams" and "networks of teams." These are new challenges, laden with many hidden surprises. But the early industrial era also had more than its share of "gotchas" encountered while people were figuring out how to harness the new technologies.

In steep hierarchies, work is broken down into smaller steps and different people are assigned to carry out these activities. They are structured according to "superior-subordinate" relationships. Everyone has a boss who determines what activities are to be carried out and how.

In a networking environment, people reach out to one another to work on whole sets of challenges in teams and clusters of teams in distributed environments across functional and organizational boundaries. Network enterprises build upon "peer-to-peer" relationships. People are expected to take initiatives, based upon their understanding of an agreed-upon context.

It has often been assumed that it is only a matter of time before computers and networking replace most people in our companies, as though people are the expendable item. Although fewer people will be needed to run our companies, this assumption of expendability is misguided.

A sober realism is overtaking our naive fascination with computers. As we understand their limitations, we are beginning to appreciate human capabilities even more. For example, artificial intelligence and expert systems have not delivered what some had promised, primarily because rule-based systems have difficulty in capturing the larger *context* in which activities must be understood.

The reemergence of interest in neural networking is indicative of a deeper appreciation of our human capability to see and respond to *multiple patterns* in real time. Instead of seeing the mind as a machine or even as a computer, neural networking starts with a more humble appreciation of the wonder of the networking capability of the billions of neurons in the human brain. Our human minds are able to see, interpret, reinterpret, and act on multiple patterns of impressions.[1] As we realize that the best databases are in people's heads, our challenge is to learn to network our visions and knowledge in new and creative ways.

How ironic that our quest for new forms of computer technology has increased our appreciation of human and team capabilities. Although people are able to communicate across the hall or around the world with the speed of light, thanks to computer networks, human distrust slows real communication to a snail's pace. Computer applications are accessible anywhere on the network, but not all departments have a common bill of materials. How are we to respond to the growing chasm between our technological capabilities and organizational lethargy?

Just as the dropping apple jolted Newton into a realization of gravity, a force which has been with us from the beginning of time, so too our technological advances are shaking the roots of our assumptions about work and work organization. In the turmoil, we are discovering a whole new set of management challenges.

## Management Challenges of the Next Decade

As Giardelli and the vice-presidents realized, their traditional bag of tricks, developed and honed during the industrial era, is inadequate for the knowledge era. They are not alone, for executives in Europe, Asia, Africa, Australia, and the Americas are facing a whole new set of management challenges:

1. How do we move beyond the extreme *fragmentation* of industrial-era companies?

2. How do we maintain *accountability* in flat, dynamic network organizations?

3. How do we support the *focusing and coordination* of multiple cross-functional task teams?

4. How do we build into the very structure of the organization the capacity for *continual learning?*

We have all experienced organizational fragmentation, where various functional departments focus only on their own tasks and ignore the concerns of others. It is clear that this fragmentation has to be bridged, because fragmented companies cannot deal with the rich complexity of global economies.

As we flatten the organization, the span of control increases. It is no longer as easy to look after all subordinates. Therefore, a new accountability strategy is needed, especially in a technically networked enterprise. Without a strong accountability strategy, it is easy for individuals and groups to go off in many different directions or get bogged down in swamp-like "group gropes."

The engineering, manufacturing, finance, marketing, sales, and service functions are being asked to work in parallel. In manufacturing, concurrent engineering is challenging design engineers and manufacturing engineers to develop products and processes together. Similar trends are emerging in the service sectors such as the changes being made in investment banking.[2] As people work more in multiple cross-functional teams, they will need to be more self-directing and self-learning. Moreover, they will need to coordinate their activities with other task teams, while also sharing their insights and experiences.

When these various task team efforts are under way, there will be a great deal of learning. Too often this learning disappears into the ether with no net to catch it. Yet it is an invaluable corporate asset. One of the challenges of the knowledge era is to capture individual and team learning on a continuing basis, making it available to others in the enterprise. "Time-to-learning" is as critical as "time-to-market."

## Key Concepts

Several years ago the press feasted on the Japanese fifth generation computer initiative.[3] It was feared they would wrestle the lead in high technology from the rest of the world by unleashing the power of the microchip through parallel processing. This discussion diverted our attention from the real challenge: to unleash the power in human minds so that, working together, we can recognize and respond to the ever-changing demands of the market.

Fifth generation management is not concerned with new ways of manipulating subordinates to one's advantage. Instead, it challenges us to rethink the basics: our values, attitudes, and assumptions about leadership, work, and time. It points to an elegantly simple understanding: We need to be in touch with ourselves—our visions, knowledge, thoughts, and feelings—and with one another in new and creative ways. And it assumes that the various functions are capable of working in parallel through virtual task-focusing teams. In short, fifth-generation management is a question of leadership. It is not preoccupied with one's own power, but with how we *empower, energize* and *enable* one another. It presupposes an integrative environment.

The word *integration* has taken on a special mystique, especially thanks to our fascination with computer integrated manufacturing (CIM) and computer integrated enterprise (CIE). CIM and CIE assume, in some people's minds, that we are headed toward the "paperless and peopleless factory."[4] Some argue that automation, combined with computers, will make it possible for a few top executives to sit in their "command and control centers" and, with the aid of a few professionals, direct the day-to-day operations of the firm. After all, the hardware and software will have been connected together in one *automated* and *integrated* whole, from board-room to shop floor. Strategic planning will be aided by executive decision support systems connected to operations planning, with orders being passed through computer-aided design systems to scheduling and numerical control programming on the shop floor.

This vision of CIM and CIE is a dead end because it leaves people out of the equation, and people are what give an organization its flexibility and creativity.

Let us take another look at the meaning of *integration*. It seems to mean everything to everyone. It is often used as a synonym for connectivity (including interoperability) and interfacing. When the terms are blurred together, confusion follows. There are clear distinctions between the three terms, as shown in Figure 6.1.

Connectivity                    Interfacing                    Integrating

Figure 6.1  **Distinguishing the discontinuity between connectivity, interfacing, and integrating**

It is one thing to connect offices or locations through telephone or computer networks and to interface applications; it is something else entirely to integrate organizations. Connectivity and interfacing leave the organization pretty much as is, while integration changes the way organizations work.

*Integration* comes from the root *integer*. An integer is a whole number. It is not a fraction. The word *integer* comes from the Latin roots *in* = in and *tangere* = to touch. An integer is that which is in touch with itself. Many think of integration just in terms of physical connectivity. This is only a portion of the challenge.

The problem in many companies is that they function as a "collection of fractions." Engineering sees only a fraction of the constraints under which manufacturing operates. Manufacturing does not appreciate the serviceability constraints the field is under. Finance does not quite realize the artificiality of its desire to continue to burden direct labor. And too often top management has only a fractional understanding of what really goes on down on the shop floor. The real task of integration is to bring together, to put in touch cross-functionally, the creative thinking within and between enterprises in order to deal with whole challenges and opportunities. Connectivity and interfacing will not solve this problem.

Many companies have very fragmented views of their futures. There is little alignment across functions. Many managers are not in touch with the talent in their own departments. Too many are asked to fight fires, perform busywork, and do as they are told—not as they think. There are fractions, fractions, and more fractions.

Although *hierarchies* have been around for ages, steep hierarchies arose in the business world in the 1880s as a creation of the late industrial era. These structures embody fractional thinking, whereby everyone has narrowly defined and mutually exclusive areas of responsibility, much as the gears of a machine each have their assigned roles.

*Network* is used in two different ways: (1) as a noun referring to a physical system of interconnecting elements, such as computer nodes and people, through electronic means, and (2) as an active verb, *to network*, to get in touch with ourselves, our vision and knowledge, and one another to deal with whole issues.

As used in this book, *integration* and *networking* complement each other. They refer to an ongoing process rather than a static state of affairs. I avoid the term "network*ed*" because it assumes that it is possible to establish a networked environment once and for all. Instead, I prefer the terms *networking, integrating,* and *integrative* because they underscore the continuous nature of integration, which configures and reconfigures people and resources. The *integrative process* puts us in touch with the whole, with one another, with customers, and with suppliers in ever-changing patterns of relationships. It also puts us in touch with our own wills, emotions, and knowledge. The integrative process is a process of human networking: networking our visions and knowledge so we can take decisive action in concert with other efforts.

A good technically networked infrastructure is fast becoming a precondition for marketplace success. Even more important, however, is our human ability to network with one another on real business and technical issues. As we get better at this kind of networking, the need for the rigid command superstructure of steep hierarchies will fade.

## From Steep Hierarchies to Human Networking

We have been plagued by those who take the official organizational chart, with its boxes and lines, too seriously. These traditional managers feel they must protect their *turf* (empire, territory, stovepipe, area of responsibility, or assignment). Their parochial interests often lead to debilitating political battles. This is why Giardelli realizes that he needs to tear his organizational chart in two.

A management strategy based on "command and control" is giving way to one centered on "focusing and coordinating" multiple cross-functional teams. As people come to understand themselves as resources capable of reaching out and participating on "multiple task-focused teams," to use Peter Drucker's term, we will be able to focus and coordinate enterprise resources more effectively.[5]

Ken Olsen, founder and CEO of Digital Equipment Corporation, envisions these changes:

> But above all, we believe that we're taking part in changing the way organizations work. From our point of view, the companies that will survive are going to move from an environment of management control to one that allows a large number of people, all using their creative ability, their education, and their motivation, to take part.
>
> Now, this change won't be easy. But it has to come. And we're convinced that computer networking will be at the heart of these changes ... and the vehicle through which these changes are carried out.[6]

Olsen understands the need to nurture and grow the creative abilities, talents, and motivation of those in the enterprise, freeing them from the constraining control systems of the past. Computer networking makes it possible to integrate whole organizations around the world, allowing them to deliver quality goods and services in a more timely and targeted manner. This becomes especially critical as the combination of time-to-market and time-to-learning becomes a key differentiating factor in the competitive environment. A sense of *timing*, not just time, is also becoming essential for market success. Bringing products or services to market quickly does not help if they are the wrong ones.

A recognition of the increasing importance of the human element in the enterprise seems to be erupting spontaneously in many different areas. A number of Europeans, such as Professor Paul Kidd, are writing about "human-centered CIM systems (HCIM)."[7] In Japan, Kazuto Togino, president of Komatsu Electronic Metals, has introduced the concept of "human integrated manufacturing" for many of the same reasons that Europeans are talking about HCIM.[8]

As Olsen has stressed, networking is making it possible to develop new forms of organization and new management approaches to put us in touch with one another and with ourselves in new and significant ways. The task of the 1990s is to build networked infrastructures and adjust our mindsets so that, working together, we will be adroit in our thinking and flexible in our actions. Olsen's vision is of an "elegantly simple" enterprise.

In contrast, the automationist approach presupposes the computerization of steep hierarchies. Communication within these steep hierarchies is, by definition, "confusingly complex" because of all the little kingdoms through which one must go to resolve an issue. Automating and computerizing existing organizations, with all their distrust, petty politics, and disjointedness, only makes the mess faster, not better.

Network organizations operate by a different set of dynamics. They may become elegantly simple organizations. At first blush, elegant simplicity sounds like a contradiction. "Elegance" implies a good deal of sophistication, while "simplicity" seems to be its opposite. Yet when automobiles changed from manual to automatic transmissions, they went to an elegantly simple driver interface. The automatic transmission is elegant and complex, but the interface with the driver is simple.

An elegantly simple organization is one that is easy for customers, suppliers, and distributors to interact with because of its sophistication. Rarely do things fall through the cracks. People do not trip over one another. Action is crisp and decisive. There is responsiveness to the market. And there is integrity, because people have to be able to count on each other's word.

## The Broadening Scope of Management

Traditionally, management theory has focused on relationships internal to the firm. Everyone's place can be clearly defined, and reporting relationships are clear. The shift to a broader enterprise perspective introduces a whole new set of dynamics.

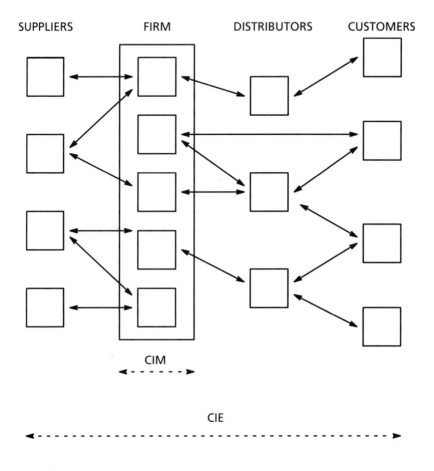

Figure 6.2 **Scope of CIM and CIE**

The relationships between firms and their partners, suppliers, distributors, and customers is one of peer-to-peer relationships (Figure 6.2). These relationships are different from the superior-subordinate relationships in steep hierarchies. Instead, the external relationships are based on trust and mutual benefit. There has to be careful listening, respect, and integrity among the parties involved.

Certainly Just-in-Time (JIT) and Total Quality relationships are not possible between cooperating partners without a good deal of openness and respect. As companies link themselves through electronic data interchange (EDI), they are starting to share long-range plans and purchasing intent, something which was unheard of just a few years ago.

This shift in perspectives is forcing a reevaluation of traditional command and control theory. It is not possible to command external resources in the same way in which internal resources can be dominated. Instead, the fine art of alliance building between peers becomes critical.

CIM focuses primarily on the interaction of functions within a firm. CIE puts this interaction within the larger context of the firm's set of relationships; it represents the extended enterprise. Computer networking both enables and demands the exchange of information within the firm and among firms. For example, aerospace firms are linking themselves in multiple networks with other prime contractors and their subcontractors, as well as with the government.

In the CIE environment, business success will increasingly depend on the knowledge resources of the firms rather than on their fixed capital. We are witnessing a shift in the sources of wealth between two eras, the industrial era and the knowledge era.

## Chapter Focuses

In order to understand this shift, we must place the discussion within a larger historical context and include the sources of wealth, types of organization, and conceptual principles which underlie the industrial and knowledge eras. These elements will be discussed in greater detail in subsequent chapters; the focus of each chapter is indicated by the chapter number in Figure 6.3.

Chapter 7 discusses the five generations of computers and managements and relates them to the historical eras. It is also suggestive of several visions of the type of organization which lie beyond the organizational bottleneck. Chapter 8 explores the attempts to computerize existing steep hierarchies. Chapter 9 looks at the conceptual principles of the early and late industrial eras, while Chapter 10 discusses those of the early knowledge era. The transition between the industrial and knowledge eras

is the focus of Chapter 11; Chapter 12 discusses ten practical considerations in managing knowledge-era enterprises.

## Historical Eras

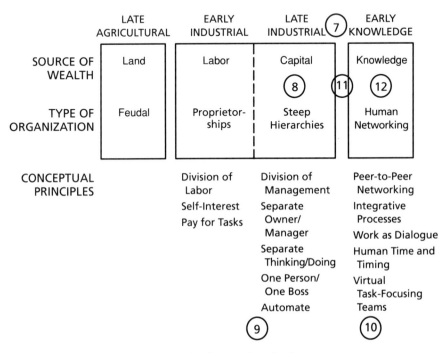

Figure 6.3  **The focus of each chapter**

This discussion picks up many of the themes introduced in the
dialogue in Book 1. The repetition of themes, or iteration of ideas, is part
of the process of unlearning, learning, and relearning basic relationships.
The shift from the industrial to knowledge eras is primarily one of
attitudes, values, and norms. It can only come through a struggle of
thought, because most of the changes are counterintuitive. We are so
conditioned by the vocabulary of the industrial era that it is often difficult
to think in new terms. We continually need to look at the past and future,
re-sorting our knowledge and expanding our visions.

# 7

# Five Generations of Computers and Management

The evolution of computers offers an interesting parallel to what we are being challenged to do organizationally.[1] Computers are breaking out of a bottleneck created by the architectural assumptions of the initial computer era. Business organizations are also up against a bottleneck created, in part, by the success of the industrial era. Can we break out?

## Generations of Computers

In the early 1980s, the Japanese, under MITI (Ministry for International Trade and Industry) initiated their fifth generation computer project. It created quite a stir and sparked similar initiatives in the United States and Europe: MCC (Microelectronic Computer Center) and ESPRIT (European Strategic Program for Research and Development in Information Technology). The five generations of computer technology are defined in Figure 7.1.[2]

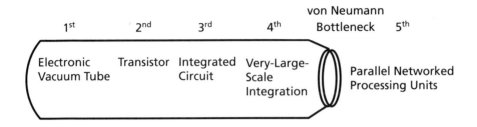

Figure 7.1 **Generations of computer technology**

Computers of the first four generations pass all information through a single central processing unit (CPU). This single CPU has been described as the "von Neumann bottleneck," named after John von Neumann, mathematician and computer pioneer.

According to von Neumann's 1945 paper, "First Draft of a Report on EDVAC (Electronic Discrete Variable Computer)," the computer needs five key components: a central arithmetic logic unit, a central control unit to orchestrate operations, a memory unit, an input unit, and an output unit.[3] It should use binary numbers, operate electronically, and perform its operations one at a time, or sequentially. COBOL, FORTRAN, BASIC, C, and other computer languages have followed this strategy of stepping through their programs in a sequential manner, although some languages are now being adapted for parallel work.

The key to the fifth generation computer, parallel processing, is in the networking of multiple processing units. In parallel processing, two or more interconnected processors simultaneously process different portions of the same application. This linking provides a new challenge: to divide the problem so that the multiple processors can work on portions of the same problem concurrently, then piece together the solution. Parallel processing is opening up a whole new frontier of exploration because of its speed.

In addition to parallel processing, networking is making it possible to run multiple applications in parallel on different computer processors by linking distributed databases together on a network. Not only the computer but also people and applications can begin to work in parallel, especially as we develop more effective user interfaces.

The computer industry is developing common windowing interfaces which allow users to open multiple windows and interact with several different applications concurrently, wherever they may be on the computer network. This makes it possible for departments to work in parallel: Design engineers, manufacturing engineers, and marketing specialists can look at the same drawings, process plans, and market projects at the same time, even if they are widely separated in distance. Through voice or electronic mail they can discuss alternatives to the design, process plans, and marketing strategy in an iterative and interactive manner.

## Generations of Management

Fifth generation computing and networking make possible new ways of working together, but organizational assumptions too often block effective use of this technology. We are still wedded to the organizational forms that evolved to meet the needs of the Industrial Revolution.

As the industrial era began, proprietorships emerged as a convenient way to organize people, resources, and technology. After about a hundred years, steep hierarchies developed. More recently we have attempted to matrix these hierarchies to increase cross-functional communication. And now we are interfacing people and applications with the use of computer-based networking.

Just as computers have outgrown their initial single-CPU architecture, so too management is facing its own bottleneck. If we can break through, then we can enable, empower, and energize the creative abilities of the people in our enterprises.

Figure 7.2 shows the five generations of management[4] and illustrates the dilemma that we face.

In the first four generations of enterprise management, raw materials and information are passed *serially* from one department or function to the next. Fifth generation management makes it possible for the functional departments to work in *parallel* through the use of multiple task-focusing teams. But in order to achieve this parallel capability, we must break through a bottleneck created by our acceptance of the assumptions implicit in Adam Smith's pin-making factory with its division and subdivision of labor,[5] reinforced by Frederick Winslow Taylor's theories of Scientific Management,[6] and Henri Fayol's fourteen principles,[7] which set the rationale for the unity of command, span of control, and scalar principles used in today's industrial-era organizations.

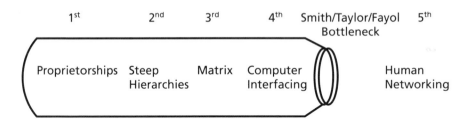

Figure 7.2 **Generations of management**

Fayol's fourth principle, unity of command, suggests that people cannot bear dual command; it is a key underpinning of the sequential operation of steep hierarchies. Fayol also emphasized division of work, authority, and responsibility; unity of direction; centralization; the scalar chain; and order (a place for everyone and everyone in his place)—all of which reinforce the rigidity and bureaucracy of our steep hierarchies.[8] The assumptions behind these principles lead to a simple calculus of importance: The higher up a person is, the more important that person appears to be, as illustrated in Figure 7.3.

This model of the calculus of importance assumes that "thinking" goes on at the top of the corporation and "doing" at the bottom; information is sucked up and summarized through executive support systems, so top management can make the right decisions. The irony of this model is that those who add value to the product are usually the least valued in the organization.

The model also supports the idea that power is concentrated at the top of the hierarchy, and it assumes the traditional series of sequential handoffs from one function to another. Research has shown that this visualization of the hierarchical model is, in most companies, a fantasy.[9] Many products and services, especially in the aerospace, automobile, and financial service industries, require a high degree of coordination among functions. Real business problems are not easily fragmented into the cubbyholes of functional hierarchies.

Figure 7.3 **Hierarchy and calculus of importance**

This realization was one of the forces leading to the initial widespread acceptance of the matrix model. Third generation management, the matrix organization, attempts to overcome some of the problems inherent in second generation management by breaking away from Fayol's unity of command, the notion of "one person/one boss." In a matrix organization, two or more managers share power over a single subordinate. This allows the organization to encompass multiple dimensions at the same time, whether they are functions, products, geographic areas, markets, or any combination of these factors. Although matrix organizations have been widely used by some companies, they have not come to terms with the underlying model of the steep hierarchy articulated by Fayol.

Stanley Davis, who in 1976 coauthored with Paul Lawrence one of the basic texts on matrix organizations,[10] now recognizes the inadequacy of this approach. Davis says that the matrix organization has "never truly lived up to its promise."[11] Although it continues in limited form, it has never adequately addressed the issue of the distribution of power. More often than not, the matrix is simply grafted onto the hierarchical structure without changing the existing system's rewards, accounting approach, or power distribution.

Davis realizes that no management approach has evolved to replace the "singular industrial hierarchy," the steep hierarchy, because we have not figured out a way to resolve conflicts among two or more bosses. Here Davis has put his finger on the dilemma we face. The one person/one boss approach is inadequate, but if this is given up, how do we manage accountability? What holds the organization together? How is responsibility assigned?

Davis suggests that the best management structure to replace the hierarchy is networking, because it relies "not on an informal web of personal contacts, but on a technological web of information handling systems."[12] Is Davis giving us a glimpse of the fourth or fifth generation organization? Is it really information handling systems that are needed, or do we not need to give visibility to the multiple cross-functional task teams that really get the work done?

Fourth generation management uses computers and networking to interface the various functions, both horizontally and vertically. This is often incorrectly called "integration" because the disparate parts of the company are connected with one another. Most of what is going on now leaves the formal organizational structure unchanged and simply adds connectivity and interfacing between the boxes (functions and departments), using translators (software) to facilitate communication and interoperability among application programs where necessary.

Ironically, as we stated earlier, we are busy stuffing third, fourth, and fifth generation computer technology into second generation organizations, steep hierarchies (Figure 7.4). To be sure, some of this technology is being introduced in matrixed and interfaced organizations, but unfortunately, these organizational modes are still hierarchical at their core.

If we hope to put advanced computer-based technology into fifth generation management organizations, we must pay more attention to the unique characteristics of integrative enterprises based on human networking. We need to find a way to break through the Smith/Taylor/Fayol bottleneck. We must develop fifth generation management capabilities in our enterprises through human networking so we will be able to leverage our knowledge much more effectively than we do now.[13]

Part of the problem in breaking out of second generation management organizations is an attitudinal one. We put too much faith in the computer and not enough in ourselves. Real integration is people dependent. It is not possible to put "integrative enterprises" on automatic pilot and expect them to run themselves.

True integration is an ongoing process; it is fragile and requires continual nurturing. It is more dependent on the values of the enterprise and the integrity of those employed than on the quality of the computer systems chosen. As cross-functional teams are configured and reconfigured, respect, trust, and honesty between people are essential. Game playing stymies effective teamwork.

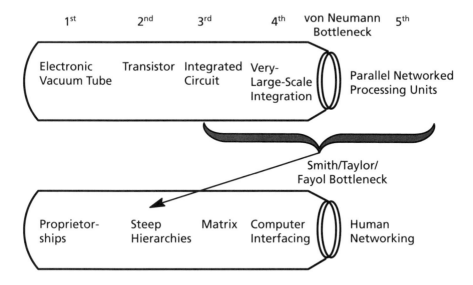

Figure 7.4 **Third, fourth, and fifth generation computer technology being grafted onto second generation management**

We have not taken our own history seriously enough, nor have we understood the major shifts between historical eras. Second generation management was ideally suited to the late industrial era, while fifth generation management will help us leverage our individual and organizational knowledge for the new knowledge era.

The first four generations of management are a creation of the industrial era. Only as we get beyond them can we expect to tap the fuller potential of both our people- and computer-based systems.

## Historical Eras

Each historical era has had its dominant form of wealth and its unique form of organization. In the West, the wealth of the late agricultural era rested in the land. People and resources were organized by the feudal system. As the early industrial era began about 1780 with the invention of the steam engine, the source of wealth shifted to labor, and proprietorships became a key form of organization. In the 1880s, with the advent of the railroads, telephone, and telegraph companies, wealth relied more and more upon capital. Moreover, as large national corporations emerged, steep hierarchies began to displace proprietorships.

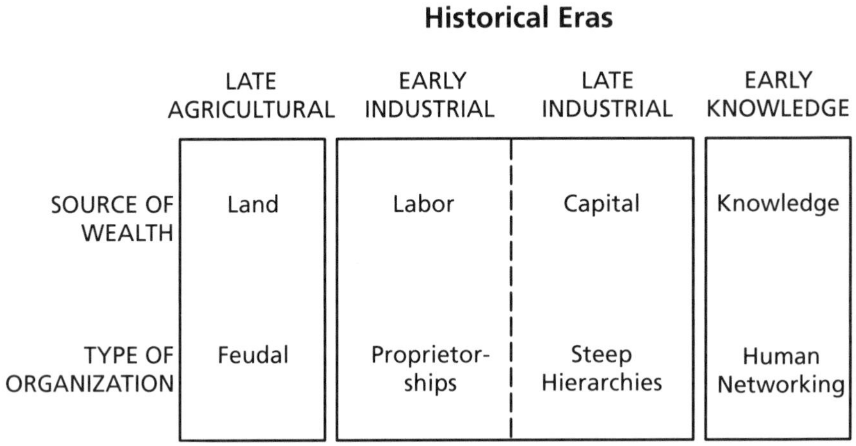

## Historical Eras

| | LATE AGRICULTURAL | EARLY INDUSTRIAL | LATE INDUSTRIAL | EARLY KNOWLEDGE |
|---|---|---|---|---|
| SOURCE OF WEALTH | Land | Labor | Capital | Knowledge |
| TYPE OF ORGANIZATION | Feudal | Proprietor-ships | Steep Hierarchies | Human Networking |

Figure 7.5  Sources of wealth and types of organizations

There was a major discontinuity between the agricultural and industrial eras, as people unlearned the old and learned to interact in new ways. New ideas of roles and responsibilities displaced the old feudal models. Now, in the 1990s, we are witnessing the beginning of another era, the early knowledge era. It is again a time of discontinuity, although we do not readily recognize the need to unlearn industrial-era values and assumptions. We are still very much under the spell of the late industrial era, and it is hard to break through the bottleneck (Figure 7.5).

The transition into the early knowledge era is not necessarily a simple or cumulative process. There are many new principles to be learned, while some of the older principles must be unlearned. The gap between the eras suggests that we will have to work as hard as Frank Giardelli and the vice-presidents to rethink our basic attitudes. Attitudes are often tougher barriers than the strongest bottle, because they are so much a part of everyday life.

During the whaling era, sailors often passed time by rigging elaborately designed sailing ships in tiny glass bottles. In many ways, the industrial era has encased us in a glass bottle. The bottle is barely perceptible because it is the only home we know. We have always expected work life to be confined and confining. We readily accept being stuffed into narrowly defined jobs, as though there were no alternative. The first four generations of management are an artifact of the industrial era. Figure 7.6 shows the interrelationship between the generations of management and the historical eras.

The knowledge era's source of wealth is not just accumulated knowledge but also our human ability to recognize new patterns and interrelate them with the old patterns that flow with us. Like detectives, we are constantly sorting out ideas, impressions, hunches, intuitions, and understanding. We are learning, unlearning, and relearning. We possess the ability to sort out significant patterns in new events. Knowledge is not something that is possessed like a commodity. Instead, it represents a capability to see broad new patterns among fuzzy old ideas and new impressions and relate them in a larger context.

What does it mean when we say that the basis of wealth is shifting from that which is "possessed as a commodity" to a "human capability"? Known facts can be possessed, but the human process of "knowledging" is a much richer and more dynamic phenomenon. This suggests that an organization that helps facilitate the knowledging process will be able to see the significant patterns in the market and respond more effectively than companies that are bogged down in routine bureaucracy.

"Knowledging" is more than just "knowing," because it suggests an active and continual process of interrelating patterns. It is more than the accumulation of and access to information, because it looks at both the known (information) and the visionary (what could be).

Shoshana Zuboff, a professor at Harvard Business School, uses the word "informate" to describe the human challenge of moving from primary experiences to working on multiple levels of abstraction while using the computer.[14] For example, as boiler-room operators shift from manually turning off steam valves to monitoring and regulating pressure at their computer terminals, they must operate through the mediation of the computer. Computer-mediated work, as Zuboff explains, challenges us to work on higher planes of abstraction, the process she defines as "informating."

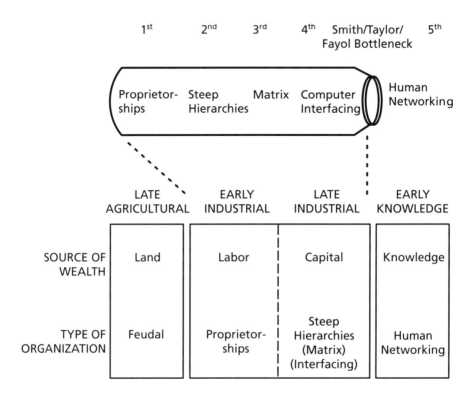

**Figure 7.6 Interrelating generations of management and historical eras**

The creation of a software package, next-generation microprocessor, new financial service, or multiaxis lathe involves both knowledge and vision. Knowledging, the basis of wealth in the knowledge era, is a dynamic and ongoing process that involves our human capabilities to see existing patterns and at the same time envision new patterns.

In the industrial era we have assumed that it is possible to figure out everything ahead of time, divide the work up among various functions, then monitor and control what is done so it meets the expected outcome. Like an ocean liner, the challenge has been to hold the effort on course, making only minor corrections for changes in winds and currents. In applying automation and computer-based solutions to the steep hierarchy, we have assumed that the task is to use these resources to phase out manual operations. Often these efforts have simply automated existing messes, making them faster, not better.

This model is out of synchronization with the changing expectations of the market. Instead of large ocean liners, we need swift runabouts that can customize solutions to particular needs. Our knowledge and capability to see patterns and nuances in patterns becomes the key asset of the enterprise.

The industrial era defined fixed resources. The knowledge era needs to draw upon variable or virtual resources to meet unique market and customer demands in a timely manner by configuring and reconfiguring the appropriate cross-functional task teams.

How much of the knowledge needed to run an enterprise can be captured in a firm's automated systems, applications, databases, and manual procedures? I have asked this question to many different groups. They almost always agree that we cannot capture much more than 30 percent. Some think it is no more than 10 percent. In either case, it is clear that the real knowledge needed to run an enterprise resides in the heads of those working there. The task then becomes one of networking the right people to handle task-focused assignments. In addition, multiple teams must be networked in order to achieve teamwork of teams. This suggests a whole new vision of what might be possible outside the industrial-era bottle.

## Looking Beyond the Bottleneck

It has been seventeen years since Joseph Harrington, Jr., published *Computer Integrated Manufacturing*, Jay Galbraith brought out *Designing Complex Organizations*, and Daniel Bell wrote *The Coming Post-Industrial Society*.[15] Each, in his own way, saw the industrial era being superseded by something new: Harrington envisioned computers linking engineering and manufacturing, Galbraith suggested that matrix organizations would bring more effective integration in complex hierarchies, and Bell predicted that post-industrial society would be organized around knowledge. Each, in his own way, was looking beyond the bottleneck.

Even though Harrington's concept of computer integrated manufacturing (CIM) has become a rallying cry for all sorts of "integration" activities, the concept will hardly sit still long enough for an agreed-upon definition to emerge. Galbraith's concept of the matrix organization has not proved to be the cure-all that was once expected because most power has remained within discrete functions. We are still struggling to understand what an organization based on knowledge instead of land, labor, or capital might be like.

Three recent publications by Peter Drucker, Stanley Davis, and Richard Nolan give some informed insights into the evolving post-industrial organization envisioned by Bell.[16]

## Drucker: Vision of the "New Organization"

Drucker expects businesses of the future to have half as many levels of management as are typical today. They will be knowledge-based and essentially self-directing. The traditional "command and control" model will have little meaning. In short, these businesses will have little resemblance to the businesses of today.[17]

Today work is done in departments or functions. Tomorrow, Drucker suggests, the activities of the business will be carried out by many ad hoc "task-focused teams." The departments will serve as bases of resources, technical and human, and as providers of standards. Instead of working sequentially, the various functions will work together in synchrony, with teams taking projects from inception to market. The emerging organization will go beyond a matrix, thus requiring greater self-discipline and individual responsibility. It will be held together by clear, simple, common objectives and coordinated like a symphony orchestra, but without a score. It will have to write its own music as it goes.

Drucker lists four challenges of these emerging information-based organizations:

1. Developing rewards, recognition, and career opportunities for specialists.

2. Creating a unified vision in an organization of specialists.

3. Devising the management structure for an organization of task forces.

4. Ensuring the supply, preparation, and testing of top management people.[18]

Drucker finds examples of his vision in large symphony orchestras, hospitals, and even the British civil administration in India. He says we can only see dimly the outlines of this new form of organization. Some of its characteristics are known, but "the job of actually building the information-based organization is still ahead of us—it is the managerial challenge of the future."[19] It is likely that we will need to learn how to structure organizations around multiple overlapping networks of teams, instead of simply spinning off ad hoc teams as needed.

## Davis: Networking Will Encompass Hierarchies

Stanley Davis expects a shift in focus from hierarchical organizations to networked ones, although "networks will not replace or supplement hierarchies; rather, the two will be encompassed within a broader conception that embraces both."[20]

What is this broader conception? Davis is only suggestive and adds that we are still struggling to figure out just what this means. He introduces into the discussion new considerations of *time* and *space.* By bringing a vision of the future into the present, present activities take on more directionality. A firm's space does not need to be physically defined by the four walls of its factory or office building, since it can extend through computer terminals right onto the customer's site. Like Drucker, Davis sees a shift from working sequentially to using multiple functions simultaneously.

What do these visions have to do with fifth generation management? First, Drucker's vision places significant new demands on the human component of the organization. Second, the efforts of multiple task-focused teams will need to be continually integrated into the total effort of the enterprise. And Davis suggests that the emerging knowledge-based organization will be built around the *network.*

Fifth generation management embodies values and attitudes that make it possible to leverage networking technology so people can remain in touch with one another in ever-changing constellations of work teams. Richard Nolan, Alex Pollock, and James Ware describe much of this shift.

## Nolan: The Twenty-First-Century Organization

Richard Nolan suggests that the bureaucratic hierarchy form of organization used by most companies today is obsolete.[21] He suggests that the organizational structure of the twenty-first century will have to take the form of a network in order to compete.

Companies that try simply to modify their existing bureaucratic hierarchies will "fall short of becoming globally cost-competitive, market-drive, or achieving a lasting competitive advantage."[22] These companies will not have the flexibility or adaptability to meet market demands primarily because of the shift from relatively stable to dynamic markets. Moreover, there is also a shift in knowledge requirements from relatively simple needs to complex interdependencies.

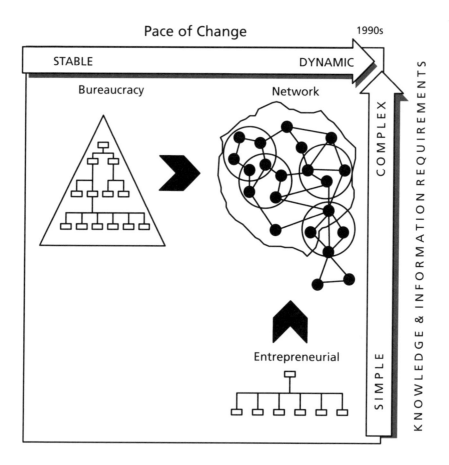

Figure 7.7 **Organization forms and environmental demands**[23]

Nolan and his colleagues picture this shift as shown in Figure 7.7. The entrepreneurial form represents first generation management. Bureaucracy, or steep hierarchy, is second generation management. The networked organization requires fifth generation management. The circles indicate multiple task-focusing teams. One of the teams involves participants from either a supplier or a customer organization. Third generation matrix organizations and fourth generation interfaced hierarchies are simply superimposed on the steep hierarchy.

Many companies are not looking beyond fourth generation management. Instead, they are busy trying to overcome their fragmentation by computerizing their existing steep hierarchies. What results can we expect?

# 8

# Computerizing Steep Hierarchies:
# Will It Work?

After two hundred years of working to divide and subdivide enterprises, we find ourselves today trying to integrate these same processes with computers and networks. In spite of the enthusiasm for computer integrated manufacturing and computer integrated enterprise, it is not easy. Why?

George Hess, vice-president of Ingersoll Milling Machine, caricatures our present industrial-era organizations as "human disintegrated manufacturing."[1] He dislikes the "fragmentation virus" affecting our organizations. Certainly the endless turf battles, the need for middle managers as expediters, and the seas of irrelevant data all give testimony to Hess's observation. But these are merely symptoms of deeper problems.

How do we begin to address the extreme fragmentation that is so common in our manufacturing and service organizations? Is the problem really with the way we organize ourselves? After all, structure is supposed to follow strategy. Yet structure too often develops a life of its own. Even a structure that has outlived its usefulness will resist the pressure to change or get out of the way. The traditional steep hierarchical corporate structure, that familiar pyramidal mobile with the boss at the top and department heads and middle managers dangling beneath, cannot cope with the rapidly changing customer demands and technological pressures of today's marketplace.

Can the imposition of computer-based technology, by itself, transform the corporate structure into one that allows the vast potential of CIM and CIE to be realized? Or must the old corporate species die to make room for the new? Figure 8.1 shows the focus of this chapter.

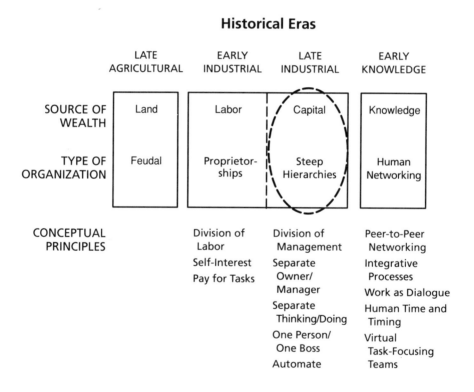

**Historical Eras**

|  | LATE AGRICULTURAL | EARLY INDUSTRIAL | LATE INDUSTRIAL | EARLY KNOWLEDGE |
|---|---|---|---|---|
| SOURCE OF WEALTH | Land | Labor | Capital | Knowledge |
| TYPE OF ORGANIZATION | Feudal | Proprietor-ships | Steep Hierarchies | Human Networking |
| CONCEPTUAL PRINCIPLES |  | Division of Labor | Division of Management | Peer-to-Peer Networking |
|  |  | Self-Interest | Separate Owner/ Manager | Integrative Processes |
|  |  | Pay for Tasks | Separate Thinking/Doing | Work as Dialogue |
|  |  |  | One Person/ One Boss | Human Time and Timing |
|  |  |  | Automate | Virtual Task-Focusing Teams |

Figure 8.1 **The focus of the chapter: steep hierarchies**

## Historical Perspective

In *The Wealth of Nations*, Adam Smith theorizes about the division and subdivision of labor, one of the key concepts of the Industrial Revolution.[2] He uses as his model a pin-making factory in which the manufacturing process is broken into a sequence of simple steps, each of which is performed by a specialist who does nothing else (Figure 8.2).

Figure 8.2  **Division and subdivision of labor in pin-making factory**

It is perfectly natural to organize the work of a small-scale proprietorship such as a small shipyard, a group making shoes, or a textile import concern according to this idea of the division of labor. The owner coordinates the various activities necessary to acquire the raw materials, divide up the work, and sell the products. Market forces determine the interplay between these and other enterprises, as suggested by Adam Smith's concept of the "invisible hand": As the proprietorships look after their own "self-interest," the general economy prospers. Government's role is to establish the ground rules for this competition.

Smith's idea of the role of self-interest is a macroeconomic concept: As proprietorships try to maximize their own positions, society benefits from optimum employment and the creation of wealth. Within an enterprise, however, self-interest often works to the detriment of the company. As each function competes to maximize its own position, it diverts resources from other vital functions, and the corporation as a whole suffers. If engineering does not devote time and expense to understanding how its designs create problems in manufacturing, resources are wasted on engineering change orders (ECOs).

Steep hierarchies are a creation of the last hundred years. They evolved out of the early industrial-era proprietorship, according to Alfred Chandler in *Managerial Hierarchies*.[3]

## The Emergence of Steep Hierarchies

In the 1880s and 1890s steep managerial hierarchies began to appear in the United States, Europe, Asia, and elsewhere. In the United States the railroads and telegraph companies needed extended management structures to span the large geographic areas covered by their companies.[4]

Chandler notes that in these companies, "The visible hand of managerial direction has replaced the invisible hand of market mechanisms . . . in coordinating flows and allocating resources in major modern industries."[5] Chandler's work focuses on this shift from the market-driven proprietorships, guided by Smith's "invisible hand," to the "visible hand" of managers who were no longer the owners of evolving firms such as Pillsbury, Procter & Gamble, Eastman Kodak, John Deere, and National Cash Register.

These firms were faced with the task of organizing their managerial ranks to coordinate high-volume production with national and international distribution. Careful planning and scheduling, as well as standardization, were critical to achieving economies of scale. Through mergers, consolidations, and other strategies, many of these companies expanded forward into distribution and back into raw materials. This "vertical integration" helped them reduce costs, increase profits, and build barriers against other potential competitors.

In other words, integration is not a new concept.

As they evolved, these firms employed middle- and top-level salaried managers to monitor and control the work of their operating units. Gradually, multiunit enterprises emerged, with work divided among the functions.

This form of organization brought many advantages. Unit costs could be kept lower through coordinated buying and distribution. The internal flow of goods between operational units could be coordinated through effective planning and scheduling. Facilities, personnel, and cash flow could be managed more effectively.

Managers within steep hierarchies had to develop whole new sets of procedures, policies, and standards to coordinate their activities. New managers had to be recruited and trained. Many activities had to be differentiated.

These needs brought about a "division and subdivision of management" that paralleled Adam Smith's earlier concept of the division and subdivision of labor, especially with respect to two key features: sequential work and narrowly defined tasks (Figure 8.3).

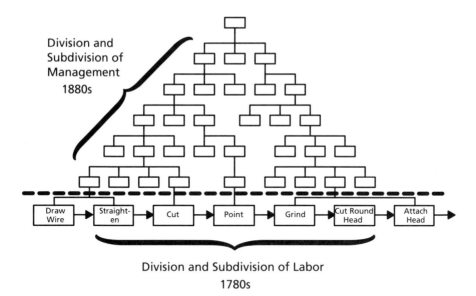

**Figure 8.3 Division and subdivision of management and labor with sequential work and narrowly defined tasks**

This division and subdivision of management made it easier to manage the growing capital resources of the firm. As a result, new accounting procedures were devised to assign costs, budget for capital investments, and allocate expenses.

New strategies were needed to support both the differentiation of the functions and the integration necessary to coordinate diverse but interconnected activities. Lawrence and Lorsch's classic study, *Organization and Environment,* traces the way the organizational structure became the key integrating influence within the enterprise.[6] Clearly articulated departmental charters and job definitions helped define who was responsible for each task. This challenge represented an attempt to establish clearly defined spheres of *authority* and *responsibility* in order to maintain *accountability.* Reward strategies and accounting procedures became key to keeping the companies focused and coordinated.

There are many examples of this process. As companies such as Pennsylvania Railroad, Western Union, Kodak, John Deere, General

Electric, and General Motors grew, their managerial hierarchies increased in size and complexity. In the 1920s, General Motors and Du Pont pioneered the multidivisional structure with autonomous product divisions. At GM, the divisions ranged from Cadillac, at the top of the line, to Chevrolet at the bottom. At Du Pont, the divisions specialized in explosives, films, fibers, and chemicals. Executives of both companies added centralized staff at headquarters to coordinate the long-range financial development of these divisions. As more and more layers were added, the steep hierarchies of today took shape.

Many of the problems we face today are the result of using the division of labor as a model for the division and subdivision of management. Even the multidivisional approaches, such as those of General Motors and Du Pont, rely on distinct functions within each division. The sequential model of functional handoffs has not changed, even within divisions, although both companies are working to change this today. Many companies are plagued by their managers' preoccupation with their turf. As information is passed sequentially from one function to another, it is lost or misinterpreted in the handoff. Decisions are made from the narrow confines of one function, without an understanding of the larger context. These problems are endemic in steep hierarchies.

## The Structure of Steep Hierarchies

Steep hierarchies may have ten to fifteen layers of management, with a complex set of operating procedures to determine reporting channels, authority levels, departmental charters, job definitions, and operating policies (Figure 8.4). Their structure is based on the assumption that *thinking* will be done at the top of the organization, *doing* at the bottom. Middle management's role is to summarize information for top management and to instruct, monitor, and control subordinates. To ensure responsibility and accountability, each person has only one boss.

Steep hierarchies work by a sequence of handoffs: Each department completes its work, then passes the results on to the next department. It is easy to see why all-encompassing bureaucratic procedures are necessary in this environment to integrate the various functions. When established procedures and policies fail to cope with specific situations, the problems are tossed upstairs to the next managerial level—a natural safety valve for the lower levels.

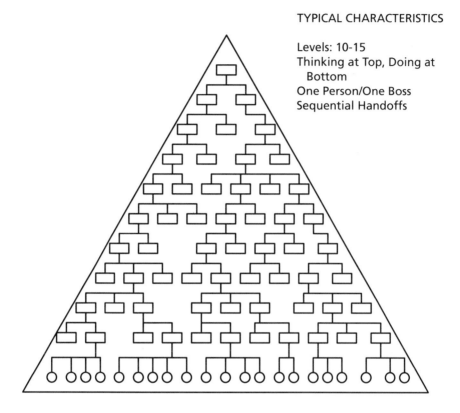

TYPICAL CHARACTERISTICS

Levels: 10-15
Thinking at Top, Doing at
   Bottom
One Person/One Boss
Sequential Handoffs

Figure 8.4  **Steep hierarchy**

Steep hierarchies in their different forms have worked well over the last hundred years. Despite their recognized shortcomings and growing obsolescence, they have proved quite useful in solving a broad range of managerial problems as they have evolved over the years.

The Industrial Revolution was fueled not only by an entrepreneurial spirit, but also by a steady flow of technological innovations. The steam engine, the spinning jenny, and metallurgical techniques helped fuel the visions of the industrialists.

The early industrial era combined the division and subdivision of labor with a system that sent work to craftspersons in their homes.[7] As concentrations of equipment began to grow in the 1880s, a shift to professional management necessitated the building of an organizational hierarchy. Functions took over responsibility for the various aspects of the firm. Each function, such as engineering, finance, marketing or manufacturing, was responsible for building up its own capabilities.

Once these functional hierarchies were defined, they could more easily absorb new technology. When a new lathe, milling machine, or steel-making process was introduced into the hierarchy, there was usually no need to change the way the organization worked. The function that acquired the improved tool or process simply became more efficient and productive.

In spite of the success of these hierarchies, there are many issues that steep hierarchies cannot handle. In their success are the seeds of their failure, and these are being noted not only by Drucker and Davis but by many other contemporary writers.[8] Part of the problem has been that while we have had many theories about hierarchical organizations, we know little about how they actually operate. For example, Teicholz and Orr see the factory as "a seething caldron of emotion, perspiration, nobility, foolishness, greed, sincerity, selfishness, idealism, vanity, and generosity." They go on to note that its "actual operation is almost impossible to diagram because it is shrouded in a fog raised by the heat of human activity."[9] This quotation may be overly dramatic, but it does point to many of the human elements overlooked in most studies of the manufacturing environment.

Robert Reich notes that America's successes have occurred principally in large mass production markets that require what he calls "superstructures of management," his term for what we are calling steep hierarchies.[10] The nation's basic industries—steel, automobiles, petrochemicals, and machinery—mastered the art of high-volume, standardized production. Now, faced with the competitive demands of a world economy that requires flexible systems in products and processes, American companies are playing a catch-up game.

Many manufacturing organizations have simply grown in an unplanned manner, like the Winchester House in San Jose, California. This Victorian mansion, built by the Winchester rifle heiress over thirty years, has staircases leading to nowhere, a chimney that rises four floors to stop just short of the ceiling, and doors that open to blank walls—all because of the owner's obsession that if the builders stopped working, the spirits of those who had been killed by her husband's rifle would come back to haunt her.

Although few if any manufacturing firms are driven by such obsessiveness, most have their share of projects that go nowhere, reports that are necessitated because one department does not trust another, and endless meetings that are held because departments do not understand or appreciate the constraints under which other departments are working. So much information is fragmented within these jumbled hierarchical environments. How can it be sorted out and made available to those who really need it? This deficiency has created a vacuum that is drawing computer-based systems into the hierarchies in an attempt to reverse the fragmentation. The explosive interest in CIM and integration exemplifies this way of thinking.

## Computerizing Steep Hierarchies

In the early days of the computer, it seemed only natural to budget computer equipment the same as other projected equipment purchases. Individual functional departments had large volumes of repetitious information to process. Computers nicely streamlined and shortened these operations. Each department wanted a computer to support its activities. Finance had accounting to worry about, manufacturing was concerned about tracking inventory, and engineering desired tools to support design and drafting. These functions pulled in both hardware and software to do work that had always been done manually. In fact, most computerization initiatives have been focused on replacing manual operations with the supposed efficiency of the computer. Few efforts have been designed to use computers in qualitatively new ways.

Another dynamic has also been at work: the politics of information management. In steep hierarchies, the information a person controls is directly correlated with that person's power base. In many organizations, information has become currency, doled out to friends and withheld from others.

Figure 8.5 shows a steep hierarchy with computer systems within various departments. Not every department has a computer; they are distributed unevenly within the hierarchy. Different functions have different styles of computing: some are very hierarchical, others distributed.

Each company configures computer systems differently. Some have these resources widely distributed; others have resources concentrated in limited areas. Still other companies have introduced different levels of computing, from large applications packages to word processing and electronic mail systems. Some have more inclusive networks than others. And, of course, the situation is changing all the time as companies add and upgrade systems and tie them together with networks, both internally and with their suppliers and customers.

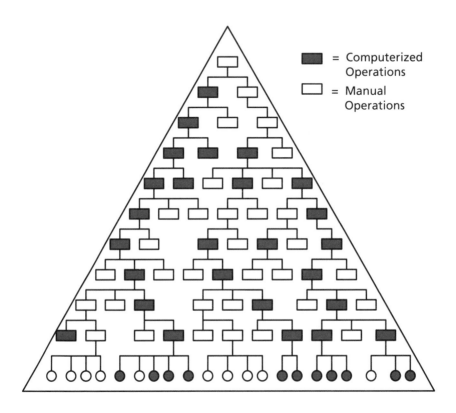

Figure 8.5 **Steep hierarchy with computer systems**

There are some important trends which cut across most companies and industries. Initially, computers thrived in the "glass houses" of the computer centers doing batch operations. Frustrations with centralized and bureaucratic MIS often led to departmental computing. Time-share computing added flexibility to these systems, as professionals used dumb terminals to access their applications and mail. We have just been through the PC wave, where everyone has wanted his or her own terminal.

Gradually, companies are moving from large, centralized, hierarchical computing to peer-to-peer computing, using local and wide-area networking to link terminals, PCs, and workstations. Windowing and client/server technology are making it easier to access files and applications anywhere on the network. Cooperative work-group computing (teamware) is spreading, as is interest in relational and object-oriented programming and databases. There is tremendous pressure from users to establish open systems, including industry-approved user interfaces.

These technological developments will make it much easier for enterprises to work in parallel, by creating multiple task teams from the different functions to deal with market and customer complexity. Unfortunately, our attitudes and understanding are not maturing as fast as the technology. It is easy to become dazzled by technology and overlook the human and organizational changes necessary to leverage this technology.

## Some Unexpected Consequences

When Deere and Company tried to computerize and integrate its Waterloo, Iowa, tractor works in the early 1980s, it encountered a few surprises. It developed a computer-based system that allowed it to track work-in-process, download programs, schedule operations, and track maintenance. It built high-bay storage capacity so it could easily store and retrieve parts. When the systems were all put into operation, they did not work as they were supposed to. Why not?

Deere discovered, after much reflection, that it had simply computerized and automated operations as they existed in a manual mode. After much soul searching, Deere realized that it had computerized the contradictions, confusion, and inconsistencies of its existing operations. Reflecting upon this experience, Jim Lardner, a Deere vice-president, recommends that companies simplify existing operations before introducing heavy computerization.[11]

Deere subsequently embarked on a "Total War on Waste," incorporating notions of Just-in-Time (JIT) and Total Quality. The interplay between CIM-related efforts, JIT, and Total Quality has enabled Deere to sort out and simplify many of its processes and, where appropriate, to computerize and automate them. Deere may be further along on the learning curve than many other companies.

In the 1970s many companies and government agencies believed it would be possible to develop what some affectionately called the "Great Database in the Sky." Surely the computer would be powerful enough to help run the entire operation. The U.S. Air Force spent millions of dollars on such an effort, only to find it an impossibility. They failed because of two unforeseen problems: first, the available hardware and software were not flexible enough; and second, they tripped over naming conventions. They found that traditional flat data files together with COBOL or FORTRAN did not provide the flexibility to interrelate multiple operations. Each functional group in the organization had its own naming conventions. They underestimated the difficulty of achieving agreement across the organization regarding the definition of key terms. They had assumed the problem was one of "bits and bytes," but they learned that the challenge was to hammer out a consistent set of meanings and a definition of key terms between people in different functions.

Two lessons stand out in these examples. First, simplify operations before automating or computerizing them. Those who naively chant "Automate or evaporate!" need to understand that an automated mess is not a better mess—just a faster one. Second, standardize terms across the organization. Without cross-functional understanding, cross-functional computerization will flounder in a sea of turf battles and unresolved definitions.

We often underestimate the complexity of our organizations. Although the organizational chart of steep hierarchies makes us think we understand the organization, the hidden networks of interrelationships, the informal organizations, the old-boy networks, and the political chit systems are major factors in running the operation.

Since George Homans's classic study *The Human Group* in the early 1950s, there has been a growing interest in how organizations actually constitute themselves in spite of their formal organizational model.[12] In order to get the work out the door, people form alliances and coalitions that cut across traditional boundaries. These "invisible" networks are often the real strength of the company, yet traditional computerization approaches are blind to their existence.

Until recently, the main thrust in industry has been to attempt to automate and computerize existing organizations with all their idiosyncrasies and contradictions. We should certainly try to make manual operations more efficient with the aid of the computer. But what happens when we do this?

## Critical Computerization Issues

As our enterprises are connected and interfaced, we face a new range of issues related to computerization and networking of business and government organizations:

1. Ownership of information

2. Managed information systems

3. Hidden assumptions and levels of abstraction embedded in software applications

4. Multiple applications with inconsistent definitions

5. Social norms about the transmission of information

6. The values and politics of organizations

These six issues are interrelated in many ways because an organization's values and style are going to influence the way it "owns" and "manages" its information resources. We will look at the six separately, then as a whole.

### Ownership of Information

In developing an information systems strategy, one of the first exercises undertaken is to determine who creates the information, who uses it, and who can update it. As database technology matures and more and more information is shared, the issue of *who owns the data* becomes even more pressing. Distributed databases and networking will force the ownership issue to the fore because more people will have access to multiple databases.

The steep hierarchy model gives the impression that each of its boxes represents a "territory" or "turf" that is "owned" by its occupant. Some companies move their employees around so often that in addressing one another, they use organizational chart box titles rather than names as their addresses. The *ownership* model of organizational thinking leads naturally to the idea that if a particular territory generates a particular set of information, that territory should own it. Thus, we take our attitude toward the organization and transfer it to its data pools.

The problem is that many data elements are key to multiple functions. For example, do the *employee* data elements belong to the personnel function that hires them, the payroll department that pays them, the management functions that assign them work, or the medical department that is concerned about their health needs? Who owns the *part number* data element? Is it engineering, which designs the part; operations, which produces it; or accounting, which costs it?

This is why so many companies have multiple employee records and parts lists. It is common to find from three to seven different parts lists in major corporations, with multiple bills of materials. Why? Because everyone wants to control and own his or her own data. The problem is further compounded when different functions use different schemes to represent the data elements. One group may use a six-digit number, another may use eight alphanumeric characters, and still another may insist on using the vendor's numbering system.

This is not only a question of consistent numbering schemes, but also of how two or more functions agree upon the definition and maintenance of key data elements—not a trivial task. A typical manufacturer has from 600 to 3,000 such data elements that are common to three or more functions. Service companies can have from 500 to 1,000 common elements that need careful tracking.

The ownership dilemma is generated, in part, because we tend to think of *data* as something that can be owned and controlled apart from its users. In reality, data is a language of communication based upon a set of conventions. Just as I cannot *own* any of the words in the English language (though I might create some), I cannot own the data in an organization. To be sure, I can control access to specific parts of the data in one database or another. But if data is to have meaning within a broader enterprise, it must be used, like the words of a language, to communicate with others.

In a language, words can be ambiguous unless the context is understood. However, it is difficult to capture both particular words and the context in a computer at the same time. Computers cannot cope with ambiguity as people can, because computers can work only with particulars. This is why, as Winograd and Flores have pointed out, artificial intelligence and expert systems have limitations.[13]

The irony may be that we are asking the wrong question. The ownership question is critical if we accept the presupposition of the steep hierarchy, where the accent is upon *ownership* of one's turf and resources. But as we move toward flatter networked organizations, there may be another approach that will help answer this question. Information management is becoming even more critical, but not in the traditional MIS sense.

## Managed Information Systems

Like a geological study, there are strata of thinking about computer systems. In their early days, the concept of "data processing" (DP) was generally accepted. The name then evolved to "management information systems" (MIS), because vendors wanted to suggest that their computer systems would allow organizations to manage their information more effectively and would provide management with their own systems. Now a whole variety of terms are being used—from decision support systems (DSS) to information resource management (IRM) to information asset management (IAM).

In theory, the change from DP to MIS made a lot of sense, as do the shifts to these newer concepts. But one reality of steep hierarchies is that as information passes up and down the organization, there is a strong tendency to *manage* and *massage* it. A function is often more interested in making itself look good than in telling things the way they are. In too many companies, even before the computer, we have had *managed information systems.*

The computer has not changed this pattern of interaction between levels. Usually MIS attempts to mirror the configuration of steep hierarchies, so they suck up information from lower levels, summarize it, and provide top management with executive decision support systems. These decisions are then communicated back down through the hierarchy to lower levels.

Many information systems (I/S) consultants have dreamed about assisting large Fortune 500 companies to develop perfect command and control centers wired to their entire enterprises. In fact, a growing body of literature deals with executive information systems (EIS) and executive support systems (ESS) built on this dream. Is this where managed information systems are taking us? Will these systems be used to "micro-manage" the plants and other functions? Or will they be used by executives to gain new insights into the multiple patterns of interrelationships affecting their businesses?

The managed information systems issue will continue to persist even as networks and distributed databases are introduced. In fact, the problem will become even more critical. Certainly, this issue is tied into the question of ownership of data. It is also tied to the values and norms of the organization. For example, if little trust exists between levels or between functions in steep hierarchies, there is going to be a greater interest in managing or massaging the information that is passed vertically between boxes.

Is it possible that the wrong questions are being asked in the MIS arena? The more appropriate questions may deal with *leveraging knowledge* rather than managing information. The challenge is to see the interrelationship of multiple patterns. Unfortunately, traditional managed information systems tend to remove all the interesting rough edges and sanitize the information so the important patterns do not show up.

## Hidden Assumptions and Levels of Abstraction Embedded in Software Applications

In a predominantly manual operating mode, we can easily see the information that is being requested and understand the interrelationships between the key pieces of data. Everything is generally straightforward and open. But when a company buys or develops its own software application, it encounters another problem, one not well documented. Because the assumptions, logic, and structure of the applications package are removed from the user, it is much harder to understand how the various elements of the program fit together.

This problem is even more acute when the application package has been developed by multiple authors over an extended period of time based on their own assumptions and experiences of how things happen in an organization. This is particularly true with many Manufacturing Resource Planning (MRP II) packages, which require extensive training to learn the forms and input syntax. Often discrepancies are found between the terminology (data elements) used in the application packages and the language customarily used by the department or function. These application packages also assume a level of discipline and consistency that is seldom found in the typical department. No wonder so many companies have stubbed their toes on MRP II packages.

Zuboff has highlighted another significant transition process.[14] She shows how workers and managers are being removed from their primary involvement with the operations processes and forced to use computers located away from the action. Computer-mediated control is a new experience for many people who find themselves forced to work at higher levels of abstraction. This is an unnatural environment to those who like to see, touch, feel, smell, and kick the processes. Certainly, computer literacy is much more than learning to type: It involves the ability to think and perceive on multiple levels of abstraction.

Most off-the-shelf application packages assume certain internal relationships between data elements that may be different from those assumed by the using organization. This leads to confusion and, in some instances, to a distrust of the systems.

These problems are compounded when companies try to interface multiple application packages. Typically, manufacturing and process industry companies have from fifty to one thousand different application packages, each with its own structure, its own set of definitions, its own internal logic, and its own inadequate documentation. Usually there is a conflict when applications from various vendors are interfaced, because data elements have different meanings or different shades of meaning in different contexts.

We face not only a question of shades of meaning in different applications, but the fact that any application represents a historically dated understanding of a problem or process. Most application programs are not easy to reconfigure; they lock us into a particular view, which may have been right on the mark when the program was written, but which may not adequately reflect subsequent changes in thinking. Later, when we wish to link up applications in organizational networks, this inflexibility causes deep consternation because of the varying shades of meaning.

At present, we do not even have a good word to describe the reconfiguring that will be necessary to get the applications in alignment with one another. Perhaps "maintenance" is close, but it generally implies the updating of existing applications. Interfacing different applications is a new challenge and a frustrating one because of the shades-of-meaning problem.

In the early 1990s many companies will find their computer maintenance budgets growing exponentially as a result of the contradictory assumptions embedded in different application packages and the push to reconfigure them to work with other applications. The problem will be ameliorated only in part by common user interface strategies such as X Windows System. Nevertheless, if applications are to reference one another, translator maintenance will be an increasing cost, especially in a networking environment.

One way to address this challenge is to grow a common and shared understanding of the key terms or data elements (entities or objects). Ingersoll Milling Machine Company, which began this process in early 1979, now has tremendous flexibility and consistency in its operations because it changed to a common data architecture.

## Multiple Applications with Inconsistent Definitions

We seldom stop to think about the ambiguity contained in everyday speech. We recognize words by their context. For example, what does the word *bow* mean? It depends upon whether we are in the navy, hunting, being polite, or dressing up.

The language used in both manufacturing and the service sector is full of this same kind of ambiguity. No wonder the maintenance portion of MIS budgets often equals 80 percent of the total. A lot of time and expense is required to figure out, document, and redefine basic relationships between the application packages.

In 1979 Ingersoll Milling Machine Company found that it had 1,300 different application programs and systems operating from 225 different computer master files full of redundant and uncoordinated data. Many of the application programs were really bridge programs that took data out of one file and fed it into others.[15] Recognizing that it could not afford to maintain this Rube Goldberg assortment of interfaces, Ingersoll spent the money and time to develop a common core data reference architecture, thereby achieving tremendous flexibility and consistency of operation.

Unfortunately, most companies do not know how many different applications they have or the extent to which they suffer from redundant and ill-defined data. This problem will become even more intense as networks spread within and between companies. People will assume that because it is easy to move information around in digital form, the battle of integration will be easily won. On the contrary, *connectivity* does not mean *integration*. Nor does it mean that everyone will understand the words used by the other departments.

For example, it is possible for me to call someone in a foreign country. If the person answering the phone speaks only a foreign language that I do not know, there will be little communication. But suppose this person speaks English, even in a faltering way. He says, "I see a bear out my window." If I were to reply, "I'd love to see a bear, please shoot it for me," what should I expect to get in the mail? A snapshot of the bear, or a stuffed bear? The telephone line provides *connectivity*, and I can *interface* using the language, but integration comes when there is an agreed-upon set of definitions and the context is understood.

Companies that are now using networks to interface different functions, such as finance, engineering, manufacturing, and field service, know well the distinctions between connectivity, interfacing, and integrating. They are also discovering how inflexible a software package can be.

It is typically assumed that if the software developers did a good job of coding, an application should remain useful for a long time. The problem is that an organization is dynamic and is constantly looking for new ways to interrelate various elements in its processes. If the application was developed using flat files or even hierarchical or networked databases, changing it will require many pointers to be moved around. This is an extremely time-consuming job, especially because many applications are not well documented and have only minimal data dictionaries.

Some companies are beginning to see the wisdom of not only developing corporate data dictionaries but also defining the interrelationship between the key elements of their data in open architectures, or data architectures. This allows different functions to use the same data (and objects, in an object-oriented application) but to process it differently, depending on the unique needs of the department.

The use of open and expandable data architectures will begin to make not just interfacing, but integration, possible. It will become clear that data is as much a corporate asset as the machinery in the factory, the point-of-sale terminals in the store, and the desks in the office. Yet this approach often runs up against the turf-ownership tendencies in steep hierarchies. Why? Because first, these data architectures are a cross-functional undertaking, and second, they require agreement among the functions on the meaning of key words in relation to one another. Our organizations are not set up to work this way. Yet this is one of the key tasks of the 1990s.

## Social Norms about the Transmission of Information

We have grown up with the social norms of "chain of command" and "span of control." We know, of course, that much communication, especially informal communication, cuts across organizational lines. Nevertheless, on paper there is one boss for each person and communication goes up and down the chain of command.

It may very well travel this route, at least formally. We know how this process filters and baffles communication, often muffling significant messages. But what happens in a networked environment where the electronic mail system makes it possible to communicate directly with everyone else, regardless of rank? Is it enough simply to copy in one's boss, or is it necessary to ask one's boss to forward the communication?

Electronic mail, computer-based conferencing systems, and videotext information resources make it more natural to network with others of similar interests across the enterprise. They put professionals on a more even level, influencing people's communication patterns and expectations of one another. Easy access to information also raises other challenges.

What happens when it is easy for one manager to look at another manager's financial results? Will this information be used for political advantage, or will the two managers use it to discover ways they can both improve?

To what extent is a boss responsible for a subordinate's communication that is sent directly to another function? How is accountability maintained? How are conflicts to be resolved? Who is liable in legal suits? What kinds of checks and balances are necessary? We must understand how these issues are changing our social norms and develop a new approach to organizational accountability.

## The Values and Politics of Organizations

Those who have held management positions in steep hierarchical organizations, whether they were in manufacturing or the service sector, know the political realities of these organizations. Long-range planning, promotions, and budgeting can bring out undesirable personality traits as managers contend for limited resources. Reward systems, which are often based on the dollar value of decision-making authority or the number of direct reports, intensify these conflicts.

Many managers have simply accepted these conditions as part of the territory. They have learned the tactics of survival. They may even have gone to courses designed to hone their political skills. After all, is their survival not based on the protection and expansion of their turf?

What happens when subordinates can easily communicate with their peers in other departments? What happens when these same subordinates can easily communicate with their boss's peers? And what happens when responsibility is no longer clear-cut? Are well-cultivated political instincts enough?

We can look at the problem another way. What happens when a company installs even the most sophisticated and technically advanced local and wide-area network systems? In a politically charged environment, will the network be used effectively? Will one department readily share significant information with other departments? Will a plant allow corporate headquarters to poke around in its databases?

Not necessarily. Where there is little trust between functions, between levels, or between a plant and corporate headquarters, the connectivity of the network is suboptimized. One government agency installed an electronic mail system, but had it "customized" to prevent communication between levels except through carefully prescribed channels.

Try an experiment: On a scale of 1 to 10 (with 10 representing total trust and 1 complete distrust), estimate the level of trust between people within a functional department, between departments, and between a plant and corporate headquarters. Responses to this query show that trust within a department usually averages 7; between functions, about 4.5; and between the plant and corporate headquarters, 2.5 or less.

Warren Shrensker of General Electric has seen firsthand the importance of trust between departments. "Without trust," Shrensker maintains, "we waste many resources checking and double-checking on each other's functions. These activities do not add value to the product, only costs to the bottom line." Shrensker explains that trust is related to the integrity of individual managers, professionals, and workers and to their reliability, predictability, and genuine interest in others over time.[16]

Many vendors sell networks, but where does a company go to increase its climate of trust? Trust cannot be bought; it has to be won over time. Integrity, honesty, and openness are the result of the way people interact within an enterprise. What incentive do people have to exercise these values when they are measured on their ability to maximize narrowly defined functional charters?

## Key Interrelationships of Computerization Issues

One of the fundamental tenets of steep hierarchies is the notion of ownership of one's turf, be it individual or functional. This is implicitly the message of the proverbial organization chart. It is small wonder that information should be managed and that political fighting should be a way of life. What value do trust and integrity have in such an environment?

As computer and networking systems are introduced, how will the enterprise begin to deal with the new dynamic of communication? How will it deal with meanings that are hidden in applications? When will it begin to get consistency of definitions between functions? Will horizontal communication be encouraged? Will trust and openness be developed? These assets are not easily bought: they must be home-grown and carefully nurtured. A computer vendor cannot install trust in a user environment.

In the process of defining an organization, implicit values are also defined. An organization is not a neutral body. Its structure shapes the attitudes and values of those involved in it. These values also shape policy, reward systems, and accounting procedures. Computer systems and networking are not neutral in their impact on the organization. They are not just more capital equipment, justified by return-on-investment formulas or hurdle rates. Their value is in the way they help all elements of the enterprise to work together. In many instances, this has still to be realized.

David Stroll of Digital Equipment Corporation suggests that computers and networking are beginning to dissolve the traditional structure of organizations, the high walls that have separated functions. This creates anxiety and uncertainty as people lose the protection of these traditional boundaries. At the same time, Stroll adds, the clock of organizational interaction is speeded up as companies are required to respond more quickly to market changes.[17] This increasing complexity adds further stress. Enterprises are being forced to interrelate multiple factors—marketing, design, manufacturing, cost, and service—in new ways. These changes are forcing functions to work more iteratively rather than just sequentially.

We are putting powerful new technology in traditional, industrial-era steep hierarchies. Either we learn to adapt to this new technology and leverage its capabilities, or we may find our companies imploding as they choke on complexity and their inability to sort out multiple interrelated variables.

The chapter began by asking whether computerization of steep hierarchies will work. The answer is clear: no.

One of the biggest problems is not in the technology but in our attitudes. As long as we persist in thinking in terms of "boxes and lines," in terms of the "ownership" of these boxes, and in terms of the "ownership" of data, collaboration between multiple functions will continue to be politicized and a climate of distrust and fragmentation will persist.

We are just beginning to recognize the right questions to ask about a fifth generation management approach that can lead to the effective leadership of flatter network enterprises. For example, how will accountability be maintained? How will knowledge be shared? How will the various functions work together and yet not trip over one another? And how do we reverse the trend toward fragmentation that is so common today?

If computerizing the steep hierarchy is not the answer, what is? The answer lies in an attitudinal shift. If we can come to terms with some of the assumptions we have been making about organizations and power, we will be able to use the resources of the computer and networking in exciting new ways. Our challenge is to rethink the conceptual principles that underlie the steep hierarchy. The breakthrough to fifth generation management will be made, not by money, but by will. The next chapter looks back at the conceptual principles of the industrial era that still confine us in the bottle.

# CHAPTER
# 9

# Steep Hierarchies: Breaking Free

Like the smile of the Cheshire Cat in *Alice in Wonderland,* integration seems elusive. When the smiling promises on the slick brochures fail to materialize in the plant, serious second thoughts set in. We are confined and uncomfortable, but we do not know how to break free.

Chapter 8 suggested that the problem is that of putting advanced computer technology in second generation organizations, steep hierarchies. But will not these organizations evolve as this new technology is introduced? No, because steep hierarchies have a life of their own. Like persistent dandelions that continue to spring up, no matter what we do, the conceptual principles of the steep hierarchies seem to permeate all our thoughts and actions. They continue to hold us captive.

The division and subdivision of labor, self-interest in one's own turf, and simple-minded tasks were convenient principles to support the transition from the agricultural period to the industrial eras, yet they still shape our thinking today. The division and subdivision of management, creation of a management group separate from the owners, separation of thinking and doing, a command structure in which each person only has one boss, the desire to automate—all these conceptual principles keep us in a full nelson.

## Historical Eras

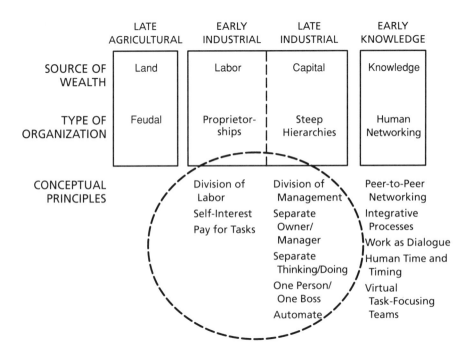

Figure 9.1 **Chapter focus: eight conceptual principles of the industrial eras**

In this chapter we will discuss these conceptual principles and the attempts to break out of them through various integration efforts. It may well be that the technology cannot overpower these principles. If so, we must find a new set of basic ideas around which to organize both the manufacturing and service sectors.

Figure 9.1 highlights the area of consideration in this chapter. We will first review the conceptual principles, then move into a discussion of the forces leading toward technical integration.

# Conceptual Principles of the Early Industrial Era

The transition from the late agricultural era to the early industrial era was accompanied by a profound conceptual shift. This shift between eras was an exciting period, shaped by the rise in scientific thought, political shifts, technological innovations, and many other factors. This section focuses on three conceptual principles that helped shape the fabric of the early industrial era: (1) the division and subdivision of labor, (2) self-interest, and (3) pay for narrowly defined tasks.

### The Division and Subdivision of Labor and Self-Interest

Two simple interrelated principles put forth by Adam Smith have become the foundation upon which the industrial era has been built.[1] These two key ideas, the division and subdivision of labor and self-interest, are simple to grasp.

Smith believed that there had been four stages of society: hunting, pasturing, farming, and the one he was ushering in, commerce. He saw his task as one of redefining economic life to help people understand that their own efforts could become the basis for the wealth of nations. He felt a need to go beyond the mercantilism of the sixteenth and seventeenth centuries, which argued that gains through international trade were the principal factor in promoting national power. He was also influenced by and wanted to push beyond the French physiocrats, who sought to establish a science of economics based on the laws of nature rather than on the concept of divine law that had supported the feudal era.

The physiocrats saw agricultural labor and land as the sources of a nation's wealth: Land combined with human labor produced bounty from the fields, creating a surplus that nourished all classes. Smith felt that this was too limited a concept. He was sure that more wealth could be generated through the proper application of labor in manufacturing, using the principle of the division of labor. At the same time, he was influenced by the physiocrats' discussion of self-interest. They believed that individuals know their own interests best, and that as they act to fulfill their interests, society is benefited. The physiocrats expounded the maxim *laissez faire, laissez passer*—that is, let things alone, let them take their course.

Smith's acceptance of this concept of self-interest was reinforced by his reading of Bernard Mandeville's *The Fable of the Bees*, subtitled *Private Greed, Public Benefit*.[2] In order to defuse the storm created by Mandeville's writing, Smith wrote that as each person "intends only his gain, he is . . . led by an invisible hand to promote an end which is not his intention. . . . By pursuing his own interest he frequently promotes that of society more effectively than when he really intends to promote it."[3]

Whereas Mandeville put envy and vanity on a metaphorical pedestal as ministers of commerce and industry, Smith chose a much more innocuous and acceptable metaphor, that of the "invisible hand," to represent self-interest. Who could be against a seemingly benevolent "helping hand" that looked after things much as parents looked after their children.

This principle of self-interest, teamed with the division of labor, would give birth to the industrial era. Labor, based on skill, dexterity, and judgment, according to Smith, could best be used under two conditions: (1) if people were allowed to follow their natural interest, specializing in those professions of greatest interest and selling their surplus in the market; and (2) if work were divided into fairly simple steps so individual workers could specialize in just one step in a larger process.

This second point was illustrated by Smith's discussion of the pin-making factory (Figure 8.2) that divided the process into eighteen steps (although only eight are shown). This division and subdivision of labor was to make it possible to easily employ the unskilled, train them in the individual steps, and thereby greatly increase the "quantity of work" produced. Smith saw three factors bringing this about. First, as each worker specialized, he or she would gain greater dexterity in that particular function; second, time would not be lost going from one step to the next; and, third, as the worker concentrated on a particular function, he or she would "invent a great number of machines" that would facilitate these efforts and "abridge" the labor content.[4]

Smith believed that division of labor would increase the workers' skill and dexterity as they repeated the same function daily. But, he was also aware that there would be a consequence: The workers would be "stupefied" by the repetition of the task, losing contact with the overall process. This would cut down on the workers' judgment, one of the key aspects of his definition of the nature of work. Smith never really reconciled this conflicting consequence of his division and subdivision of labor. History has shown that in some instances the division of labor has enhanced a worker's skills and dexterity, but in many others it has stupefied the worker.

Smith had a broad view of the interaction of the various components of the economy. He understood that capital formation was essential for the investments necessary to develop manufacturing concerns and to pay wages. He also figured in the rent that could be generated by the use of land. These two elements, land and capital, when combined with productive labor, would provide the basis of an expanding economy. Capital formation became essential to the development of the later industrial period.

In a historical context, Smith's principles made sense. Since Smith's time, though, their importance has become so exaggerated in our minds that it is hard for us to see their growing obsolescence.

Although Smith also dealt at length with the role wages were to play in his economic model, it was Charles Babbage who developed a more precise approach for relating wages and tasks. Babbage, best known for his development of the digital computer, had a profound impact on thought regarding the ways in which work should be organized and rewarded.

## Pay for Narrowly Defined Tasks

Babbage's *On the Economy of Machinery and Manufacturers*, published in 1832, helped establish a scientific approach to the study of management.[5] Concerned with the design and manufacture of machinery, its use, and the organization of labor, Babbage reinforced the work of Smith and anticipated themes that would later be articulated by Frederick Taylor.

Babbage clearly believed that a worker should be paid only for the task performed:

> *The master manufacturer, by dividing the work to be executed into different processes, each requiring different degrees of skill and force, can purchase exactly the precise quantity of both which is necessary for each process; whereas, if the whole work were executed by one workman, that person must possess sufficient skill to perform the most difficult, and sufficient strength to execute the most laborious of the operations into which the art is divided.[6]*

Like Smith's division of labor and self-interest, Babbage's payment for narrowly defined tasks made sense in the context of the times. Processes were generally well known and easily divided into simple steps. It made sense to pay only for what a person did, not for what he or she knew. This approach was also easier to administer because it could be related to clock time: the worker would agree to give up a specified amount of time for an agreed wage. As the division of labor was extended to the division of management, the same pay strategy was extended to staff professionals and to the middle levels of the steep hierarchy.

For hourly workers through middle management, we still largely operate on Babbage's principle of payment for narrowly defined tasks. This approach makes less sense today, however, because now we rely more on people's knowledge and awareness of how operations are interrelated.

The gap is growing between Babbage's pay-for-tasks approach and the approach that is needed in the knowledge era. We need a compensation system that recognizes not only knowledge but vision and skill in focusing on and responding to the themes of the market, whether from a marketing, engineering, manufacturing, finance, or service perspective. The Japanese recognize and reward people for three qualities: will, emotion, and knowledge. *Will* is a measure of engagement; *emotion* or *heart* determines, among other things, the quality of interaction with others; and *knowledge* involves memory and vision.

In summary, the three conceptual principles that made the early industrial era possible—division of labor, self-interest, and payment for tasks—must be redefined to fit the knowledge era. These principles are preventing us from being able to leverage the full potential of the technology and human capabilities of the knowledge era. We cannot overcome them by simply ignoring or forgetting them, because they will not easily let us go. They are so much a part of the intellectual woodwork of our thinking that, without a conscious rethinking of their role, we cannot get free. At the same time, we also have to come to terms with the conceptual principles of the late industrial era.

## Conceptual Principles of the Late Industrial Era

Around the 1880s, the growing size, complexity, and geographic extent of corporations ushered in the late industrial era and its characteristic organizational structure, the steep hierarchy. In addition to those of the early industrial era, five new conceptual principles characterized the late industrial era: (1) the division and subdivision of management, (2) the separation of ownership and management, (3) the separation of thinking and doing, (4) the notion that each person should have just one boss, and (5) the drive to automate.

## Division and Subdivision of Management

Some argue that managerial hierarchies are as old as human history, having arisen in military, political, and religious forms; however, this overlooks the difference between steep and flat hierarchies. Anthropologists point out that most tribes, clans, and family farms have had surprisingly flat hierarchies: the Roman Catholic Church, for example, has only four levels. Nevertheless, many accept the idea that steep hierarchies are a natural part of life.

The impetus toward steep hierarchies began in industries that spanned the continent. As railroads, telegraphs, and telephones spread, companies discovered a need to develop duplicate structures in diverse geographic locations. Each unit needed a general manager, functional managers, and direct reports to summarize information, pass on orders, and monitor activities.

Figure 8.3 illustrates the development of the management infrastructure as it was built above the division of labor. It shows how we became wedded to the box-and-line model. Each box is seen as being owned by its incumbent; the lines show the accepted channels of communication. No wonder many corporations have spent millions to carefully define management jobs and departmental charters. If the company is to be competitive, the organization must run like a clock; every function is expected to mesh with the others, like so many cogs in a series of gears. This is possible only when everyone knows his or her place.

This organizational system, which our business grandfathers and grandmothers thought of as "integration," is at the heart of many of our problems in today's large enterprises. When each of the functions is preoccupied with hanging on to its narrowly defined charter and looking out for its own self-interest, it is not surprising that ideas fall through the cracks or drown in a sea of politics. Managers retreat into their foxholes, protected by barbed wire (Figure 9.2).

Large organizations need some division of responsibility, of course, but the lines between functions should not represent unscalable walls. We will need to think of the areas as much more blurred and fuzzy, and indeed overlapping. Instead of treating marketing, research and development, finance, engineering, manufacturing, process control, service, human resources, and MIS as little empires unto themselves, we must realize that there is substantial overlap in their concerns. Each of the functions is really a resource center for the entire enterprise.

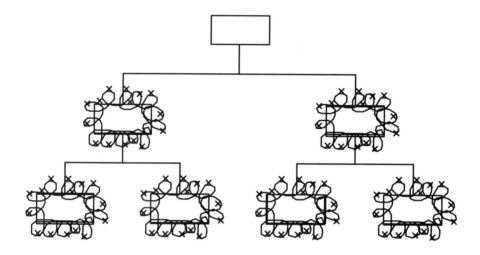

Figure 9.2 **Foxhole management**

## Separation of Ownership and Management

The industrial era is characterized by advances not only in technology but also in legal doctrine. The interplay of the two is critical. The corporation has evolved over the last few centuries. It was established in English law at least as early as the fourteenth century, when it applied primarily to religious bodies, towns, and guilds, both craft and mercantile.

Gradually the legal principles of the corporation were defined: it could hold property, sue and be sued, and endure beyond the lives of its members. The first corporations were established by grant from the king. In many ways, they served as a device by which royal power was both administered and expanded. These early corporations were often granted monopoly rights to a particular area or economic field of activity.

In the sixteenth and seventeenth centuries, the corporate concept was expanded to allow for joint stock trading. This made it possible to concentrate capital for the economic expansion of the corporation and added a new dimension to the purpose and role of the corporation.

Whereas the charters of the early corporations allowed private persons to serve public purposes, nineteenth-century charters became instruments by which private groups used the corporation for their own interests. When some of these interests became excessive, legislation such as the Sherman antitrust laws of 1890 began to set limits on them.

With the growth of the modern corporation, especially in the latter part of the last century, there arose the industrial bureaucracy, characterized by its hierarchy of functions and authority. Management was professionalized and there was a proliferation of written rules, orders, and record keeping.[7] Some corporations, striving to integrate mass production with mass distribution systems, found that they needed well-defined areas of responsibility and well-defined procedures to coordinate their diverse activities. The bureaucracy, the organizational chart, the departmental charters, and the job descriptions were the integrating structures of these large corporations.[8]

Thus proprietorships of the early Industrial Revolution gave way to the steep hierarchies of the late industrial era. Capital could now be concentrated and expended to extend the power of the enterprise. Accountability could be maintained through the structure of the hierarchy.

Direct involvement of the owners lessened. As professional managers took responsibility for the daily affairs of the corporation and ownership was diffused, the influence of the stockholders receded. The board of directors, representing the owners, was not involved in the daily activities of the corporation in the same way the proprietor had been.

The modern corporation does not have built into its structure the same types of checks and balances that the U.S. Constitution has built into the structure of government. Some scholars have bemoaned the fact that the corporation does not maintain the democratic traditions we expect in the political arena. But many others admire the corporation because it can quickly take decisive action. This has been important in developing the goods and services that have contributed to our rising standard of living.

Even so, many now worry that the corporation is not responsive enough to rapid changes in the marketplace. To compete in a global economy, companies need shorter product life cycles, concurrent engineering, greater cross-functional coordination, and external coordination with suppliers and distribution channels.

The bureaucracy, essential in the era of mass production, is now getting in the way in the era of "mass customization," to use Stanley Davis's term.[9] Mass customization requires functions to work together closely so that 20 percent of a core product can be redesigned to meet different customer expectations.

The classic integration of the vertically defined corporation is not the integration we are seeking today, which involves putting the diverse parts of the corporation in touch with one another so products and processes can be developed in parallel rather than sequentially. Boards of directors should understand that their responsibility is more than fiduciary, and should challenge top management to break down the artificial boundaries between functions. Some chief executives, like Jack Welch of General Electric, have already taken steps to remove bureaucratic cholesterol by "delayering" their corporations and moving toward flatter network organizations.[10]

In short, as proprietorships shifted to corporations and bureaucratic management began to dominate the steep hierarchy, the seeds of inflexibility were sown. This inflexibility has been amplified by separating thinking and doing.

## Separation of Thinking and Doing

Frederick Winslow Taylor, in recounting the origin of scientific management before a special congressional committee in 1903, told of having gone to work at Midvale Steel Works in 1878. As a lathe operator, he participated in limiting output to about one-third of what it might have been, which was the custom of the time. This "soldiering," under the piecework system, allowed operators to restrict the flow of work.[11]

Later, after his promotion to "gang boss" in this machine shop at Midvale, the workers asked him not to be a "piece-work hog." He explained that as an operator, he had not broken a single rate set by the group but that, as a supervisor, he intended to get more work out of them.

Taylor's first-hand experience in the machine shop convinced him that it was necessary to gain control of the production process. To this end, he believed that scientific data had to be used to separate planning and doing:

> Thus all of the planning which under the old system was done by the workman, as a result of his personal experience, must by necessity under the new system be done by the management in accordance

*with the laws of science. . . . It is also clear that in most cases one type of man is needed to plan ahead and an entirely different type to execute the work.*[12]

Taylor considered the most prominent single element in modern scientific management to be the "task." He and his colleagues, Frank and Lillian Gilbreth, envisioned the tasks of every worker being fully planned out by management at least one day in advance. The planning office was to provide complete written instructions as to what was to be done, how it would be done, and exactly how much time was to be allowed for each task. If the worker fulfilled the instructions within the allotted time, he or she would receive a bonus of from 30 to 100 percent of the base pay.

Taylor believed that under this new system the workers would "grow happier and more prosperous, instead of being overworked." But to achieve the separation of thinking and doing, a "mental revolution" would be necessary. "Both sides [management and labor] must recognize as essential the substitution of exact scientific investigation and knowledge for the old individual judgment or opinion . . . in all matters relating to the work done in the establishment."[13]

Robert Reich sums up Taylor's contribution: "This separation of thinkers from doers was the apogee of specialization: Planning was to be distinct from execution, brain distinct from brawn, head from hand, white collar from blue collar."[14] The separation of thinking and doing was a natural outcome of Taylor's desire to increase specialization through simplification of individual tasks, to use predetermined rules to coordinate these tasks, and to monitor and control performance. Each level of the organization had its planning assignment.

Although they were resisted at first, Taylor's principles spread throughout American industry following World War I, then were accepted in Europe and even in the Soviet Union, where Lenin heartily embraced them. Rules and plans multiplied within every large organization. Top management was responsible for the "strategic plans" of the enterprise. Middle management formulated the "operating rules," and "standard operating procedures" were established for the lower levels.

Taylor's approach was, in effect, an extension of the principles established by Smith and Babbage. Taylor believed he was establishing a scientific foundation for the Industrial Revolution. His approach made sense in the drive toward large-scale mass production, especially when companies were assumed to be structured like machines. Just as every part of the machine had its function, so each department was to follow the sequential steps specified by the overall plans.

Thus industry developed a system of rigid job classifications, work rules, and narrowly defined departmental charters. Monitoring and control systems set up to ensure conformity to these plans, such as cost accounting, inventory control, and financial reporting, were supposed to give top management overall control of the system. Each person was assigned his or her area of responsibility, and lines of authority were clearly specified on the organizational chart.

While Taylor reinforced the thought of Adam Smith on the shop floor, it was Henri Fayol and a few others who articulated this same type of thinking for management.

## One Person/One Boss

Henri Fayol, a Frenchman, rose to the position of managing director of a large coal mine, Comambault, in 1888. At that time, the firm was on the verge of bankruptcy. When he retired in 1918, it was in an extremely strong financial position. Fayol attributed the success of the firm to his system of management, which he described in *General and Industrial Management*, published in 1916 and translated into English in 1929.[15]

Fayol identified five components of management: planning, organizing, commanding, coordinating, and controlling. Although he and Taylor developed their ideas independently, they reflect a remarkable similarity of spirit. In his work, Fayol emphasized division of responsibilities (leading to specialization of functions), authority of position (boxes), unity of command (one person/one boss, where each person reports to only one boss), and the scalar chain (the gangplank principle with the lines on an organizational chart indicating the chain of command).

Clearly the underlying notion was that the chain of command would be the mechanism of integration within the enterprise. With highly specialized roles tied together by the chain of command, each role and function could be planned, organized, coordinated, and controlled. Communications would go through prescribed channels, people would perform and be evaluated on their narrowly defined tasks, and authoritative leadership would be the norm.

Other authors of the era reinforced these same ideas. In 1937 Lyndall Urwick wrote the following:

*The considerations which appear of greatest importance were that there should be clear lines of authority running from the top into every corner of the undertaking and that the responsibility of subordinates exercising delegated authority should be precisely defined.*[16]

Undoubtedly, Urwick was reflecting his experience in the British army during World War I as much as his experience as a manager in a chocolate candy company in the 1920s.

Two American counterparts of these two Europeans were James Mooney, a vice-president and director of General Motors, and Allan Reiley. Reflecting the same general line of thinking as Fayol's and anticipating Urwick's approach, Mooney and Reiley wrote:

*The subordinate is always responsible to his immediate superior for doing his job, the superior remains responsible for getting it done, and this same relationship, based on coordinated responsibility, is reported up to the top leader, whose authority makes him responsible for the whole.*[17]

These three writers were in agreement that specialization and departmentalization were essential and that the chain of command was capable of integrating the various activities. As Paul Lawrence and Jay Lorsch point out, these ideas of authority were implicit in the legal definition of the corporation: "They were rooted in the traditional concept of the master-servant relationship, which had been carried over to the employer-employee relationship."[18]

The influence of Fayol, Urwick, and Mooney is evident in most enterprises. The concept of the chain of command and the idea that each person should have only one boss seem bred into us. Yet those who work within this model have an uncomfortable sense of a gap between theory and real life: the miscommunication, the politics, the "back-stabbing," and the cracks through which information falls attest to fundamental problems. Somehow, in spite of it all, human nature and ingenuity often rise above the conditions to get the job done. As Jay Galbraith has noted, "Informal organization processes arise spontaneously and are the processes through which the organization accomplishes most of its work, despite the formally designed structure."[19]

There is a growing awareness that division of labor, functionalization, and specialization often lead to extreme fragmentation. Chester Barnard, in his 1938 classic *The Functions of the Executive*, was one of the first to question the notions that were leading to organizational fragmentation.[20] For example, he explored the five bases upon which an organization can be specialized: (1) the place work is done, (2) the time it is done, (3) the people with whom it is done, (4) the things upon which it is done, and (5) the method or processes employed. He noted that on the surface, specialization seems straightforward, but when these factors are introduced, it becomes more complex.[21] For example, many companies continue to struggle with the competing interests of product lines, geographic responsibility, and industry orientation. To which aspect of this equation should one be more loyal?

Functionalization and specialization also seem to be getting in the way as companies try to build more flexibility into their operations. As more and more companies realize they must compete in a world market, customer responsiveness becomes critical, not only to survive but also to build market share and profitability. These companies suffer from rigid work rules on the shop floor as well as from narrow-minded functional managers who are more interested in their own success than that of the enterprise.

Industry observers have taken issue with the shallowness and rigidity of the Smith/Taylor/Fayol bottleneck. In his work *Administrative Behavior*, Herbert Simon points out the ambiguities of the seemingly straightforward notions of work specialization.[22] Robert Reich observes that a more flexible system of production "cannot be simply grafted onto business organizations that are highly specialized for producing long runs of standard goods."[23] Peter Drucker teaches that "top management is a function and a responsibility rather than a rank and a privilege," as would be suggested by the steep hierarchy model. Moreover, he points out that "people are a resource rather than a cost," and "the purpose of a business is to create a customer."[24] And George Hess, a practical, hands-on manager, speaks of the "human disintegrated manufacturing" characteristic of so many of our steep hierarchies.[25]

In spite of their shortcomings, the conceptual principles underlying the steep hierarchy seem to be anchored in concrete. They have withstood the assaults of Douglas McGregor's classic work on Theory X and Y, *The Human Side of Enterprise*, published almost thirty years ago,[26] as well as those of more recent authors such as Robert Hayes and Steven Wheelwright, Tom Peters, and Stanley Davis.

The irony is that technological developments may themselves force more profound organizational changes than all the theorists combined. For example, the conventional wisdom has been that computers will enhance the overall efficiency of steep hierarchies. It should be clear by now that simply computerizing steep hierarchies leads to a spaghetti-like mess of interfaced systems: inflexible and incompatible.

As time and timing, particularly time-to-market and market timing, become the factors that distinguish the market leaders, the need to put people and processes in touch in dynamic ways is ever more pressing. Networking can help facilitate this process of communication, but unfortunately we are still seeking the magic solution or the major innovation that can do our work for us. We are still under the spell of the promise of automation.

## Automation

The concept of automation has a long history. The early Greeks, seeking freedom from the routine toil and drudgery of labor, conceived of devices that might take over certain tasks. The word *automation* is derived from the Greek word *auto-matos*, meaning "self-acting." It refers to an apparatus, process, or system that is capable of operating by itself in an unassisted manner.

Aristotle, in *Politics*, foresaw an automated shuttle and harp capable of working or playing at word of command or in intelligent anticipation:

> *There is only one condition on which we can imagine managers not needing subordinates, and masters not needing slaves. This condition would be that each [inanimate] instrument could do its own work, at the word of command or by intelligent anticipation, like the statues of Daedalus or the tripods made by Hephaestus, of which Homer relates that, of their own motion, they entered the conclave of Gods on Olympus, as if a shuttle should weave of itself, and a plectrum should do its own harp-playing.*[27]

Today, Aristotle's vision is being realized. Engineering drawings are transformed into post-processed tool paths and sent out over distributed numerical control (DNC) systems directly to the machining centers. Some flexible manufacturing systems (FMS) are close to being instruments that can do their own work like the statues of Daedalus. They are backed up by other systems that can help schedule processes and products. Given these developments, can we expect the continuation of this process until all of manufacturing is totally automated? Does this not make it easy to equate automation and CIM, with CIM being the total connection of all automated activities?

Some authors, such as Teicholz and Orr, have chosen to define CIM as if it were a natural continuation of the automationist tradition:

*Computer-integrated manufacturing (CIM) is the term used to describe the complete automation of the factory, with all processes functioning under computer control and only digital information tying them together. In CIM, the need for paper is eliminated, and so also are most human jobs. CIM is the ostensible evolutionary outcome of computer-aided design and drafting and computer-aided manufacturing (CADD/CAM).*

*Why is CIM desirable? Because it reduces the human component of manufacturing and thereby relieves the process of its most expensive and error-prone ingredient. . . .* [28]

This definition is an excellent example of the automationist point of view taken to its logical conclusion. It implies that the enemy is the human element, because it is "error-prone." Paper and people, the two variables that do not lend themselves to consistency and predictability, will be removed by CIM. But what is the underlying assumption of this definition? It is routine work. In the Teicholz and Orr conceptualization of CIM, routinized processes are handled by hardware and software, not people.

Also implicit in this definition is a focus on the factory floor, where the most direct labor takes place. But what about the interaction between marketing and engineering? Is it outside the scope of CIM? It is probably excluded in Teicholz and Orr's definition. Certainly their choice of topics in the *Computer Integrated Manufacturing Handbook* shows a clear focus on engineering and manufacturing.

Is there a place in CIM for the other functions, such as marketing, sales, finance, and service? Are the people there also to be replaced by automation because they are "error-prone"? It may seem so, but there is more to the story. It is one thing for Aristotle to envision the automated shuttle; it is another to bring it about throughout all functions in an organization. We are clearly not anywhere near there yet. Aristotle envisions an automation in which managers will not need subordinates and masters will not need slaves.

Two of Aristotle's ideas have particularly influenced the way we interact with one another. The first is the *master-servant* relationship; the second deals with the ancients' disdain for labor *or* work. The master-servant principle is embodied in our organization and in labor laws concerning agency and ownership. This idea is most clearly manifested in the notion of employer-employee, a modern term for the old master-servant idea. This notion assumes that the master or employer has the right to be arbitrary, to decide without consulting the servant or employee. There is a lot of precedent and legal doctrine surrounding management prerogatives that are embodied in labor-management contracts and laws.

A disdain for labor and work (these terms are being used synonymously) was built into the Greek language. To them, work was a curse and nothing else. Their name for work, *ponos,* has the same root as the Latin *poena,* meaning "sorrow." For the Greeks, *ponos* was colored with the same sense of a burdensome task that we feel in the words *fatigue* and *travail.* Hesiod defined happiness as a life free from work. According to Homer, the gods hated humankind and out of spite condemned men and women to a life of toil. The Greeks deplored the mechanical arts as brutalizing the mind and making it unfit to think about truth. Even free artisans and craftsmen were scorned as hardly better than slaves. Such intolerance was natural in a society where most heavy labor was done by slaves.[29]

Nevertheless, the old Western prejudices remain in assumptions about job design, training, authority, and responsibility. People still believe that the higher a person is in the hierarchy, the more important he or she is. Often those professionals and workers who add the most value to the product are the least valued in the organization. Even though direct labor costs now constitute only 2 to 15 percent of total costs, the drive to automate persists.

Several tentative conclusions can be reached at this point. First, automation is one way to deal with the negative connotations of work and labor as toil. Laborers are not expected to be thinkers; they do not have the leisure. Therefore, they have to be trained and closely supervised, or so we are taught by the tradition carried on by Charles Babbage, Frederick Winslow Taylor, and others. When Teicholz and Orr speak of labor as "error-proneness," are they not reinforcing this centuries-old prejudice?

Second, the thinking behind the master-servant model also assumes that the former does the thinking and the latter the doing. Why should we ask labor or even some professionals their opinion about what is going on? Are they not supposed to do only what they were trained to do? This might have made sense in Taylor's era, which was characterized by routine production processes. But it makes less sense when companies are faced with the need to continually change and upgrade their technologies, forge closer links with their suppliers and customers, manage for quality and excellence, and deal with shorter product cycles.

Two consequences result from this prejudice against labor and from the master-servant model: (1) middle-level professionals and labor are not taken seriously as thinkers, and (2) professionals and middle managers are to be replaced if possible with automation so their "error-proneness" does not muck up the works.

This line of reasoning, in turn, leads to two fundamental problems:

1.  We fail to listen to and benefit from the insights, knowledge, and visions of those who are actually doing the work.

2.  Automation often reduces the flexibility of the organization, especially at a time when flexibility is most needed.

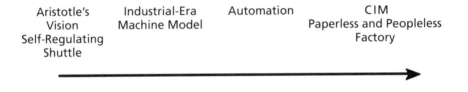

Figure 9.3 **Automationist's linear view of CIM**

Automation has an important role to play, especially in addressing routine tasks, but there is a growing shift toward nonroutine activities, where teams of professionals and managers must be supported, not eliminated.

Aristotle's concept of automation has continued to evolve into the industrial era's "machine model," in which all parts of the organization mesh like clockwork gears.

As our thinking evolved, we first spoke of hard automation, then soft automation, and now CIM, the supposed "paperless and peopleless factory." Figure 9.3 illustrates this evolution.

The problem with this linear thinking is that it misses the critical dimension of integration. The automationists are doing us a disservice to equate total automation with CIM, because CIM is something qualitatively different from a paperless and peopleless factory. It makes more sense to think of CIM and CIE as a partnership between people and technology.

In the CIM literature there is tension and a great deal of uncertainty as to whether CIM is heading toward the "paperless and peopleless" enterprise, or whether "integration," assisted by the computer and networking, will enable people to work together. In most manufacturing establishments, the direct labor base is shrinking as are management ranks. Many companies that once maintained eight to fifteen levels of management now find they can operate with four to six levels. Our enterprises of the future will produce more with fewer people, but each person will be more valuable. Since there is always room for new and dynamic companies, new employment opportunities will replace the jobs that fall to automation.

## Automation and CIM

To be sure, a lot of money has been spent on industrial automation, often with good success. Flexible manufacturing systems are proving their worth in a good many installations. The slash is coming out of CAD/CAM, as engineering departments send parts programs directly to numerical control (NC) equipment on the shop floor and as they learn the rules of design for assembly (DFA). Bar coding is spreading. Companies are finally obtaining the training required for successful MRP II efforts. In the service sector, airlines are making money from their computer-based reservation systems, banks are extending their automated teller machines, and distributors are putting terminals on their customers' premises.

The picture is anything but black and white. The landscape is a patchwork quilt of successes together with numerous unpublicized failures. With these general successes, is it not a matter of time before interfacing becomes integration? Yes and no. Third and fourth generation computers will be used long into the future, even as fifth generation computers become more commercially viable. These successes represent isolated accomplishments within the hierarchy rather than true steps toward integration. We can expect the old ways of organization to persist well into the next century.

Given the hold that the conceptual principles of the early and late industrial eras still have on our thinking, it is not surprising that we should want to computerize and network our steep hierarchies. However, although computers and networking may be flexible, there is an inherent inflexibility in the thinking underlying steep hierarchies, and this is a significant source of the problem.

Bill Lawrence, plant manager of the Texas Instruments facility in Sherman, Texas, remarked during an Automation Forum meeting that he regretted investing $3 million in a state-of-the-art computerized high-bay storage facility.[30] Even though it provided great flexibility to move work in process in and out, it was of less value as the company moved to a Just-in-Time approach. He now wishes that money could be available to invest in the training and education of his plant personnel.

In 1987, Lawrence's facility received the prestigious LEAD Award (Leadership and Excellence in the Application and Development of CIM) from the Computer and Automated Systems Association of the Society of Manufacturing Engineers, in part because of the human climate of openness and trust that he created. Certainly he was trying to break out of the attitudes of the industrial era, although the web of capital investment decisions made over the years did not make it easy. In many ways, Lawrence's values and approach are unique. Most managers are still "CIMizing" their steep hierarchies.

This trend can be seen in the "reference model" being developed by a wide variety of groups in the United States, Europe, and Japan. The Factory Automation System of Computer Aided Manufacturing–International (CAM-I); the U.S. Air Force's Factory of the Future project; the Purdue Workshop's Reference Model for CIM; the International Standards Organization's Technical Committee 184, Working Group 5's model; the National Institute of Standards and Technology's Automated Manufacturing Research Facility; and even the European CIM/Open Systems Architecture model all, in their own ways, focus on interconnecting the technologies of various levels of the organization.

The working notion is that of hierarchical control. Even though the structures being modeled are not hierarchical, this approach tends to cast them in a hierarchical mindset (Figure 9.4).

The two key words related to this structure are *hierarchical* and *control*. The model presupposes the steep hierarchy and assumes that the key concept is control, with orders coming down from the top and information filtering up, much as they have done for the past hundred years in the manual mode.

**Levels:**

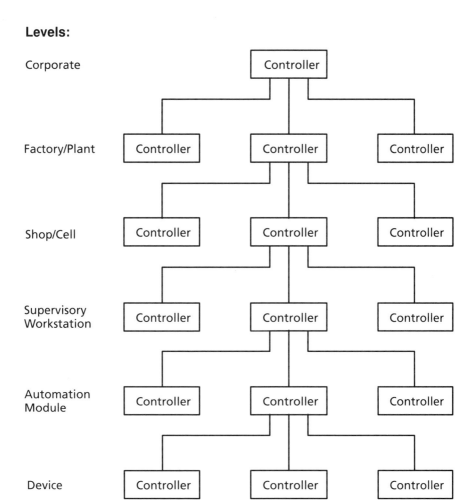

Figure 9.4 **Typical hierarchical control system**

Many people are working on standards so that there will be well-defined protocols between levels and so that equipment from different vendors will fit into one structure. Industry's search for more open standards, to allow for interoperability, has given a strong boost to UNIX, Manufacturing Automation Protocol (MAP), Technical and Office Protocol (TOP), Initial Graphics Exchange Specification (IGES), Product Data Exchange Specification (PDES), Electronic Design Interchange

Format (EDIF), various graphic interchange standards, and X/Open. These efforts will continue to grow in importance as connectivity and interoperability become central issues.

### Integration: An Evolving Concept

Computer integrated manufacturing is a marvelously vague concept that defies easy definition. The father of CIM, Joe Harrington, Jr., who coined the term in 1973, studied the way computer applications were beginning to penetrate the engineering and operations functions of manufacturing organizations. He realized that a good number of the major manufacturing functions were "potentially susceptible to computer control."[31] He also recognized the human impact of CIM, stating that "the functions of management at all levels will undergo a major change."[32]

Ten years later, by the time Harrington wrote his second book, *Understanding the Manufacturing Process*,[33] he had broadened his concept of CIM to include the entire manufacturing company. He considered manufacturing a "monolithic function." This second book discussed how the functions could interact as a seamless whole.

Harrington was helpful to Dennis Wisnosky and Dan Shunk in designing the U.S. Air Force's Integrated Computer Aided Manufacturing (ICAM) program in the mid-1970s, and their work, in turn, influenced Harrington's second book. The ICAM program was visionary in showing that a new approach was necessary to achieve integration in manufacturing firms. Wisnosky and Shunk developed a "wheel" to illustrate the architecture of their ICAM project and to show the various elements that had to work together (Figure 9.5). They were among the first to understand the web of interdependencies needed for integration. Their work represents the first major step in shifting the focus of manufacturing from a series of sequential operations to parallel processing. The ICAM program has spent over $100 million to develop tools, techniques, and processes to support manufacturing integration and has influenced the CIM project efforts of many companies.

The growing use of the word "architecture" is itself a recognition that various activities are interrelated and should be coordinated. Companies are now developing material architectures, information systems architectures, data architectures, and distribution architectures.

The Air Force's ICAM program recognizes the role of data as central to any integration effort. Data is to be common and shareable across functions. This concept still remains ahead of its time, because most major companies will not seriously begin to attack the data architecture challenge until well into the 1990s.

**Figure 9.5  U.S. Air Force's ICAM architecture**[34]

The ICAM program recognizes the need for ways to analyze and document the major activities performed within the manufacturing establishment. The Structured Analysis and Design Technique methodology, developed by Douglas Ross of Softech, was adapted for the ICAM program with his help.[35] It is called ICAM DEFinition methodology 0, or $IDEF_0$. The ICAM program also recognizes the importance of being able to identify the key information items (data entities) that should be captured, architected, and managed in an integrated manner. This has led to the creation of ICAM DEFinition methodology 1 for data architectures (IDEF$_1$), with the support of Dr. Robert R. Brown of Hughes, Stewart Coleman, and Dan Appleton of DACOM.

The need to simulate events in time led to the development of a simulation language, called ICAM DEFinition 2, or IDEF$_2$, from work primarily done by Pritsker & Associates. These IDEF methodologies have found widespread use, especially in the aerospace industry; they are now spreading to other industries as companies work to integrate diverse functions.

In response to this challenge, the ICAM program and the National Institute of Standards and Technology (NIST, formerly the National Bureau of Standards) also initiated the Initial Graphics Exchange Specification (IGES), which uses a neutral file format to enable CAD drawings to be translated from one vendor's system to another's. Roger Nagel, then of the NBS, Philip Kennicott of General Electric, and Walt Braithwaite of Boeing provided the first version of IGES. IGES has proved to be extremely important in integrating information from dissimilar CAD systems, and has undergone continual improvements under the leadership of Brad Smith of NIST.

NIST has taken responsibility for the continued evolution of IGES and has added a new initiative, also inspired by Air Force work, called Product Data Exchange Specification (PDES). PDES is intended to be a more intelligent and structured file format that transmits not only graphic representations, but bills of material, form and features, tolerances, test specifications, and the like. PDES is expected to grow into an internationally recognized standard called Standard for the Transfer and Exchange of Product model data (STEP) as part of the Department of Defense's Computer-aided Acquisition and Logistics Support system (CALS).

It is likely that the IGES and PDES efforts will become more significant as the Electronic Data Interchange (EDI) movement picks up speed. EDI, at this point, is primarily concerned with the ordering and invoicing cycles between companies and their suppliers, although its horizon is broadening fast. As experience is gained with EDI, there is a growing desire to include technical data interchange (TDI), which consists of product and process specifications like PDES, so that work can be bid on and managed between prime contractors and second- and third-tier suppliers. EDI and TDI are harbingers of the kinds of interorganizational integration challenges that loom on the horizon. They also illustrate how companies will communicate with one another based on their strategic alliances.

At about the same time as Harrington and the Air Force's ICAM staff were rethinking the intraorganizational elements of integration, John Hall was independently sketching out the first wheel for the Computer and Automated Systems Association (CASA) of the Society of Manufacturing Engineers (SME). This wheel has evolved from an engineering and operations perspective to one that involves the entire enterprise. The latest iteration of the CASA wheel[36] includes not only the engineering and manufacturing functions, but also marketing, finance, strategic planning, human resource management, and general management (Figure 9.6). It also recognizes the role of information resource management and communications (networking) along with common data.[37]

The CASA/SME CIM wheel is built around integrated systems architecture, which encompasses information resource management, communications (networking), and common data. In most manufacturing companies, there is very little architecture in the way the functions interact, and there is very little common data.

The ICAM and CASA wheels are significant in that they represent initial attempts to focus on the interaction among and between functions. John Hall has told me that as he was developing the CASA/SME Wheel he was aware of the inadequacy of the traditional hierarchical organization to foster effective collaboration between functions.[38]

There is, however, a growing awareness that CIM is too limited a concept, especially with its emphasis on computers and manufacturing. More and more, there is a desire to take an enterprise perspective which includes a recognition of the important contribution people play. This is why the CASA wheel is now called the *enterprise wheel*. For many of same reasons, Computer Aided Manufacturing International (CAM-I) in Austin, Texas, is supporting a working group attempting to define the outlines of computer integrative enterprises.

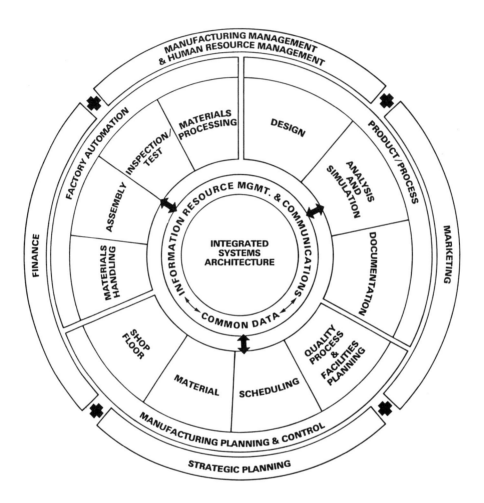

Figure 9.6 **CASA/SME CIM enterprise wheel**

## CIM and People

Where do people really fit into these models? In most of the reference models, there is almost no discussion of the human element. In a few there is an awareness that people have to be accounted for, but it is unclear how to do this. For example, the European ESPRIT CIM/OSA (European Strategic Program for Research and Development in Information Technology, Computer Integrated Manufacturing/Open Systems Architecture) project description booklet includes the following paragraph:

> From these short descriptions of the key points governing the CIM philosophy, it must be stressed that the human still plays a dominant role in its realization and execution. **The human operates and programs computers.**
>
> S(He) is involved in the complicated information transfer structures (communication equipment, information definition, and data transfer software). It is unthinkable that the design, manufacturing and installation processes could be handled without human participation. The current state of the art is still such that people are the dominant factor in this total process. **The point is that we had better make sure that in all our automation plans and strategies, the person is not forgotten.**[39] [Emphasis added.]

It is a step in the right direction when Kidd and others introduce the idea of human-centered CIM into the European CIM discussions. But is an admonition not to forget the human element adequate? Is technology destined to remove the human element? We may feel badly about this, so we remind ourselves that humans can at least operate and program computers. Luckily they will continue to have a role—at least for a while.

Joseph Harrington, Jr., saw CIM as a "control and communication structure." He felt that the competitive pressures of the marketplace would challenge companies to begin the process of reintegration:

> The term computer integrated manufacturing does not mean an automated factory. People are very much involved. New skills are required at the working level, and, of course, in the supervision of the working level. New skills are certainly involved at the next higher level, the planning and control level. Additionally, the managerial function changes radically. At least half the present functions of top and middle managers are removed to the data processor and the true functions of managers—innovation; management of people, money, and legal affairs; the selection of objectives and policies—become full-time regimens for the manager. It appears, too, that the day of the specialist is passing. The managers of tomorrow must be multi-specialists (not generalists). **Thus, a new kind of manager at all levels is required.** The impact of computer integrated manufacturing falls

*as heavily on the man as on the machine, a situation surely to be met with reluctance, if not outright opposition in many quarters.*[40] [Emphasis added.]

Harrington makes it clear that he does not see CIM as simply automating the factory as proposed by Teicholz and Orr. He foresees more involvement of people in the process, with much of the machine-tending work done by the computer at the work cell, allowing professionals and managers to be more innovative and to concentrate on managing people, money, objectives, and policies. He advocates "multispecialists" in place of narrow specialists or even generalists. As CIM changes the way traditional functions work together, this recognition will play an even more important role. In the future, cross-functional team members will need to be multispecialists as they work in virtual teams in virtual organizations, in much the same spirit as that of the task-focused teams of Drucker.

Implicit in Harrington's concept of CIM is an awareness that the computer will assist with the routine, freeing laborers, professionals, and managers to focus on the nonroutine. In his own way Harrington agrees with Olsen and anticipates Tom Peters's idea of the need to thrive on chaos.[41]

Interestingly enough, a working group of the Czechoslovakian Academy of Sciences produced a study in 1965 stating that computers would help free people from their machine-tending chores, pushing them into more involvement with planning and innovation, functions that require a higher level of creativity.[42] One way to encourage this ability was to enhance the artistic, dramatic, and musical environment. The theater and concert house were seen as important sources of creative inspiration. If Harrington is right in stating that there is a qualitative shift in the roles of laborers, professionals and managers, then the Czechoslovakian insight is right on target. In fact, if Harrington is right, we are going to have to rethink both our cultural and educational foundations. A stimulating and creative environment may well be a significant factor in encouraging innovation in the workplace.

Harrington's thesis concerning this shift in roles has been confirmed in studies done jointly by Nolan, Norton and Company (NNC), an information systems consulting firm, and Digital Equipment Corporation. NNC reports that three-fourths of a typical company's resources are used to transform information about products and processes and one-fourth to transform raw materials into finished goods. Thus our approach to structure and organization has to be qualitatively different from that of the industrial era.[43]

Zuboff also understands the limits of the hierarchy in an "informed organization." She believes that if we cannot come to terms with the new conditions of work, we will find "knowledge and authority on a collision course."[44] Knowledge represents our ability to see information from different levels of abstraction, while authority represents the power of the position within the hierarchy.

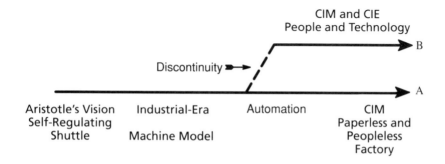

Figure 9.7 **Discontinuity in shift to CIM partnership**

This means that CIM is not a linear descendant of Aristotle's notion of automation. Instead, there is a discontinuity in the process. CIM and HCIM represent a new partnership between people and a computer-based, networked technology that enables professionals and managers to interact in new and more dynamic ways (see Figure 9.7).

In Figure 9.7, Teicholz and Orr represent track A, the automationist point of view. Harrington, on the other hand, recognized that CIM sets us on a new course, represented by track B. By implication, Harrington raises this question: How can we change the quality of interaction between functions so there is more innovation and creativity? He highlights the idea of multispecialists—people with knowledge and skill in several areas—rather than specialists. He implies that there is a need for in-depth capabilities tempered with a broad understanding of the interplay of functions.

In spite of Harrington's thoughts, the reminder in the ESPRIT CIM/OSA booklet, and Lawrence's remarks, the trend is to impose CIM on the steep hierarchy. It seems as though the automationist tradition has the upper hand—perhaps because of our preoccupation with technology. Thus the shift from CIM to CIE will require a fundamental rethinking of industrial-era conceptual principles. We need a new set of conceptual principles to support the emerging knowledge era, especially if we hope to achieve a break with the automationist mentality and free ourselves from the confinement of second-generation management. The next chapter explores the conceptual principles of the early knowledge era.

# 10

# Human Networking: Self-Empowering

In spite of all the noble words in corporate annual reports about people being the corporation's most important asset, the industrial-era mentality tells us that it is only a matter of time before our positions are automated out of existence. Reactions to this threat have taken many forms: participative management, job enlargement, job redesign, sociotechnical systems, employee involvement, and Quality of Work Life. These efforts have attempted to develop more meaningful task assignments. Their success has been limited, not because they are wrong in their vision and values, but because the task is so large and the vested interests are so well entrenched.

What is needed is a set of conceptual principles that redefines the central role of professionals—including managers and workers—as they work alone and on multiple teams. These conceptual principles should help us use the 70 to 90 percent of the knowledge needed to run the enterprise which is still in our heads. To leverage this valuable reservoir

147

of knowledge, skill, and experience, we must create working conditions under which our learning, insights, vision, and motivations can be more effectively utilized. This chapter focuses on five principles, highlighted in Figure 10.1 from the perspective of the historical eras.

These conceptual principles are not new creations but rather are reflections of an understanding of the fundamental nature of our humanness. In order to appreciate the significance of these principles, we must first look at the pressures being exerted upon steep hierarchies from both business and technical sources.

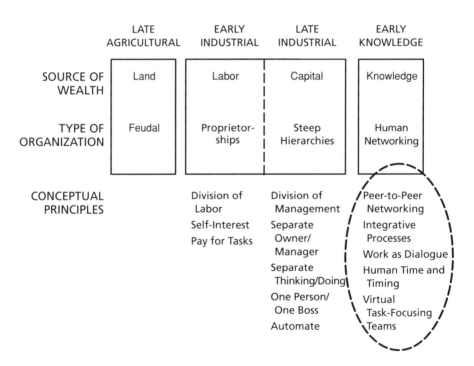

**Historical Eras**

|  | LATE AGRICULTURAL | EARLY INDUSTRIAL | LATE INDUSTRIAL | EARLY KNOWLEDGE |
|---|---|---|---|---|
| SOURCE OF WEALTH | Land | Labor | Capital | Knowledge |
| TYPE OF ORGANIZATION | Feudal | Proprietor-ships | Steep Hierarchies | Human Networking |
| CONCEPTUAL PRINCIPLES |  | Division of Labor<br>Self-Interest<br>Pay for Tasks | Division of Management<br>Separate Owner/Manager<br>Separate Thinking/Doing<br>One Person/One Boss<br>Automate | Peer-to-Peer Networking<br>Integrative Processes<br>Work as Dialogue<br>Human Time and Timing<br>Virtual Task-Focusing Teams |

Figure 10.1 **Chapter focus: conceptual principles of the early knowledge era**

## Steep Hierarchies under Pressure

Recognizing the energy-sapping effects of top-heavy management, many corporations, such as General Electric and Ford, are "delayering" themselves and cutting management positions. Executives are learning to lead with fewer levels of management below them.

At the same time, companies are producing more with less direct labor because of better work methods and automation. Depending on the industry, the typical cost of direct labor is now 2 to 15 percent of total costs. The trend toward a flatter hierarchy (Figure 10.2) is attributable not so much to automation as to business factors—the realization that our organizations are overstaffed and that layer upon layer of paper pushers and report expediters make the organization sluggish and unresponsive to the market.

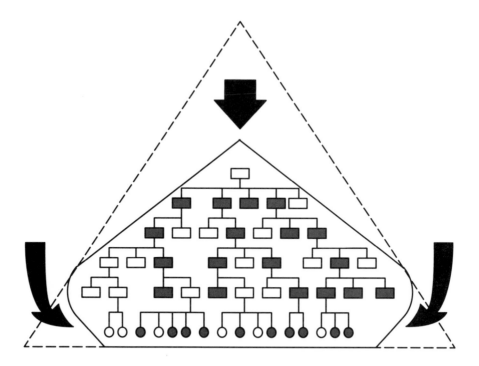

Figure 10.2 **Steep hierarchies under pressure**

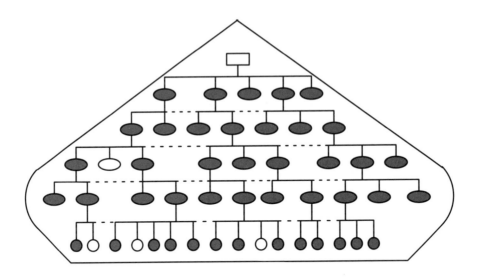

Figure 10.3 **Shift from boxes to people as resource centers in human networking enterprises**

What happens when we flatten the hierarchy? We get a little less of the same thing. Even though there are fewer levels of management, people still suppose that their box is sacred territory which can be defended at all costs. Organizational flattening only treats the symptoms; it does not fundamentally redefine relationships between people and functions in the organization. Functions still work sequentially, making decisions from fragmented perspectives.

Suppose, instead, we were to think of ourselves and our positions within the organization not as fixed little empires, but as resources available to others. If we were to see ourselves not as boxes but as nodes in a network, not as cogs in a gear but as knowledge contributors and decision points, our support of one another would increase dramatically.

To shift from rectangles to ovals in a drawing is one thing, but it is something quite different to emotionally and intellectually accept the changes this implies. It is wrenching to give up the comfort of known job boundaries and established reporting relationships. When we first see ourselves as resources in a network of other people, we cannot help but feel vulnerable. Yet this vulnerability brings challenge and excitement to the work environment.

We are beginning to understand that it will take resources from many functions, working together, to distinguish and respond to patterns so that knowledge-era organizations will have the necessary market resiliency. Organizational learning and the ability to synthesize information are essential. Management must draw upon these multiple resources to perform tasks, much as a conductor draws on the instruments in an orchestra or a coach mentors a basketball team.

Figure 10.3 symbolizes this change by replacing the boxes by ovals. To be meaningful, a switch in attitudes and expectations is also needed. The boxes of the traditional hierarchy have come to represent the turf that is "owned and controlled" by the position. The ovals represent a "capacity and knowledge" resource that is available to join with others in order to deal with the multiple challenges of the enterprise.

In the network enterprise, each position, or oval, represents a person with capabilities, skills, and experience. Instead of mutually exclusive tasks (jobs) and departmental assignments (charters), enterprises blend the talents of different people around focused tasks (Figure 10.4). Thus individual talents, knowledge, experience, and aspirations become more important resources in network enterprises than they ever could be in steep hierarchies.

Thanks, in part, to ready access to computer network infrastructures, companies are using more cross-functional task teams. These teams may appear under many different names: project teams, concurrent engineering teams, competency teams, account teams, network teams, bid teams, task forces, and steering committees. The idea of using teams is not new. Alvin Toffler has been writing for years about "ad-hocracy," the use of short-term task forces,[1] but it has been hard for many executives to conceive of organizations with the randomness that an ad-hocracy suggests.

Instead of a random ad hoc approach, we need to structure an increasing amount of the enterprise's work around well-defined multiple cross-functional teams, even if executives may worry about maintaining focus and coordination within such a fluid organization. Nevertheless, we know we must experiment—because, as Leslie Berkes suggests, the pyramidal organizational structure is no longer working.[2]

How do we find cohesion and structure in a fluid and dynamic environment? One way is to understand the conceptual principles that can help us to lead and manage knowledge-era enterprises.

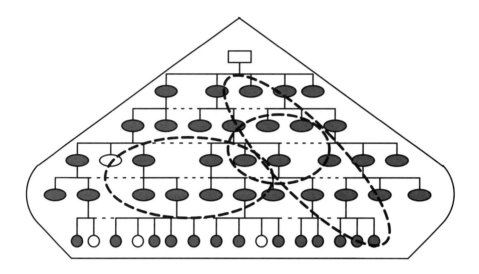

Figure 10.4 **Designating cross-functional virtual task teams**

## Conceptual Principles of the Early Knowledge Era

Although the exploration of knowledge-era principles will be new, what they recognize will not be. Was gravity created when Newton discovered it? Did the sun only stop revolving around the earth when Copernicus proposed his heliocentric theory?

I suggest that there are five conceptual principles of the early knowledge era: (1) peer-to-peer networking, (2) the integrative process, (3) work as dialogue, (4) human time and timing, and (5) virtual task–focusing teams. To understand these concepts, we will explore each theme individually, then look at their interrelationships. This is part of a reinterpretation process we will need in order to work our way out of the constraining legacy of the industrial eras.

### Peer-to-Peer Networking

Peer-to-peer networking has three aspects: technology, information and people. The technology of peer-to-peer networking allows each node to communicate directly with every other node, without having to filter through a hierarchical arrangement. Peer-to-peer information assumes that people and applications have ready access wherever the information may be located. And peer-to-peer people networking assumes that individuals have access to one another's knowledge wherever it may be in the enterprise. In all three instances, we have moved beyond the superior-subordinate attitude of industrial-era steep hierarchies.

In the early days of computing, different processors were expected to communicate hierarchically. With the development of minicomputers, the advantage of peer-to-peer computing became clear: any node can talk to any other node. All the major computer companies are now building this capability into their systems; this makes it simple to configure and reconfigure resources on the network.

Peer-to-peer information access is a major challenge. It is one thing to be able to connect computers together on the network, but it is quite another to support interoperability between dissimilar operating systems. In addition, even though client-server computing is allowing us to reach any other node in a network with ease, we face major hurdles in interfacing multiple applications.

Over the years companies have developed hundreds of applications on different computers. As we network these computers, the natural tendency is to want to interface the applications as well, so that we can share common information. Unfortunately, applications written at different times have used different naming conventions. One of the biggest problems we face is that various applications may use different words to mean the same thing, the same words to mean different things, or different shades of meaning for the same words. This problem was discussed in Chapter 8.

The most significant change that peer-to-peer networking brings is in the way people in the enterprise interact with one another. The superior-subordinate relationship of the steep hierarchy assumes that a higher level is an indication of superiority. It may indicate superiority in rank, but it does not guarantee superiority of knowledge.

If we can begin to envision the resources of the enterprise arranged in a large circle, as was discussed in Book 1, it will be easier to think of tapping into the resident knowledge, wherever it may reside, as we form multiple task teams. Each of the functions becomes a resource from which talented people can be drawn together.

In the industrial era, as teams are formed, the members are sometimes told to "protect our department's interest." Moreover, members of the teams often compete with one another to show how clever they are. At times it may be necessary to have every department equally represented on megateams. These behaviors mitigate against effective teamwork, because as team members put one another down, they become mired in the politics of the organization and do not actively contribute to the success of the project.

Suppose instead that we were told by our managers to do our best, that we really wanted to learn from one another, and that each team had only those resources needed to get the task done. The quality of work within and between teams would be greatly enhanced.

Peer-to-peer networking assumes that there will be teamwork of teams. Small, well-defined and well-staffed teams will meet with one another periodically to share their learning, insights, and challenges. We will cross-fertilize one another's efforts. We will develop a rhythm of meeting which allows us to work on the particular, without losing sight of the larger context. And as the team members work together and learn from one another, we will be refreshing and renewing our knowledge and visions.

Peer-to-peer networking allows us to pull people together to work cross-functionally on market opportunities, instead of parsing the various aspects of those opportunities into stiff and rigid steep hierarchies, as the dialogue in Book 1 indicates. This allows us to size up a problem's patterns and make this learning available to others in our company.

Peer-to-peer networking does not homogenize people into bland commonality. Instead, it sharpens our perceptions of one another's talents and abilities. We learn to value differences and to play off each other's strengths. We become more important as individuals as we participate on multiple teams, because our knowledge and talents are sought after by the other members.

Our natural leadership abilities are challenged and nurtured when we are continually being asked to assume leadership or support others' leadership. Each team needs a talented project leader. Over time this role will rotate to different people. I may be the project leader on one team, while on another I actively support another's leadership.

New arrangements of local and wide-area networks are making possible dynamic peer-to-peer collaboration between people, processes, and companies. Applications can be run through the network, putting the power of the mainframe on the desktop. Text and graphics can be shared in new ways. People can work interactively, passing information back and forth in an iterative manner while developing ideas, instead of becoming bogged down in turf warfare and in managing the sequential handoffs of paper-based systems.

Peer-to-peer networking assumes that as we network, we add value based on our thinking, observing, knowledge, and vision. Managers, professionals, and employees are no longer cogs that must mesh together, as in a machine in a steep hierarchy—we are knowledge contributors and decision points, or nodes, within the network.

H. Chandler Stevens describes this shift to networking in a short poem:

*I'd rather be a node in a network*
  *Than a cog in the gear of a machine.*
*A node is involved with things to resolve,*
  *While a cog must mesh with cogs in between.*[3]

As we picture ourselves as nodes or decision points within the network, we will sense our own empowerment. Empowerment is not like carrying a credit card; it must come from within to be effective.

Peer-to-peer networking assumes that people are not superior or inferior; each has something of substance to add to the overall output. This assumption contradicts the Greek notion of the inferiority of human work. On the contrary, work brings excitement and challenge and is the basis of growth.

A peer-to-peer model of networking requires a different coordination strategy from that of the traditional hierarchical organization; otherwise, indecision will rule the day. As people make decisions in a networked environment, there has to be some commonality of context. We need to understand how our own activities are going to fit into a larger whole and how to draw upon common information resources—knowledge—so that we can see significant patterns, adding value through our own insights and wisdom.

Peer-to-peer networking does not eliminate the hierarchy; it just recasts its role and function. Companies still need some levels of authority. There are times when decisive leadership from the top is necessary. But executives of the flatter hierarchy move away from our preoccupation with the prerogatives of "decision making." Instead, we find we get better results when we actively listen to our teams, ask challenging questions, define the context for the teams, and build our resources.

We also need to be in touch with one another in meaningful ways so that we can deal with complexity and act decisively in support of the larger organization. This suggests that "being in touch" is more than just being able to reach another person on the network; instead, it implies that the integrative process is multidimensional and continuous.

## The Integrative Process

In a modern enterprise, people and processes are not set in concrete; they are virtual resources, available when called upon. Constant adjustments are necessary as the enterprise responds to ever-changing customer expectations, market conditions, government regulations, competitor activities, and supply strategies. In a fluid environment, as teams are configured and reconfigured, the challenge is to continually "reach out and touch" the thinking of others in order to identify and act upon significant patterns.

In fact, seeing the significant patterns together as teams is the challenge of any enterprise. Too often, different departments see portions of a pattern and act as if they have seen the whole. Technical networking provides us with the connectivity across functions we need in order to see, reflect upon, and act on these patterns together.

The integrative process requires us to be in touch with the key patterns inside and outside the enterprise. It involves perception, judgment, and the will to act: this is why the role of people is very important. The integrative process is not something that is fixed; it requires continual dynamic reconfiguring of ideas, people, processes, and resources.

Among the most critical ingredients of the integrative process are the knowledge and values that those in the enterprise accumulate over the years. This knowledge makes it possible to see, interpret, and act upon significant patterns. Unfortunately, this knowledge is woefully underutilized in most enterprises because of the internal logic of steep hierarchies, whose accounting and reward systems have no way to value them.

Traditional management strategies are out of place in a networked enterprise. They do not encourage workers and professionals to build learning capabilities or to develop the ability to see significant patterns and align resources rapidly.

This is why the use of the word integrated creates a false sense that one arrangement will serve for all time. Business ideas evolve, technologies evolve, capabilities evolve, and people grow in their understanding and knowledge, so it makes little sense to develop hard-and-fast walls between functions, operations, or people. To be successful we need to spend time getting to know the human capabilities, experiences, knowledge, and values of the others in the enterprise.

New developments in organizational development (OD) theory are aiding in this process. Instead of thinking that the task is to figure out a needed change, unfreeze the organization, institute the change, and then refreeze everything, OD now supports continuous change.[4]

What is important is not just the storage of bits and bytes on hard disks connected by networks; it is the knowledge of the people in the enterprise and our ability to bring this knowledge to the task of seeing, interpreting, and acting decisively on significant patterns. This is why we call our new age the early knowledge era, rather than the information era. In this era, work recaptures its natural meaning.

## Work as Dialogue

What is work? We began our discussion of automation with the Greek attitude toward labor and work. This described not what work *is* but one culture's attitude toward it. In this section, a more fundamental examination of work itself is in order.[5]

Work is part of our everyday experience, yet it can be elusive in its meaning: we know what it is—until we are asked! Of course, it is exertion, what we get paid for, the result of our efforts, being in operation like a machine, and the application of energy to accomplish an altered state of affairs. But what is the essential character of work?

The answer to this challenging question is critical, because our attitudes toward work and its organization have shaped the context in which we perform every day. Does "Work is exertion" tell me what it is? Does "Work is what we get paid for"? "Work is being in operation like a machine"? "Work is a measure of energy applied"? "Work is the result of the effort"? Only partially!

In the industrial era, there seem to be three notions that have shaped our thinking about work: (1) it is effort or travail, (2) it is being in operation like a machine, and (3) it is what we get paid for. Why should these three definitions predominate? As the industrial era began, Newtonian physics was still the rule, with its orderly universe operating like clockwork. As early as Descartes, the machine was the major reference model. People were fascinated by figuring out how the pieces fit together. They also had to content themselves with receiving compensation for giving up their time to work for someone else.

In the industrial context, these notions fit nicely with the idea of the division and subdivision of labor. Each activity was to fit into the larger whole like a cog in the gear of a machine. The natural task was to become expert at the routines so that the enterprise operated like a well-oiled machine.

No wonder the need to introduce bureaucracy and routine has been a major management challenge in the industrial era. Certainly the automationists have accepted these ideas and want to use CIM to perfect their vision.

The "physics" of organizations continues to rely more on the outdated notions of Newton than on the newer principles of Heisenberg and Einstein. Even though the rigor and determinism of Newtonian physics has given way to the indeterminacy of Heisenberg or the nonlinearity of the new physics of chaos, we are still trying to build into our manufacturing and service organizations the same mechanical routines.

Such experts as Drucker, Beer, Trist, Peters, Briggs, and Peat speak of the turbulence, the uncertainty, and the chaos of the environments in which our firms operate.[6] Nevertheless, we have not really understood the new physics from an organizational perspective. This is unfortunate, because it means that we continually misappropriate our technology and human resources, trying to arrange them in configurations that are inappropriate for the tasks at hand.

Human energy remains bottled up in organizational structures that allow little room for true human creativity. A new wave of management literature speaks of human empowerment: Waterman's *The Renewal Factor* and Kanter's *The Change Masters* as well as a growing discussion on high-performance systems.[7]

Let us return to the question at hand: *What is work?*

When you and I work, we are involved in a *process* of doing something in time. We are engaging in a series of acts that have a pattern, in much the same way that a piece of music consists of a series of notes arranged in a particular pattern. The creations of the pattern become the *products* of the effort. Work then involves *processes* and *products* (Figure 10.5).

In the process of working, we are giving expression or form to our visions (the future which is in the now), enhanced by our knowledge (the past which flows with us). The quality of the process of giving expression is very much dependent upon our ability to listen to the themes being expressed and to respond accordingly. Our work is also dependent upon the quality of our visions and the knowledge we have available. In other words, our ability to listen (present), see (future), and remember (past) must play together in the process of work.

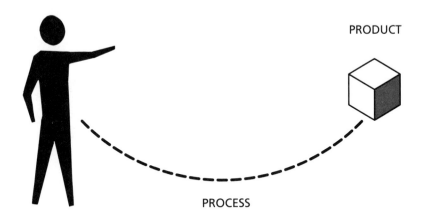

Figure 10.5 **Work involves process and product**

The product of the effort embodies the thoughts and ideas of the process. The result is the *expression*—literally, "pressing out." That which is inside us presses out. We give birth to new arrangements, new patterns, new conditions. When we see what we have done, we may be either inspired by its quality or depressed that it does not match our vision and knowledge of what it might have become.

We can see both the process by which we express ourselves and the product of that expression (Figure 10.6). As we see what we have done and how we have done it, we can choose to repeat the process or to improve and alter it, thereby altering the resulting product. We do this all the time. The process may be building, scheduling, writing, researching, coordinating, or arranging. The products may be widgets, schedules, reports, research findings, task team efforts, or meetings.

Work has a more fundamental meaning than whether we get *paid* for our time, one of its classic definitions. There is human engagement and expression in work, wonder and uncertainty, and a striving to give expression. As we press out these ideas in ourselves, the excitement of discovery, exploration, and accomplishment seasons our work experience.

We grow as we are able to master a process and see the results of the effort embodied in the product.

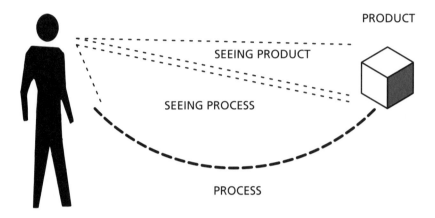

Figure 10.6 **"Seeing" the process and product**

The traditional concept of work in the industrial era has little understanding of this simple and natural process. Instead, people are expected to fit into a small portion of a larger process. We are trained to do something and are told not to deviate from the established procedures. Our visions are considered unimportant and liable to get in the way. Our knowledge is of little real value. Instead, we are to put ourselves in a predetermined setting and perform our rote skills.

This system is based not on trust but distrust. In fact, many of the activities in our industrial-era enterprises are there not to add value but to check and double-check whether people have been performing their assigned tasks. Distrust is a natural corollary of the division and subdivision of labor; it is built right into the fabric of our organizations and cannot be overcome by exhortations to be more trustful.

There is a significant difference between work in which we are engaged—listening, visioning, and remembering—and work in which we are just doing what we are told. Most jobs in industrial-era companies are defined in ways that make it hard for both the worker and manager to see the entire process. Industrial-era jobs do not give people a clear understanding of the nature of the product. A significant part of the process and the product is locked into a black box, out of sight of the individual contributor (Figure 10.7).

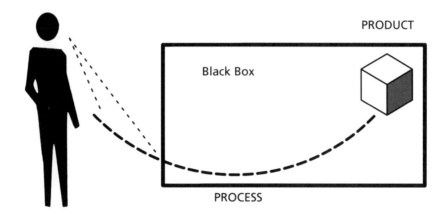

Figure 10.7 **Portion of process and product hidden**

Is it any wonder that workers take a short-sighted approach to the process and the product? Changes made to their part of the process may not be compatible with other portions of the process, with downstream consequences that surprise everyone. As a result, process and product configuration management is a difficult and thankless task in many organizations.

Work is then an activity involving a process of expression and an evolving product. The existence of a product sets up an anticipation pattern of how the product may vary in the future. Once something is created, we wonder how it may be improved. The product is not an isolated entity but the statement of an effort at a particular point in time. It is, in essence, an invitation to *dialogue*.

For example, companies may produce a product, then vary it in subsequent product offerings. If the product hits a responsive chord, there is a sense of excitement as new versions are brought to market. For example, Ashton-Tate set an expectation pattern in motion with dBase I; the product has grown since then through additional iterations.

What is the value of a well-executed process? What is the value of a well-designed product? Both can bring satisfaction, recognition, and a completeness to the effort which both challenges and inspires. This is also part of the dialogue.

In producing something, from a musical score to a bookshelf, we see the process and the product not in isolation but within the larger horizon of our visions and knowledge. Our mastery of the process and the resulting product inspire us to want to use our skills, vision, and knowledge to bring out variations on the product by varying our techniques. This is really a *self-dialogue*, combining vision and knowledge in a dialogue with ourselves and others. When we are engaged in a process that is creative, innovative, or experimental, what we are learning becomes available for future efforts. As we master the process, we find our vision broadened and we are encouraged to create bolder visions (Figure 10.8).

Notice the integrative process involved in work. We need to be *in touch* with our vision and knowledge dynamically as the product is being developed. Before we can make something, we envision what is to be made. This vision is of a future state of affairs, but it is very much here in the present as it guides us in our projects.

A vision without knowledge is unrealizable. Knowledge gained from past study, training, and experiences becomes a resource which stays with us. Our visions and our knowledge come from two sources: (1) our own experiences, training, and studies; and (2) the collected experiences and knowledge of the culture of which we are a part, whether they were gained at home, in school, or through the media. As we reach out and share experience, knowledge, and visions with one another, we are involved in human networking. This is more than simply connectivity between people; in a concrete sense it involves our ability to interrelate our vision and knowledge in a creative manner.

Networking not only is an individual process; it also involves the person in a community of others. Too often engineers will get fancy in a new design rather than using listed parts and techniques. This creativity can unnecessarily add to inventory and introduce complexity into the manufacturing process. Engineers should stay in touch with the material and manufacturing constraints of their organization. This is the dynamic side of the integrative process, of being in touch not only with one's own vision and knowledge, but also with the vision and knowledge of the larger organization, which may be articulated in its strategic plans, budgets, market analyses, engineering standards, and operating norms.

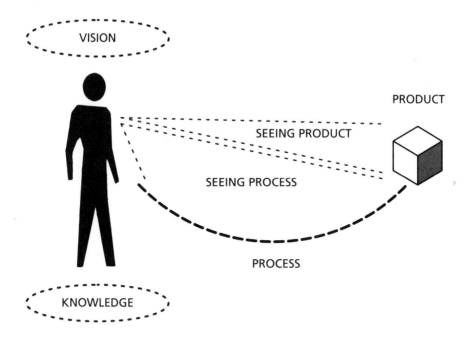

Figure 10.8 **Work as dialogue: using vision and knowledge to shape process and product**

Work involves not just one process and one product, but a continual process of producing many products and variations on these products. Feedback from the process is important in order to improve it; feedback from the use of the product will add knowledge and vision as it is attempted again.

Work is an iterative process, never conducted in a vacuum. Instead, it is very much a creative process when it is viewed as a whole. When work's wholeness is stripped away, as it is in so many industrial-era jobs, the worker or professional feels like a prisoner in the present, without the right to have a vision or recognition for the knowledge he or she has accumulated over the years.

Notice the creative elements in the work process. As we make, build, write, or coordinate, something is created. We are also adding to our vision and knowledge. We create in our minds the possibility that we can do something similar to what someone else may have produced. This becomes part of our vision and accrues to each individual's knowledge.

Work is a *transitive* verb: We make something.

Work can also be a *reflexive* verb: We make ourselves as we work.

Our vision and knowledge are being enriched. Our work is also creative for others because it challenges or adds to their visions and knowledge.

In its essence, work is a *form-bestowing activity*.[8] It empowers. It not only forms products, it also informs the worker (vision and knowledge) and informs or inspires others (their visions and knowledge). The actual product produced is only one aspect of the overall work effort (Figure 10.9).

As shown in Figure 10.9, work is a multifaceted activity. We (A) are producing not just one item but six. We are involved in a process (1) that results in a product (2). We see the process and product, and it inspires our vision (3) and adds to our knowledge (4). Another person (B) also sees what was done and the resulting product, which adds a dimension to this person's vision (5) and knowledge (6).

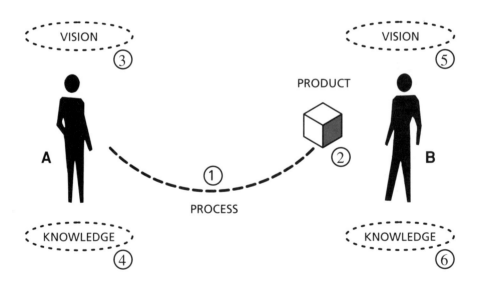

Figure 10.9 **Work as dialogue with self and others**

We (A) gain recognition not only through seeing our own process and product, but through being seen by the other person (B). We may discuss the process and the product with someone else and together see aspects that neither of us had seen individually. We learn together and add further information to our knowledge. This is work as dialogue.

Suppose we are craftspeople who have mastered an entire process. What happens if this process is divided into a number of steps (Figure 10.10), as in Adam Smith's pin-making factory? The worker (A) loses an overview of the entire process. The product is also hidden by the fragmentation in the process. Work ceases to be a dialogue; instead it becomes drudgery.

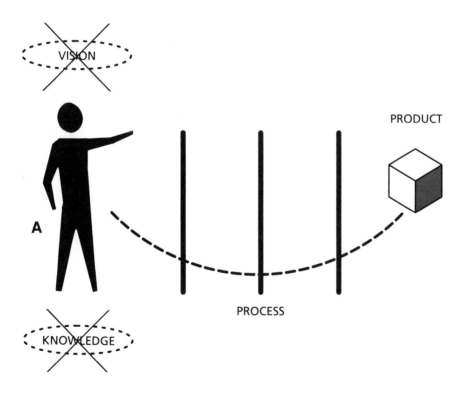

Figure 10.10 **Production process cut into tiny steps**

There is no excitement, no wonder. There is nothing that inspires people's vision or accrues to their knowledge. And there is no meaningful recognition, because it is hard to see what any individual has contributed creatively.

In fact, what is desired in this system is not creativity, but conformity to the established procedures. Supervision will be needed to make sure these people conform to the company's procedures and goals. Workers are told to leave their vision and knowledge at home and just follow the process instructions. These people are out of touch with the *wholeness* of the operation. They are no longer involved in an integrative process but in a fraction of a process.

The whole strategy of the industrial era has been to fragment the work process so that few can see the overall process. Time and motion studies, the industrial engineer, and work standards are concrete embodiments of this approach, this fractionation with which we are presently struggling as we seek to empower one another. Little wonder that under these conditions people feel "stupefied," to use Adam Smith's word. This is the Achilles' heel of the industrial era, its tragic flaw.

Seeing and responding to patterns is the process of dialogue. Work, in fact, is a continual dialogue with a vision of what is to be made, knowledge of how to make it, and the creative results of a combination of the two in active engagement with the elements of the mind and nature. Work cannot be understood apart from a fresh look at the nature of human time.

## Human Time[9] and Timing

As the industrial era progressed, timing increased in importance. The time clock, the stopwatch, the run time of machines, and the timing of activities became ever more important.

Ten to thirty years ago, the concern was with cost: Get cost out of the product. Today time is the concern: Get time out of the product. Timing is even more critical today in terms of time-to-market, windows of opportunity, and cycle time. The automobile companies want to bring new cars to the market in one to three years instead of the historical four to six years. Cycle times in computers are constantly decreasing: the CPM systems of the 1970s ran at 4.7 MHz, while newer workstations run at 25 to 100 MHz.

With our preoccupation with clock time, we have overlooked a dimension of time that is equally as critical—human time. Human time is an essential part of what it is to be human. Clock time assumes a past, present, and future, each separate from one another. Human time assumes that the past and future are integral to the present. There is a wholeness of time from the human perspective. Yet clock time has given us the impression that there is a separation between our past and future.

Clock time is omnipresent. It is easy to think about. It is obvious. It is everywhere we look. We have assumed that clock time is the only type of time there is. This is a fatal mistake.

It is not surprising that the industrial era and the modern timepiece have grown together. In any enterprise, events must be synchronized. When one activity depends on another, proper coordination is essential. Precision has become even more critical in the computer world, where activities have to be timed to the microsecond. In terms of time as synchronization, the clock is essential to coordinate a large variety of activities. It lets us divide events into several categories—those that come first, second, and so forth. Would the division and subdivision of labor be possible without it? Hardly. But what is clock time?

Is not clock time a series of moments? Past, present, future: these are the three parts of time. But how do they relate?

We think of clock time in spatial terms. This simple model has shaped our thinking in a more profound manner than most of us realize. It leads to the following assumptions:

The **past** is left behind. There is physical separation.

The **future** has not yet arrived. There is physical separation.

If the past is left behind and the future has not yet arrived, we have access only to the now. We are disengaged from the past and the future. There is a physical separation between ourselves and the past and future. The only thing that really matters is the present.

The past is behind us, so it is best forgotten. If something is done poorly, there is always an opportunity to correct and improve it. It is best to try to forget what has been done and get on with the activities at hand.

The future is still to come; its shape can be influenced when it gets here. Planning is the way to try to shape and influence it. Therefore, it is only proper to engage in long-range or strategic planning as a way to decide how to allocate resources. But at the same time, because the future is out there, separate and distant, if we do not plan as carefully as we should, we can always correct things when the future becomes the present, or so we suppose.

In short, conventional wisdom tells us that the past has been left behind us, the present is now, and the future is way out ahead of us. Typically, we mark time by the hands on the clock. The minute hand points to the present, the now. What is behind the hand is the past, and what is to come is the future.

We view time with the use of a spatial model because of the convenience of showing "before" and "after." This spatial view of time gives us the impression that the present is all we have access to. Does Figure 10.11 correctly represent clock time?

Have we now solved the question: "What is time?" It would seem so, unless someone were to ask, "How long is the present?"

The length of the present should not be difficult to calculate, or is it? Using this century as an example, we know that ninety-two years have gone and there are seven to come, so the present must be this year. But we know a month has gone and ten are on their way. So, of course, it is this day. Perhaps. But fifteen hours have gone and there are eight to go, so it must be this hour, this minute, this second, this nanosecond, this picosecond, this . . . and so on.[10]

Could it be that the present is so infinitesimally short that it does not really exist? Or is the present so minute that it is trivial? If so, we really live either in the past or the future—but that does not seem right. So what is clock time?

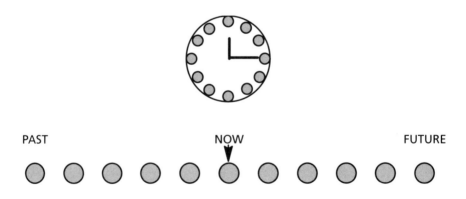

Figure 10.11 **Clock time**

St. Augustine once said that he knew well what time was—that is, until someone asked him.[11] He was reacting to Aristotle's notion that "time is the number of movement in respect to before and after."[12] Figure 10.11 represents Aristotle's definition in a spatial manner. Time is a series of moments that can be numbered in relation to those which have come before and those which will come after. Is this clock time?

Yes, as we understand clock time, Aristotle's definition is perfectly adequate. And from a pragmatic point of view, it works! It allows us to coordinate and synchronize events most efficiently. But it has not answered the question of the length of the present.

William James's *Principles of Psychology*, published in 1885, describes some studies he conducted to determine people's perceptions of how long the present seemed. He concluded that the present is typically perceived to be twelve seconds, a figure that suggests attention span rather than time itself. But James also said something much more significant: "The past flows with us."[13] These two ideas, the span of attention and the idea that the past flows with us, are the keystone in understanding human time.

When we are designing a new part, identifying a new metallurgic process, or defining a new service, our span of attention encompasses a *now* that lasts twelve seconds or one hour—time when our immediate attention is focused on the activity at hand. But the designing or developing process does not occur in a vacuum. We call upon knowledge gained in past studies and through experience to shape the product or process. Those things that we studied in the past stay with us as a resource.

Technically, it is our anticipation of the future and remembrance of the past that are present in the now with us. The discussion of work as dialogue illustrated this point (see Figure 10.8). The design of products and the creation of services are done because we anticipate in the present their expected future implications for the marketplace.

Examples of the past flowing with us abound in our companies. Engineering drawings are still around. Invoices, part numbers, process routings, and customer profiles are still with us, as are data on purchases, inventory usage, maintenance work orders, process settings, and order transactions. This information may be well ordered and readily accessible, or it may be like Fibber McGee's closet, piled high with the door forced shut.

Individuals, like companies, also have information that flows through time: training, education, experiences, or notes in a little black book. This information may be more or less readily available, depending on how well it was grasped, categorized, and arranged in memory.

The future is not really *out there*; like the past, it is very much here in the present. An enterprise's future is determined by its expectations, shared vision, values, and norms. But whether these elements are clear, or a jumbled mess, they are very much a part of present reality.

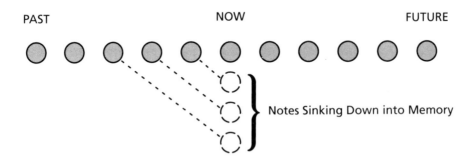

Figure 10.12 **Perceiving the pattern of music in human time**

Human time can be more clearly understood by examining our perception of music. Music is a series of notes, one following another. In terms of clock time, at any point in a symphony we are listening to a single note or chord. Notes already played have been left behind. Notes not yet played are still somewhere out in the future. But is this really the way we experience music?

When we listen to music, each note seems to sink down into our consciousness, allowing us to grasp patterns and themes (Figure 10.12). Suppose we are listening to Beethoven's Fifth Symphony. If we were to hear the first three notes, would we know the theme? No. But when we hear the fourth note, suddenly the pattern becomes clear: dit, dit, dit, dum!

What happens to the first three notes when we hear the fourth? They are not left behind, as they should be in clock time, but instead sink down in our consciousness as, in human time, we grasp the pattern. At this point, our sense of expectation is awakened. We anticipate that future notes will have some relationship to those just heard (Figure 10.13).

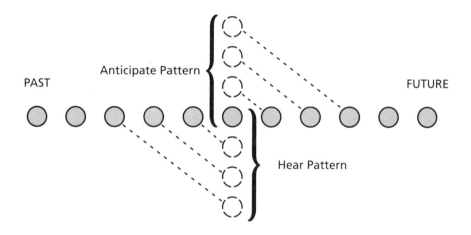

Figure 10.13 **Anticipating the patterns to come in human time**

Certainly clock time is an important backdrop for human time, but notice how in human time we grasp patterns that have occurred in clock time and begin to anticipate patterns that will occur in the future. Remembrance of the past and anticipation of the future are immediately present in human time.

Indeed, without this human capability, Beethoven's Fifth would be just a jumble of notes. But we know from experience that it is anything but a jumble. The Fifth is brilliantly built upon the first four notes. At times our anticipation is confirmed; at other times it is surprised. This is what gives it its delight, and what involves us in the piece in a meaningful and significant manner: our natural ability as humans to retain what we have heard, perceive significant patterns, and anticipate those to come.

Is this not what an experienced machinist does as he operates a drill press? Changes in the pitch of the drill signal a pattern that the machinist recognizes, so a dull drill is changed. Unless he anticipates what can follow the pitch change, he will not take timely action. A skilled financial advisor can pick up patterns in the market, even if they are faint and diffused, and give sound advice.

### The Past: Living Remembrances

Our ability to grasp significant patterns in music, as well as in other experiences, is a function of our previous learning, experience, and familiarity with a given subject. We draw upon this experience and knowledge to help interpret and understand these patterns. For example, if we have learned to play the piano, studied composition, or played in a band, that knowledge can help us to hear the themes in Beethoven's Fifth Symphony (Figure 10.14).

The availability of knowledge depends upon how well we have mastered the piano lessons or composition classes. Experience with a band would also help. If we paid attention and discovered patterns in our activities, our ability to match those patterns with the ones at hand will be greatly enhanced. By knowing Beethoven's Fifth, we will have a greater appreciation for Gershwin, and we can understand what Miles Davis and Oscar Peterson are trying to expand upon in their music. There is a lesson in this: Live in the past, the present is too late!

Of course, we cannot live in the past, but what we do in the present becomes part of the past, which flows with us. Thus the present is the portal into the past. If we have sorted out and arranged our thoughts and experiences, they can become a resource to help us live more effectively in the present. If we have done a slipshod job, the past can be an anchor weighing us down rather than a buoy keeping us afloat.

Like individuals, companies also live in human time. Those companies that have sorted out their engineering standards (a pattern), their parts-listing schemes (another pattern), and their classification and coding of drawings (still another pattern) know the value of these resources in the present. Those who have not will find themselves adding new parts, increasing inventory, and generally adding to the complexity of their operation because they did not live well in the past.

Notice how little thought we typically give to our companies' *legacy*, the knowledge that is distributed among file drawers, in hundreds of different databases, and in the hands and eyes of our experienced professionals. It is this legacy that is really the key asset of an enterprise. Unfortunately, our accounting friends have not found an effective way of auditing and valuing it. If they had, we would quickly understand how important past actions are to our present reality.

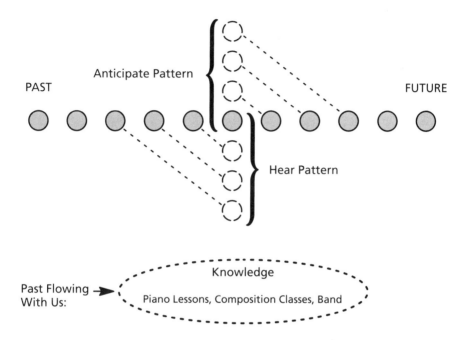

Figure 10.14 **Drawing upon knowledge to see and anticipate patterns**

To some, the legacy is a two-edged sword. Our accumulated knowledge is valuable because we can use it to discover new patterns—the source of learning and the basis for more knowledge. But we must continually arrange and rearrange it in significant patterns to use it. This takes time and energy; however, if we just throw things into the hall closet, the mess will live on to haunt us.

Many companies feel burdened by their old ways of doing things. They wish they could simply leave their outmoded policies and procedures behind and start fresh. Unfortunately or fortunately, the past flows with us. The only way to deal with it is to reinterpret it, to rearrange the patterns, and to sort out the twisted jungle of "ways of doing things." This book, in fact, is an example of an attempt to reinterpret the past and sort it out.

Our anticipation of future patterns will be very important to the way we attend to the present. If we envision starting up a new product line in the custom semiconductor sector, wholesale banking, or custom valves, the steps we take today will largely determine its future outcome.

### The Future: Living Anticipations

Think again of the music analogy. The skill and care with which we listen to Beethoven's Fifth is conditioned not only by our past knowledge, but also by our anticipation of becoming a conductor or concert violinist or having a nice dinner after the performance. Our future vision is very much in the present, an important factor in the attention we give to the Fifth or any other activity (Figure 10.15).

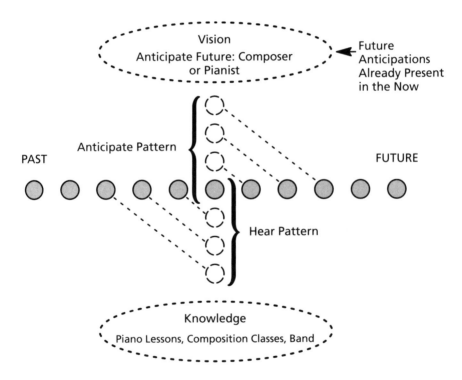

Figure 10.15 **Future vision influences ability to see and anticipate patterns**

Music is meant not only to be listened to but also played. A pianist envisions a piece while she or he is playing. Through the creative process, the texture of the piece is expressed and enriched by the pianist's knowledge and skill. This vision is what motivates his or her attention to the piece. But what is envisioned may also be a piece of music brought up from memory. The dialogue between the envisioned piece and the actual keyboard performance is where the performer's creativity is expressed.

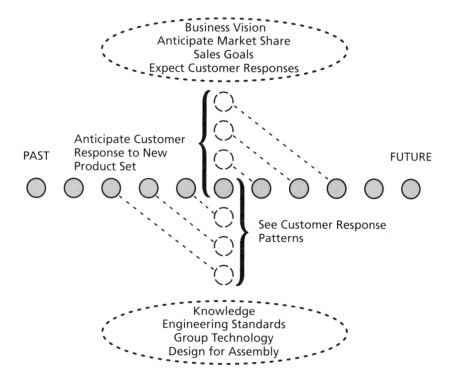

Figure 10.16 **Enterprise's business vision and knowledge help it to see customer response and anticipate future responses**

What is true for an individual is also true for an enterprise. Its ability to see patterns of responses from customers, to anticipate trends, and to draw upon its own collective knowledge in light of its business vision will influence its competitive success in the market. The better the enterprise is able to draw on these resources, business visions, and knowledge and attend to emerging patterns, the more likely it is to be a significant participant in the market (Figure 10.16). This is especially true today because the windows of opportunity come in all shapes and sizes and at random times; therefore, discerning patterns becomes even more challenging.

The enterprise must become more flexible, adaptive, and in tune with the market signals; otherwise it will miss many opportunities. Figure 10.17 illustrates the typical product decision cycle.

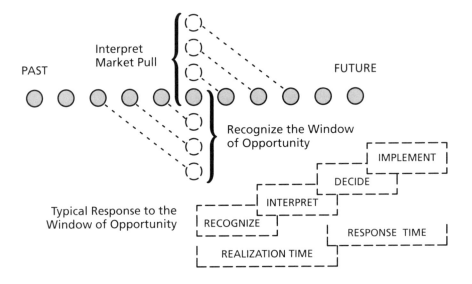

Figure 10.17 **Response process to window of opportunity**

The process of recognizing the patterns that indicate the opening of a window of opportunity usually takes time. Then the signs have to be interpreted, and decisions must be made and implemented. It is not enough for only one function of the organization to "see" the patterns: most of the functions must identify the appropriate responses almost concurrently, given the capabilities and constraints of their organizations. They must make sure there is alignment between the signals of the market and the capabilities and resources of their company. We have all run into a situation where marketing and sales have sold something that does not exist, with no idea as to whether it can be produced. Engineering takes it on as a challenge, and manufacturing rises to the occasion to beat the odds. Quality function deployment (QFD), a method of sorting out customer expectations, is helping to remove the ambiguities in this sequential approach.[14]

The functions must grasp, understand, and jointly interpret the many and various marketplace experiences of actual and potential customers. Rather than developing a wide variety of products to meet different operating conditions, it makes more sense to develop a robust design that can operate over a wide range of conditions. For example, one part of Japan runs its electricity on sixty cycles, the other part on fifty cycles; a product to be used there must be capable of operating in both zones.

Listening to the market is certainly much more complex than listening to one piece of music. In fact, it may be more like listening to ten or twelve different pieces at once. Without good statistical sampling techniques and QFD, it is hard to unscramble the significant patterns.

The interpretation of "customer expectations" can be further complicated if there is inadequate alignment between the functions' visions and their knowledge. If there is no agreement about the business's mission or critical success factors, each function will look at customer patterns from a different perspective. This leads to a key set of questions: What is adequate alignment between visions? How is it achieved? Who is responsible for bringing it about? A corollary set of questions deals with core alignment of functional knowledge. What is minimal alignment of this knowledge? How is it developed and achieved? How much effort does it take?

The alignment process is critical for management if the functions are to see and respond quickly to customer signals as the windows of opportunity are opening (Figure 10.18).[15]

Paul Lawrence and Davis Dyer's landmark study, *Renewing American Industry*, points out the varying temperaments of the functions that make them tend to pull in different directions.[16] For example, engineering loves complexity, whereas finance prefers simplicity. Marketing is generally unconstrained in its interpretation of market needs, while manufacturing is strongly constrained by its existing equipment.

Typically, marketing determines customer needs, translates them into specifications, and hands off the information to engineering, which designs the product. The product designs are then given to manufacturing or process engineering to produce. Once the product has been sold, service is responsible for supporting and maintaining it. Notice that all these activities occur in sequence.

On the other hand, suppose that the various functions work together in an iterative manner from day one to review the marketing, product, process, and service considerations. Will the final outcome meet the customer's expectation better? Will the product be robust in design and easily serviceable? Will the designs have picked up the pattern of themes of multiple customers? Will the product also reflect the proper customer aspirations? In short, will it be in tune with the market? More often than not, the answer will be yes.

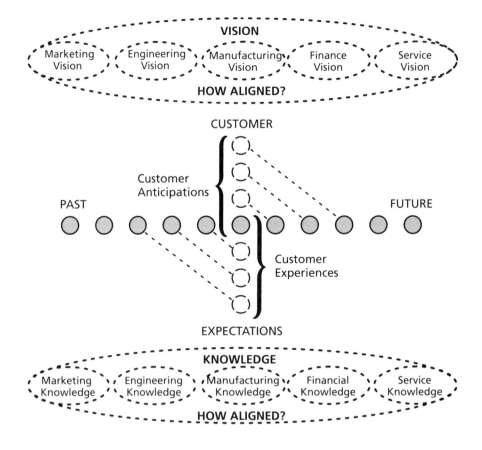

Figure 10.18 **Alignment of visions and knowledge**

There are already examples of concurrent or simultaneous engineering where design and manufacturing engineers are developing next-generation products and processes together in an iterative process.[17] Each function is able to explain its visions and constraints to the other. Other companies have combined marketing and product development in an attempt to get quicker and better alignment. Still others are doing co-engineering between two separate companies: as one company designs its new product, the second company develops the process for building it. These efforts cut the length of the product cycle.

Often companies use project management for cross-functional coordination. Project management will be critical to human networking because the dialogue between the functions is iterative and parallel; this capability makes it possible for the companies to take decisive and well-timed actions that strengthen their market presence.

The interplay between work as dialogue, human time, and timing is what gives a company its strength. An enterprise's interaction with the market is not just passive listening; it is listening to and playing the music at the same time, the way jazz musicians pick up a theme and work with it. The theme aligns their vision; then each musician interprets the theme based on his or her individual knowledge. As they play, they inspire and challenge each other to new combinations, new modes of expressing themselves around the basic theme; yet they play with discipline and emotion because of long hours of practice.

The same thing can happen within a company that listens to the themes of the marketplace. As the functions learn to work in parallel, they improve their timing, reduce cycle time, and improve quality and time-to-market. The alignment of their vision and knowledge allows them to discern significant market patterns, and their individual abilities add creativity and uniqueness to their response as they shape their market strategy, product design, process strategy, and service capabilities concurrently. Often finance and personnel are also involved in these efforts. In working together as cross-functional task teams, each function considers the constraints under which the other functions operate, often finding ways around some of them and avoiding unnecessary engineering change orders.

Figure 10.19 illustrates the dialogue possible when the different functions are in touch with their aligned visions and knowledge and can act decisively. Communicating on a peer-to-peer basis, the team can quickly resolve issues and maintain market rhythm. By identifying and chartering well-composed, cross-functional, task-focused teams, they can recapture in a "crafts-team" many of the virtues that once characterized the craftsperson.

No one person can master all the intricacies of a complex set of operations, but a well-developed team can. This is what Drucker was suggesting in his *Harvard Business Review* article.[18] Making pins or shoes is something an individual craftsperson can do alone. But electronic or discrete parts manufacturing requires more skill and knowledge than any one person can master. Modern insurance and banking require many different technical capabilities. We need to be able to draw on the multiple talents in an enterprise to put together virtual task-focusing teams.

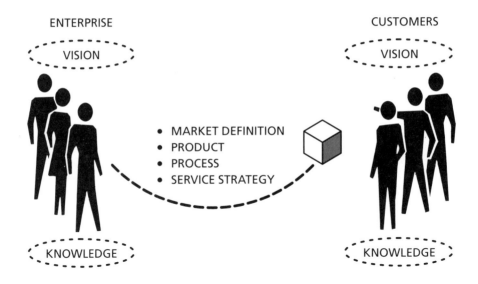

Figure 10.19 **Task-focusing team developing concurrently its response to customer expectations**

## Virtual Teams

There are two concepts from the world of computer science that may be of help in our activities: multiplexing and virtual memory. *Multiplexing* refers to the parallel transmission of more than one message over a single line. Humans can multiplex their attention from one project to another—that is, they can shift their focus from one task to another in short order.

The word *virtual* is defined as "being such in force or effect, though not actually or expressly such." "Virtual" has the connotation of being unreal, yet a virtual resource is very real. Something that is virtual is an available and adaptable resource. The concept of *virtual memory* has made it possible for computer systems to run much larger programs than their physical memory would allow by swapping blocks of information into and out of random access memory as needed. As far as the program is concerned, the entire program and all its data are fully accessible, if not in physical fact, in virtual fact. Companies such as Prime Computer, Digital Equipment Corporation, and IBM have used this concept effectively in their computer operating systems.

Now, how do we take these concepts and apply them organizationally? We may have to move to virtual teams in virtual organizations, teams which can multiplex their focus, in order to shepherd multiple projects through the organization.

### Virtual Enterprises[19]

In steep hierarchies, assignments are hard-wired with fixed areas of responsibility. The hierarchy assumes that someone else knows what everyone should be doing and that assignments can be made all the way down the chain of command. The functions are predetermined and people are stuffed into the appropriate slots. Such an organizational structure lacks the flexibility and adaptability to respond to the multiple demands put on organizations today. On the other hand, when people are seen as resources available to support others, rather than as owners of narrowly defined boxes, they become virtual resources.

Virtual enterprises are built upon their ability to define and redefine multiple cross-functional teams (Figure 10.3) as needed. These teams may include not only members of the company, but also persons from vendor or client companies. Virtual enterprises rely more on the knowledge and talents of their people than on the functions. Their managers, professionals, and workers can multiplex their attention to multiple projects with different sets of project members during the course of a day, month, or year. At one point they can be dealing with operational questions, a short time later they are working on planning exercises, and then they may shift to personnel matters. They can also see the interconnections between these seemingly different disciplines. Moreover, these teams do not need to be co-located.

Research studies indicate that geographically dispersed teams can often work as effectively as co-located teams, if not more so. A dispersed group must communicate more explicitly, requiring clarity of thought, whereas co-located groups often tend to communicate haphazardly. Dispersed groups also periodically find ways to communicate face to face.[20]

Virtual enterprises are an evolution of what some have called "open organizations." It is really not an accident that there should be so much interest in the International Standards Organization's Open Systems Interconnection (OSI) networking models and X/Open, an industry coalition dedicated to stimulating the development of portable software. Whereas the industrial-era model tried to cover all contingencies with bureaucracy, policies, procedures, job descriptions, and departmental charters, the new understanding is to create a common core, extending it as the need arises. UNIX, for example, is built around a clearly defined kernel that can easily be extended.

If we hope to use this flexibility, we must not define the enterprise in spatial terms, as the hierarchical organizational chart does. Instead, we should use the principles of "human time" as an organizing principle for allocating responsibilities.

It is also important to understand the idea of "work as dialogue" in conceptualizing the operation of the enterprise. People need access to their own visions and knowledge as well as to the core vision and knowledge of the virtual teams. These resources are what allow the people in the enterprise to maintain their individual and team focus, see significant patterns, and respond accordingly.

The hierarchical model assumes that the main task is to divide up the production operations and assign persons rigidly to take care of individual functions. In contrast, the virtual enterprise treats groups of activities as projects, with teams working in an iterative and parallel manner to form a collage of teams. The management of the virtual enterprises then supports the teamwork of teams.

Virtual teams arise through assignment and volunteers. They are intentionally kept as small as possible, making it easier to get work done. They do not need to have representatives from all the functions, because the interplay of the teams ensures focus and coordination. The teams can deal with multiple challenges, from assessing market changes to championing new product development using approaches such as QFD. These teams are expected first to clarify their own assignment so there is focus within the group, then to tackle the assignment. They are also expected to undertake projects in such a way that their learning accrues to the larger enterprise. Time-to-market is made possible through time-to-learning.

Enterprises deal concurrently with multiple themes. Major and minor themes are played out at the same time, as well as noises and background static that may divert attention from the key themes. Some themes or patterns are picked up by one group and others by other groups. Groups are challenged to see the interrelationships between the various themes, because they may provide some very important clues as to the best market, product, or service response.

We are involved in a process that is more than passively listening to music or to themes from the market. We are also participants in the process, creating themes of our own which influence those of others in the marketplace, whether they are customers or competitors. This is part of work as dialogue; when an enterprise creates a product, it also creates in the vision of a competitor the possibility of creating a similar product. There is a great deal of room for proactive involvement in this process by all participants.

### Virtual Teams as Task-Focusing Teams

Drucker writes of "task-focused teams." It is better to speak of "task-focusing teams," because each team will have to do its own focusing, rather than relying on an external executive. Top management might establish certain parameters, but the more detailed focusing will be done by the team itself.

The primary objective of task-focusing teams—virtual teams, as we have been calling them—is to discern the themes coming from the market, from the competition, from suppliers and partners, and from within their own company. They must then design products, processes, and service strategies to support the products throughout their life cycles. By working together, on a peer-to-peer basis, they can iterate possible solutions until they develop a mature and market-ready plan.

These virtual teams are the crafts-teams of the enterprise. They embody work as dialogue, using human time and a strong sense of market timing.

## Interrelating the Five Conceptual Principles

The five conceptual principles—peer-to-peer networking, integrative process, work as dialogue, human time and timing, and virtual teams—are clearly interrelated. They are summarized in the next two figures, which are two-dimensional spatial representations of a very dynamic process of expression and dialogue.

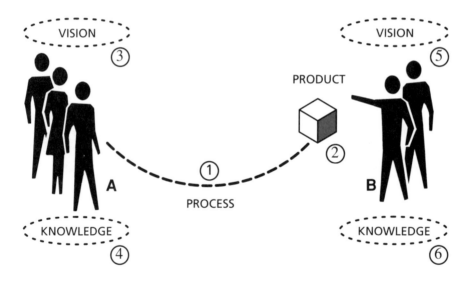

Figure 10.20 **Virtual teams**

Networking of vision and knowledge allows virtual teams to see the patterns of the present and to express their own patterns. Human networking involves drawing upon visions and knowledge to develop quality actions in the present, in concert with a team. These teams of professionals are charged with recognizing, interpreting, deciding, and implementing responses to windows of opportunity that will meet both the customers' expectations and the teams' enterprise vision (Figure 10.20).

Virtual team (A) defines, develops, and runs the process (1), which produces the product (2). The team draws on its individual and collective knowledge (4), then designs and produces the product in dialogue with its vision (3), which provides the context within which to focus their activities.

The customers (B) see the product (2) and the way it was produced (1) as exemplified in the process. As they think of how it may be used, they access their knowledge (6) and consult their visions (5) of what they would like.

Notice that there is communication among and between the virtual team members (A) as they listen to and anticipate the expectation patterns of the customers (B). This puts them in dialogue with the market. The virtual team members communicate in the present, tap into their individual and collective knowledge, and enter into dialogue with their visions. This is human networking (Figure 10.21).

While the virtual team members (A) may use their technical networking infrastructure to work in parallel on the project, they must also tap into their own experiential knowledge, knowledge of their company, and knowledge of their culture—that is, public scientific knowledge. The virtual team members also have access to their own personal visions, the visions of their group, the visions of their company, and the visions of their culture to inspire them in their work.

Human networking represents a dialogue with the past, which flows with us; the present, in which we act; and the future, which is also in the present. The quality of this dialogue determines the appropriateness of the processes and products produced by the virtual team. This dialogue is more than just a cognitive exercise; it involves our values and emotions. They play an important role in tempering our visioning, knowing, and acting.

The five principles can only work together if there is strong leadership throughout the enterprise. If people at all levels rise to the occasion, they can help to define the enterprise vision and add to its knowledge base. Strong leadership will be especially important on the multiple task-focusing teams. As we enter the knowledge era, virtual enterprises will shift focus from "control" to "commitment," from "monitoring" to "motivating," and from "commanding" to "conducting."

Leadership involves conducting, coaching, and mentoring: A conductor brings forth the best talents of an orchestra; a coach builds capabilities and confidence; and a mentor shapes talent. Knowledge-era enterprises are a composite of orchestras, basketball teams, and jazz combos. Perhaps they are more like jazz combos, because the rules are often more fuzzy and ambiguous than those governing an orchestra or a basketball game. Jazz combos know the basics, but they can take a theme and innovate creatively.

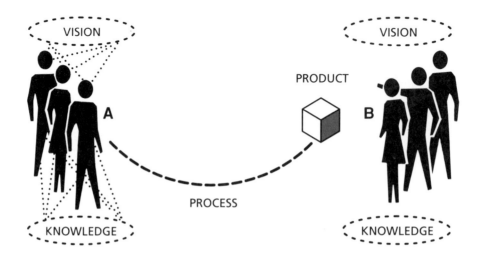

Figure 10.21 **Virtual team and human networking**

A new management strategy is needed for the knowledge era—one that can pick up on the themes of the market, technology, and human visions, and intertwine them into a score that catches the market's attention. Instead of "management by command" we move to "management as dialogue." If work is dialogue, so is management. If managers, professionals, and workers are resource centers with knowledge that can be tapped, the challenge is to involve and focus their efforts. By working together, we can empower one another. We can master the confusingly complex, because we are using an elegantly simple model based on work as dialogue and human time: human networking.

Evidence is mounting that this is the way to go. Computer-based networking technology with fiber optics of over 100 megabytes per second is making entirely new organizational structures possible; studies in neural networking and chaos are helping to move us beyond the machine model of organizations;[21] the research of Jessica Lipnack and Jeffrey Stamps of The Networking Institute shows the power of geographically distributed teams;[22] and the groupware scholarship of Robert Johansen shows the power of teamwork.[23] There are other indications that the time is right for a shift to human networking.

A new generation of professionals is growing up with the technology of networking. Natural clusters of interest arise spontaneously on computer bulletin boards and conferencing networks. User groups are pulling together people from diverse backgrounds around common themes of interest. People are networking not because they are told to, but because of natural interests. They are initiating relationships rather than waiting to be assigned to a particular spot.

Some of the seeds of change were planted years ago. Hayward Thomas, former president of Jensen Industries and former plant manager at Frigidaire, redefined Frigidaire's manufacturing organization in the late 1950s. He used round organizational charts resembling medieval chain mail, where many small steel rings are interlocked to build a structure of great strength.[24] Frigidaire's large factory used hundreds of small teams working as a coordinated whole. Unfortunately, the experiment was not sustainable because Frigidaire was changed by General Motors, which wanted to recentralize operations in a hierarchical manner. But other companies, such as Procter & Gamble and Heinz, have a long tradition of using small teams with great effectiveness.

Today design engineers are working together with manufacturing or process engineers across town or around the world. They can call on materials specialists in a third location to help cost their projects. Marketing can participate as part of the team in the development of new product ideas. These groups, working together from diverse locations, can design, build, and market products and services to meet real customer needs. Each function is a resource available to work in parallel with other resources in a give-and-take mode, iterating ideas back and forth on the network. In a similar manner, investment banking or insurance companies pull together teams from across their companies to work on multiple issues. These changes are empowering individuals, teams, and enterprises in new and creative ways. Ultimately, professionals at all levels will find empowerment through self-empowerment. When we realize that we are the authors of our own work and when we can thrive on the tension between our vision and knowledge, we will find empowerment.

There is a clear transformation occurring from the industrial era to the knowledge era. The next chapter looks more closely at the key shifts implicit in this transition.

# 11

# Confusingly Complex to Elegantly Simple Enterprises

What if our CEO were to tear up our organizational chart and ask us to re-define basic relationships, as happened in Book 1? Could we put the confusing complexity of our present organization aside and develop an elegantly simple core understanding of its basic relationships?

How do we move from second generation steep hierarchies to fifth generation human networking? How do we overcome the complexity of industrial-era organizations and discover the simplicity of the knowledge era? How do we initiate such a transition?

Certainly the transition cannot be bought from a systems integrator. True, there are companies that can install local and wide-area networks, interface one application with another, and help develop a unifying data architecture. But the real transition comes only when we look more deeply at the conceptual frameworks in which we operate. In order to break out of the confining quarters of second-generation management, we will need to shift our attitudes and approaches. Figure 11.1 shows the focus of this chapter.

## Historical Eras

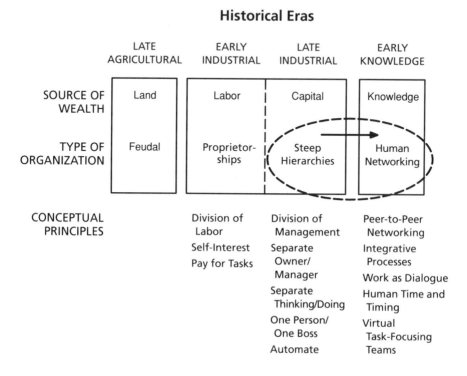

| | LATE AGRICULTURAL | EARLY INDUSTRIAL | LATE INDUSTRIAL | EARLY KNOWLEDGE |
|---|---|---|---|---|
| SOURCE OF WEALTH | Land | Labor | Capital | Knowledge |
| TYPE OF ORGANIZATION | Feudal | Proprietor-ships | Steep Hierarchies | Human Networking |
| CONCEPTUAL PRINCIPLES | | Division of Labor<br>Self-Interest<br>Pay for Tasks | Division of Management<br>Separate Owner/Manager<br>Separate Thinking/Doing<br>One Person/One Boss<br>Automate | Peer-to-Peer Networking<br>Integrative Processes<br>Work as Dialogue<br>Human Time and Timing<br>Virtual Task-Focusing Teams |

Figure 11.1 **Chapter focus: the transition from steep hierarchies to human networking enterprises**

If they are to form an acknowledged basis or core understanding, the knowledge-era conceptual principles must strike a chord of intuitive acceptance. Is it more natural to work as superiors and subordinates or peer to peer? Is it more natural to hide in a box or to serve as a knowledge resource in a network? Is it more natural to follow orders we do not fully understand or to engage in work as a dialogue, which encourages us to use our vision and knowledge? Is it more natural to try to mesh our activities in a synchronized set like clockwork or to have access to an understanding of the company's vision and collective knowledge? Is it more natural to struggle with the inflexibility of automated processes or to participate in the discovery process as part of a task-focusing team?

## The Basics: Space and Human Time

The industrial and knowledge eras have different starting points. The industrial era is built using a spatial model of reality, while the knowledge era rests on an understanding of the interplay between human time and clock time.

Space is an easier metaphor to understand. It is easier to see what is up and down, back and front, left and right. It is easy to show relationships between things and people using spatial diagrams. This is why the organizational chart is so seductively simple. It gives us the illusion of understanding how the organization works. It is much harder to see changing relationships over time, because no spatial diagram can easily capture what is going on. Yet our humanness unfolds itself in time, not space. We live in human time, at the intersection of our visions and knowledge. It is our dreams and remembrances that fuel our activities and give them content and texture. It is the tension between the two which motivates us.

The transition from a model based on spatial relationships (lines and boxes) to one based on time (human time and clock time) is the essence of the transition. There is a newness and an oldness to this transition, because in some ways we are recapturing the involvement and engagement of the farmer and craftsperson of the preindustrial era.

The farmer was very much engaged in a dialogue with the land, the seasons, and the weather. Vision and knowledge, timing and action, were woven into the fabric of the farmer's life. A craftsperson was engaged with materials and processes, visions and knowledge, customer reactions and feedback. But in the industrial era, fragmentation of processes denied many access to their knowledge and visions. Dialogue stopped.

In the knowledge era, we plant our ideas in the fields of technology; our craftsperson has become part of a cross-functional, task-focusing crafts-team in a network of teams. Vision, knowledge, and a sense of timing are as important today as they were centuries ago.

## Transition in Management Models

Figure 11.2 suggests some of the elements involved in the transition to human networking. We will first work our way around the outside of the box, then look more specifically at the transition between management models. Although the discussion may give the impression that we are engaged in an "either/or" dialogue, this is not the intent; the contrasts are sharpened to bring the alternatives into relief.

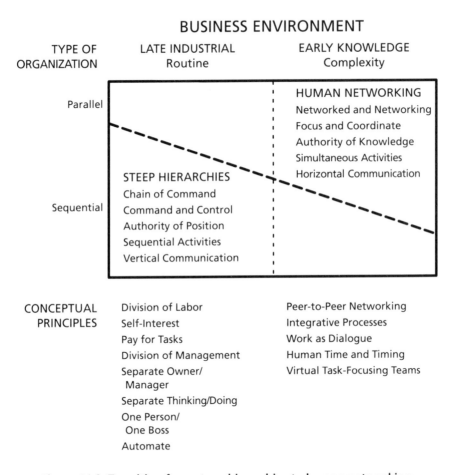

Figure 11.2 **Transition from steep hierarchies to human networking**

Figure 11.2 suggests a number of interrelated themes raised in previous chapters. They include:

1. The transition from the *industrial* era to the *knowledge* era.

2. The transition from *routine* to *complexity*.

3. The transition from *sequential* activities to *parallel* iterative activities.

4. The transition from industrial-era *conceptual principles* to those of the knowledge era.

5. The *management shifts* in structure, control, authority, and communication.

The diagonal line in Figure 11.2 is not drawn from corner to corner. Human networking enterprises will still have hierarchical authority structures, although they will be much flatter. Some activities will continue to be sequential and routine. There will still be some division and subdivision of labor, with certain tasks remaining narrowly defined. Top management will still have overall responsibility for the strategic direction of the enterprise, and vestiges of the chain of command and automation will survive.

## Navigating the Transition

The transition from steep hierarchies to networking enterprises does not involve moving or even eliminating the boxes. This has been management strategy for decades: when something does not work, move the boxes, decentralize or centralize.

What is the source of the drive for change? Does it start with the CEO and management committee? Possibly, but often they are too preoccupied with "big issues" such as capital investment decisions to really understand what is going on within the organization. Does it come from middle management? Unlikely, because even though they see the issues, they do not have the power to implement the change. Does the information systems community lead the charge? Probably not, because they are too tied to the technology to have adequate leverage with the organization.

The next transition will probably come through a coalition of interested parties within the enterprise. Ideally, this coalition should include key persons from engineering, manufacturing, finance, service, information systems, personnel, human resources, organizational development, and other interested parties. In many companies the unions will have a major role to play in helping facilitate the change. But the transition will not arrive simply because we have computerized our steep hierarchies.

Terry Winograd and Fernando Flores, in their book *Understanding Computers and Cognition,* have questioned our blind belief in the power of the computer.[1] Their book reminds us that without understanding the "whole picture," the gestalt or the organizing pattern, a computer application is extremely limited. For example, attempts to capture an expert's knowledge in an expert system are limited, because it is one thing to identify a specific sequence of steps captured as rules, but it is quite something else to identify the whole context in which an expert thinks. An expert has power because he or she can see the multiple relationships in an event and adjust for new contingencies and unexpected changes.

This leads us back to a consideration of Figure 11.2. We will take each of the five points we have mentioned and discuss them in relation to the transition process.

## Transitioning from the Industrial Era to the Knowledge Era

We have two choices: stay within the industrial-era mindset and computerize our steep hierarchies, or refocus our thinking toward the integration that is possible through human networking. The first choice will not overcome our organizational bankruptcy. The second choice will add value to past investments and increase future investments.

It is often said that the purpose of CIM is to get the right information to the right people at the right time to make the right decisions. Certainly this is a real and important process, but there is more to do than just create, move, store, and process this information. It is the human element that is able to see the Pareto charts, the histograms, the customer profiles, and the business graphics, and to understand how the patterns interrelate. Because we can grasp the organization's vision and understand its history, we know what to look for. It is the larger context, derived from human time, that makes it possible to see the patterns, even the fuzzy and obscure ones.

Our automationist mentality has led us to think we can capture everything in databases. Although databases are becoming indispensable to modern business, the human capability to see and act on patterns related to the larger context and mission of the organization is an essential complementary capability. It is our human knowledge bases that are our real assets. We need a strategy that recognizes and appreciates our human capability to see and anticipate, to expand our visions and share them, and to learn and capture this learning as a shareable resource within the enterprise. This is why time-to-learning is as significant, if not more so, as time-to-market.

When we refer to human capabilities and the human element, we are not advocating a "humanistic" approach. Too often people want to build "niceness" into an organization and encourage "participation" because it is the right thing to do. What often happens, however, is that these philosophies are superficially applied to industrial-era organizations. Even Maslow's "hierarchy of needs" and McGregor's "Theory X and Theory Y" are not adequate because they have not come to terms with the underlying assumptions of the industrial era.[2] McGregor pointed us in the right direction, although Maslow had little empirical foundation for his theories.

In the knowledge era, people will not necessarily be nice to one another. It is more important to have honest and open dialogue about the real issues, patterns, challenges, technologies, and business opportunities of the enterprise. There will still be politics, distrust, misunderstandings, disagreements, and fights over scarce resources at budget time. Trust must be won through the integrity of those in the company. If people understand the company's visions, it is because there is openness and honesty. If the enterprise learns to learn from its experiences, it is because it has interest in the thoughts and ideas of its members and not just self-interest.

The transition to the knowledge era is not a transition to a utopian or humanistic paradise. It puts people in touch with real problems and challenges, although with a more holistic understanding of their context. This is part of the alignment process, the discourse through which real understanding arises. People in the knowledge era are expected to be tempered by a realism that is capable of seeing the patterns of the past, the present, and the future.

We constantly stand at the "intersection of the timeless with time," to use T. S. Eliot's phrase.[3] We must use our ability to see and hear the patterns of the music, whether it is played in the marketplace of the business world or the laboratories of the scientists. We are also called upon to make our own music in order to capture the market's attention.

The transition from the superficiality of the industrial era to the humanly demanding knowledge era challenges us to confront ourselves as people in new and exciting ways. As Ken Olsen suggested, we may find that being in touch with our creativity, our knowledge, and our motivation has a profound value in and of itself, as well as affecting the bottom line.[4]

## Transitioning from Routine to Complexity

When the future is much like the past, organizing for routine makes a great deal of sense. But when curve balls, unexpected tunes, and kaleidoscopic technological changes are the order of the day, a strategy for dealing with complexity and variety is in order.

The real siphon of a company's profits is not work-in-process (WIP) but decisions-in-process (DIP). It is those countless little decisions that are made half-heartedly or not at all that sap the strength and inspiration of an enterprise. Many good ideas are put on hold so long, waiting for the politics to settle down, that when it is their day they look like flat tires. Decisions-in-process have to be made even when boundaries are fuzzy and information is scant.

It is not a coincidence that we should be experiencing a birth of widespread interest in the subject of chaos. James Gleick's *Chaos: Making a New Science* attempts to make available to the average person the intricacies of fractals.[5] The challenge is to find the patterns in chaos. The beauty and regularity in the irregularity of the Mandelbrot set is most intriguing. It is not surprising that Tom Peters should have named his latest book *Thriving on Chaos.*[6] In a related vein, there is growing interest in "fuzzy set theory": working with patterns that are not easily distinguishable.

How often have we heard, "If only we knew what the customer really wanted"? The concept of "the customer" is an abstraction. This customer is really a composite of many different customers with wide-ranging needs who reflect a variety of expectations and interdependencies. Often it takes perceptive marketing to discern the faint fuzzy visible patterns. We also need a good sense of timing so that we can act decisively at the right moment. A company cannot be successful being dead right at the wrong time. Too much too late hardly pays the rent.

It is for these reasons that enterprises need honest and open dialogue. The truth is often buried in the confluence of a variety of human perceptions. Only through the give and take of hard dialogue can it be discovered. This is why organizations that rely on the authority of knowledge, rather than the authority of position, often succeed where others fail. For example, Digital Equipment Corporation has a culture that values the notion of "push-back." When someone makes a statement or takes a position, others are expected to push back until the truth of the matter is discovered. It does not matter what rank the person has. Without respect for the truth of the matter, it is hard to deal with complexity. A push-back is not a put-down, but signifies an openness and a willingness to stick with the issue until the truth is known. Other organizations call this "peeling the onion," or the "five-why routine." These are examples of the authority of knowledge.

The transition, then, from routine to complexity is a transition in attitudes, perceptions, and expectations. It is not a black-and-white issue, but should be thought of as a continuum. Some companies characterized by a great deal of routine can continue to be very effective in narrowly defined market niches. Many others long for the old days when they could run economic order quantity (EOQ) formulas, instead of having to worry about lot sizes of one.

## Transitioning from Sequential to Parallel

Working sequentially isolates people and processes from one another. Each function has its role to play but lacks an appreciation of the constraints the other functions live under. It is easy to blame another function for not understanding or failing to carry out instructions, especially if one is removed from the other function's daily worries.

We have built an educational feeder system that contributes to the fragmentation of the enterprise. Engineering schools provide engineers. Industrial engineering departments supply IEs. Many manufacturing engineers come up through the ranks, although this is changing now. Those in finance live in and come from their own worlds. Marketers have their own pedigrees, and so it goes. It is very rare to find an effective interdisciplinary program feeding the manufacturing industry.[7]

As we begin to work more in parallel through such efforts as concurrent engineering, a new set of dynamics is initiated. This does not mean simply that the functions operate concurrently, but that they work together. Spatial or temporal proximity is not essential, thanks to the power of networks and common windowing formats.

Working in parallel requires more discipline than working sequentially. In a sequentially run company there are usually old timers at the interfaces who are wise and seasoned enough to translate the output of another department into the idiom of their own. They are the uncelebrated heroes of our corporations, the ones who have ensured that "as designed" and "as built" bear some resemblance.

Companies such as Delco-Remy are rediscovering concurrent engineering. This idea, developed in the 1950s but lost in the centralization trend of the 1960s, is now being rejuvenated. Design, manufacturing, and industrial engineers are working shoulder to shoulder to design both products and processes. This leads to easier-to-manufacture designs and better-quality processes. This is only the start in the trend toward working in parallel, elbow to elbow or over a network.

We also find that companies are beginning to work in parallel. As one company designs a new automobile, its equipment contractor is concurrently designing the transfer line upon which it will be built. The second company can do this only because it has prepared itself over the last ten years by unifying its database, building discipline into its organization, and moving to a project management approach. This allows the contractor to change the design of its transfer line dynamically as the auto maker's new designs emerge. This development is significant because it is the only way new-car cycle times can be cut from five years to two or less.

Companies experiencing the challenges of Electronic Data Interchange (EDI) are only now beginning to create webs of networks that will eventually allow them to work together in parallel. It is becoming easier to send orders and invoices electronically; the real challenge will be to transmit the geometry, typology, tolerances, and forms and features to the supplier community electronically. Technical Data Interchange (TDI) is being developed under the banner of Product Data Exchange Specification, which is to become the International Standards Organization's STEP (Standards for the Transfer and Exchange of Product model data) standard. The use of an increased networking bandwidth between primes and subcontractors will explode, perhaps exponentially. The U.S. Department of Defense's (DOD) Computer-aided Acquisition and Logistics Support (CALS) system is helping to speed this process along. The DOD has asked that after 1990, its prime contractors supply it with design specifications in digital rather than paper form, or allow it access to the primes' databases with this information in it.

The signs are clear that we are moving more quickly than most realize toward working in parallel. It will require a different mindset: one that is willing to examine the assumptions underlying the industrial era and contribute to developing a new set of principles.

## Transitioning the Conceptual Principles

Thomas Kuhn, in *The Structure of Scientific Revolutions,* discusses the process and role of paradigm shifts.[8] We are at the threshold of such a shift today. But there is no guarantee that we will make the shift satisfactorily. It is not inevitable. It will depend upon our own perceptiveness, intuition, integrity, and creativity. So much of the future must be created by us through our own efforts.

We can no longer afford the petty isolation of sequential work built on the division and subdivision of labor and management. Simplistic self-interest, taking our box on the organizational chart as something that we own exclusively, will go the way of the buggy whip. As Drucker suggests, we need new pay and reward systems that will nurture and grow individual and collaborative knowledge resources.[9] Bureaucracy has a role, but it is much more limited. We need to be both thinkers and doers to become simultaneous leaders and followers—mentors, teachers, and learners—as we work together on self-focusing task teams using automation within a reasoned context. If we can change the focus of the exercise and put people into the center of the equation, we will pull in the appropriate technology to help us get the work done.

## Transitioning to New Structures

Drucker, Davis, Nolan, Zuboff, and others suggest that the "new organization" will require new structures with different control, authority, communication, and accountability strategies. Now that we have worked our way around the outside of Figure 11.2, let us look at the two lists within the figure, comparing the differences between steep hierarchies and human enterprises point by point (Figure 11.3).

### "Chain of Command" to "Networked and Networking"

Henri Fayol's fourteen principles are based on his experience as the managing director of the Comambault mining company in France in the early part of this century.[10] At about the same time, Taylor was developing his theories of "scientific management." Taylor focused on the shop floor and worked up, while Fayol began with the board of directors and worked down. As Taylor developed a strategy for defining and directing direct labor, Fayol theorized about planning, organizing, commanding, coordinating, and controlling management's responsibilities.

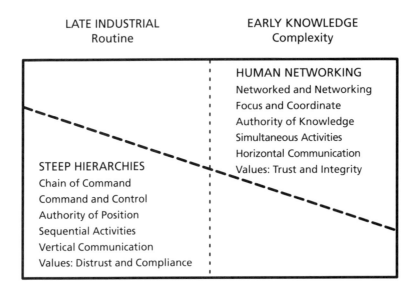

LATE INDUSTRIAL
Routine

EARLY KNOWLEDGE
Complexity

HUMAN NETWORKING
Networked and Networking
Focus and Coordinate
Authority of Knowledge
Simultaneous Activities
Horizontal Communication
Values: Trust and Integrity

STEEP HIERARCHIES
Chain of Command
Command and Control
Authority of Position
Sequential Activities
Vertical Communication
Values: Distrust and Compliance

Figure 11.3 **Management shifts**

These ideas were ideal in a time when markets changed slowly, many companies were geographically isolated, and the introduction of new technology progressed at a modest rate. They are no longer adequate in an era of global markets, geographical integration, and accelerating technology.

Today, the mere existence of a networked infrastructure in an organization does not guarantee that the organization will leverage its resources. An extensive road, telephone, and telegraph system makes it possible to communicate, but it does not ensure that we will communicate meaningfully.

Networking is an ongoing process of reaching out and getting in touch with others to get tasks done. As we become nodes in a network—knowledge resources—we tap into this available knowledge and our effectiveness increases. Instead of being confined by the chain of command, we can go directly to sources of knowledge, whether they are inside or outside the enterprise.

When a friend joined Digital, he was told a good news–bad news story. The good news was that he had 120,000 people working for him. The bad news was that they did not know it. It was up to him to figure out how he could best network himself and build working alliances.

### "Command and Control" to "Focus and Coordinate"

The steep hierarchy has a "command and control" structure, with orders originating at the top. To take initiative, a worker or professional lower down in the organization must first get his or her boss's blessing. Knowledge and wisdom are supposedly embodied in the years of experience represented by those at the top.

This thinking has been based on the "calculus of importance": the higher up in the organization, the more important the person, as measured by number of direct reports, budget approval authority, and access to the power centers. Too often this model degenerates into not *what* but *whom* a person knows.

The irony is that managers grow skillful at giving orders but never learn to ask perceptive questions or listen carefully. A question is considered a sign of ignorance unbefitting one's rank in the organization. This attitude stifles significant communication. It is a hundred small decisions made throughout a company that cause it to earn or lose money, rather than the occasional "important" big decision coming from on high. But if the culture does not support careful listening prompted by probing questions, the enterprise will atrophy.

Network enterprises with fewer levels of management face significant new challenges: How do we ensure that all levels of the enterprise are focusing on the key critical issues? How do we ensure coordination between interrelated efforts? How do people get rewarded when there are fewer levels?

A team's focus will depend, to a great extent, upon understanding its context. The enterprise's vision and knowledge base provide this context and become important determinants in the focusing process. As teams come to understand this context, they will do their own focusing. Karl Weick's *The Social Psychology of Organizing* has a wonderful description of self-directing teams.[11] As parts of their tasks are solved, the teams shift their focus to other interrelated aspects. The power of the task-focusing team lies in its freedom to shift its focus as needed, to zoom in on particular aspects of a problem and zoom out to see the whole picture.

In organizations that use multiple task-focusing teams, the teams will need to interact, like the themes in a well-developed piece of music. Part of a team's responsibility is to help grow the enterprise's vision and knowledge base; the team's learning becomes a valuable resource for other task-focusing teams.

As these teams learn to interact effectively, they will gradually become the lifeblood of the organization, their fast-paced activities giving flexibility and agility to the enterprise. Task-focusing teams are not the same as autonomous or ad hoc teams. The concept of the autonomous team suggests a disconnect between the team's efforts and the life of the larger organization. As the Sociotechnical Systems community was developing its approach, it found it necessary to carve out some space for its teams to operate, free from the traditional constraints, assumptions, and bureaucracy of the steep hierarchy. The term *ad hoc* suggests teams that are not an integral part of the working organization, merely afterthoughts designed to correct malfunctioning systems. They are provisional and transient.

Membership on task-focusing teams may be provisional, but the use of teams is structured into the daily operation of the enterprise. Thus teams need clear discipline, well-established expectation patterns, and project management skills to guide them as they sort out multiple interrelated activities, timing their efforts to achieve desired ends.

### "Authority of Position" to "Authority of Knowledge"

Within steep hierarchies, position and authority are defined by boxes and lines: the higher up the position, the more powerful it is. The prerogatives of position legitimize an arbitrary attitude with subordinates. Superiors need not listen; they merely monitor and control subordinates.

Given narrowly defined tasks, subordinates are supposed to know what to do. They are not required to be creative, only to accept the rules of the game, knowing that it is only a matter of time before they advance to the next rung. As the steep hierarchies are "delayered," what happens to the subordinates' expectations? With fewer layers, promotions come more slowly. Are people content to wait longer to advance? What happens to morale and motivation?

Authority of position works well for organizing routine tasks, but can it handle complexity? Customer needs do not come in Lego-like packages. The development of the next-generation disk drive involves physics, chemistry, engineering design, and process control, all at the same time. The logic of the market requires enterprises to use their cross-functional knowledge resources to develop an overall response strategy.

Authority of knowledge is fast becoming more important for success in the marketplace. This is not knowledge doled out in tiny bits like currency, but knowledge available to all. As steep hierarchies are replaced by multiple task-focusing teams, the individual's knowledge becomes both more important and more accessible, and a lack of knowledge can no longer be hidden behind the walls of organizational boxes. People quickly learn who has knowledge and who will share it. They are the ones who become key players on task-focusing teams.

The organization that believes in authority of position is likely to want to automate and computerize as many processes as possible, giving top management access to executive decision support systems. As Winograd and Flores remind us, we can only automate and computerize specific information we have acquired in the past.[12] We cannot automate or computerize the context—that is part of our human understanding.

Enterprises based on the authority of knowledge are messy. Neither knowledge nor tasks come in neatly wrapped packages. One person's knowledge overlaps with others'. Some people have deep resonance in their knowledge, others are fast learners, and still others turn off their thinking sets.

Authority of position is based on defining and arranging assignments so that even those with the least common denominator of knowledge have a reasonable chance of success. By overeducating a person, then underutilizing his or her talents, companies hope that the assigned tasks will get done. But an organization built on the authority of position is a slow learner because the barriers of the rigid structure act as learning baffles. Good learning does not go on between levels, since superiors are "supposed to know," even if they do not. Too often we find the pretext of knowing, rather than genuine knowledge. This attitude is quickly becoming a luxury most companies cannot afford; it is unrealistic to expect people at all levels to know more than their subordinates.

On the other hand, if the enterprise is built on the authority of knowledge, we must take one another seriously and discover what others really know. Managers must get to know their subordinates' capabilities, aspirations, and experiences. This will also require a greater appreciation of individual differences. In fact, we are only beginning to understand what it means to value differences in background, tradition, education, gender, and age.

Knowledge is more than just knowing something. It comes in a variety of forms:

Know-how—procedures that get things done

Know-who—key resources to call upon
Know-what—the ability to discern key patterns based on knowledge
Know-why—understanding the larger context, the visions
Know-where—where things can and should happen
Know-when—a sense of rhythm, timing, and realism

Much of this knowledge will remain in the heads of those in the enterprise, although significant portions can be captured and sorted into applications, databases, and procedures. For example, the discipline of classifying and coding engineering drawings makes possible group technology. Phase review procedures coordinate orderly cooperation between functions. Customer profile databases help in customizing products and services.

### "Sequential Activities" to "Simultaneous Activities"

A great deal has already been said about the shift from the sequential to the parallel, concurrent, or simultaneous mode of operation. The challenge is to develop a culture which supports the establishment of core teams that are free to draw on knowledge resources wherever they are found within or outside the enterprise.

Enterprises will be successful if these teams are able to customize 20 percent of the product, leveraging the 80 percent that has already been developed. Through the use of group technology, parametric design, manufacturability rules, expert systems, and service considerations, we should be able to effectively utilize already existing resources.

### "Vertical Communication" to "Horizontal Communication"

The shift to horizontal communication should be an obvious one, especially as we see people not as turf owners but as knowledge resources within the network. There will still be vertical communication, of course, but the predominant communication will be horizontal in nature as the core task-focusing teams leverage knowledge wherever it may be in the enterprise.

Horizontal communication in a networked environment is freer and more fluid, with few bureaucratic barriers; it also facilitates serendipity, where key patterns may be unexpectedly discovered. Perhaps a request from one team to another will provide a clue to the pattern the other team is trying to discern. If we see our work as dialogue, we will stay open to discovery, observe the interplay of multiple patterns, and achieve our visions.

### "Distrust and Compliance" to "Trust and Integrity"

Distrust seems built into steep hierarchies. The fragmented structure breeds mutual distrust among functions. It is common to hear people complain of how another department throws information over the wall. Robert Hall, together with a group from the Association for Manufacturing Excellence, has been studying the "functional silo" problem.[13]

Manufacturing must double-check the drawing it just received from engineering. Sales feels it must recount the inventory because it does not believe finance's numbers. These activities do not add value to the product, just cost, but they are endemic to too many enterprises.

In the knowledge era, trust and integrity are critical. When people work closely together as resources in a network and as members of task-focusing teams, it quickly becomes obvious who can be trusted and who cannot. Do we share our thinking, our visions, and knowledge with those who we know will misuse them?

Digital expects its people to "push back" until the truth is known; each person is expected to "do the right thing." Hewlett-Packard asks its plant managers to locate their offices right on the plant floor where they are easily accessible. These policies engender honesty, trust, and openness. But these values are fragile and hard-won. A few key people can easily torpedo a climate of trust and integrity without even realizing what they have done.

Integration efforts are delicate and easily disrupted, especially if the atmosphere of trust fizzles. We know of instances where companies that made remarkable strides toward CIM had their efforts turn sour almost overnight when management was changed or the company was bought.

Technology by itself is hollow; this is why the integrative process must involve both technology and values. Even if the company controllers cannot assign a quantitative value to trust and integrity, these qualities are no less significant to the enterprise. Just because we cannot touch or count them does not mean they are not real.

## Two Examples of the Transition: Managing with Blurry Boundaries

Consider two examples of the shift in thinking we will need as we enter the knowledge era. The first example is from the United States, the second from Denmark. They illustrate the thought patterns that move a company to a new understanding of its business.

Jim Lardner, vice-president of Deere and Company, has suggested the need to reduce a company's "complexity index."[14] He was reflecting on the real experience of Deere as it ran into difficulties trying to computerize and automate its Waterloo, Iowa, Tractor Works in the early 1980s.

Lardner realized that Deere had to reduce the confusion, contradictions, and inconsistencies that had crept into its processes over the years. Rather than building high-bay storage and automated work-in-process tracking systems, why not get rid of the WIP? Rather than pushing material through the plant, why not go to a Just-in-Time pull system? Rather than inspecting quality into the product at the end of the line, why not design for robustness and get control over the processes so that quality would be ensured?

These changes required an elegance and sophistication that could not be bought from an outside vendor. Deere initiated its own efforts to reduce its complexity index. Its CIM, JIT, and Total Quality efforts simplified procedures while developing a more elegant understanding of how the various processes fit together and interact. Deere came to appreciate the interrelatedness of a wide variety of factors.

As companies attempt to unravel specific problems, serendipity can play an important role, as a second example shows. A Danish textile manufacturer was faced with the onerous task of taking yearly inventory. Traditionally, workers unrolled all the bolts of cloth and measured them. This was tedious and time-consuming.

This Danish company explored ways to measure the thicknesses of the bolts to compute their length, but found that some were wound more tightly than others and the widths of the cores varied. They reasoned that if they could get the core makers to standardize their cores, they could weigh the bolts and thereby compute the length. They then started bar-coding the bolts. This made it possible to put bar code readers at the wholesale warehouses, giving them an indication of downstream consumption and allowing them to cut their inventory by fine tuning production to market demands.[15]

What started out as an annual inventory measuring issue led ultimately to a more elegantly simple way of doing business. As the company followed the thread of the problem through its own organization and to its distribution network, it found that many departments needed to adjust their procedures. It also discovered that it operated within a web of networked and interrelated issues and opportunities.

These examples are echoed in many other manufacturing and service enterprises. Banking finds itself in a web of networked interrelationships, as do insurance companies, distribution supply houses, and mining companies. The Japanese trading companies, the *Sogo Shosha*, are masters at working in a web of interrelationships.

We cannot afford to continue playing the superficial power games that sap the strength from so many enterprises. Unfortunately, our educational systems have been more successful in pitting one student against another than they have in creating conditions where students can learn to learn from one another in networking enterprises.

Some may argue that human networking requires too much of people. They are not interested in doing anything more than getting a fair day's pay. We have been conditioned well by the industrial era to expect little from our narrowly defined jobs. But attitudes are changing. Jack Welch, Jr., chairman and CEO of General Electric Company, has explained that GE's drive to downsize and delayer is targeted not primarily at cutting costs but "at liberating, facilitating, [and] unleashing the human energy and initiative of our people." Cutting out the layers of management removes "all the dampers, valves and baffles" that have stifled human creativity.[16]

Downsizing and delayering, by themselves, do not release human creativity. Executives need to be as accomplished in building up people and putting them in touch with themselves and one another as they are in tearing down walls and removing layers of management.

The confusing complexity of the industrial era's steep hierarchy is due primarily to its superficial appreciation of human creativity. It is an artificial construct, useful in its time but fast becoming a lumbering dinosaur in an era where lean, agile, action-oriented enterprises are a necessity. The transition to the elegantly simple idea of the knowledge era requires an understanding of human time and work as dialogue. We must release the pent-up human energy in our enterprises.

Figure 11.4 summarizes the model of the human networking enterprise. Virtual task-focusing teams are interacting with suppliers of finances, people, materials, and technology. They are also dialoguing with distributor networks and with customers. Their efforts, held together by their visions and knowledge, are responsive and quick.

The transition to fifth generation management is a process of leading and responding to people and opportunities. It is very much a human-centered process because it recognizes our natural ability to develop visions, to remember, and to act decisively. The final chapter presents ten practical considerations for managing more integrative and elegantly simple enterprises.

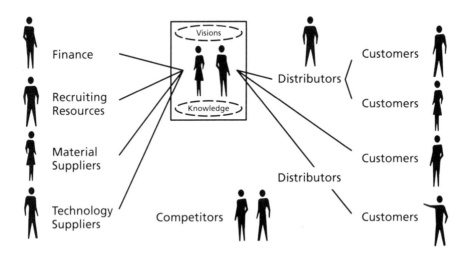

Figure 11.4 **Human networking enterprises**

# 12

# Managing Human Networking

Frank Giardelli, CEO of Custom Products and Services, is able to send shock waves through his staff by tearing his organizational chart in two. Our journey from the confinement of the steep hierarchies to the spaciousness of human networking has been a slower and more deliberate process. We have had to work our way through the Smith/Taylor/Fayol bottleneck. We now face a new challenge. How do we manage fifth generation enterprises?

The old rules of thumb no longer apply. Instead of worrying about "commanding and controlling" the enterprise, we now must "focus and coordinate" multiple-task teams. How will we build a climate of trust and openness? How will we learn the unique strengths of our people? And how will we engender accountability and learning?

Fifth generation management is not something we are easily taught. It has to come from within, as a result of discovering the power of our own insights, emotions, and ability to see new patterns. We are not only listening to the music; we are the music. This final chapter focuses on ways we can use the new source of wealth—knowledge—to build effective human networking enterprises (Figure 12.1).

We find that management by question is much more effective than management by command. Questions engage us in the matter at hand. They put us at the intersection of our visions and knowledge, human time and clock time. Questions spark growth, insights, and clarity; it is this creativity that gives an organization its long-term viability.

In human networking, not everything is entirely new. Some of the hierarchical organization remains. There are still boards of directors, presidents, vice-presidents, and directors. There are still managers, professionals, and employees. Collective bargaining still exists. The wage and hour laws are still a part of the environment. Departments continue, people still have individual assignments, and there is still dull and boring work.

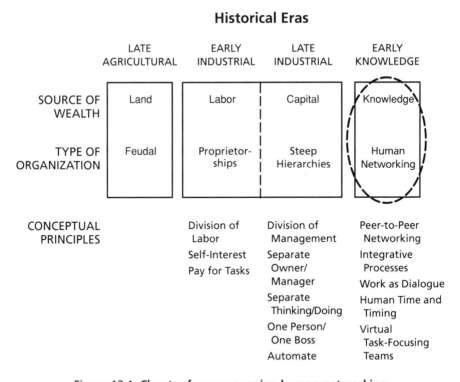

## Historical Eras

| | LATE AGRICULTURAL | EARLY INDUSTRIAL | LATE INDUSTRIAL | EARLY KNOWLEDGE |
|---|---|---|---|---|
| SOURCE OF WEALTH | Land | Labor | Capital | Knowledge |
| TYPE OF ORGANIZATION | Feudal | Proprietorships | Steep Hierarchies | Human Networking |
| CONCEPTUAL PRINCIPLES | | Division of Labor | Division of Management | Peer-to-Peer Networking |
| | | Self-Interest | Separate Owner/ Manager | Integrative Processes |
| | | Pay for Tasks | Separate Thinking/Doing | Work as Dialogue |
| | | | One Person/ One Boss | Human Time and Timing |
| | | | Automate | Virtual Task-Focusing Teams |

Figure 12.1 **Chapter focus: managing human networking**

There is, however, a qualitative difference. Organizations are much flatter. They are networked and networking. The president, vice-presidents, and others are working much closer together as teams. The quality of human interaction is much higher. Women are likely to find that they are particularly well suited for management responsibilities in these networking enterprises. In fact, more companies will move women into management ranks because it makes good business sense; they have excellent networking skills.

Instead of working sequentially in isolated departments, cross-functional resources are combined to work on large and small projects in parallel through task-focusing teams and through teamwork of teams. Costing is done by project rather than by burdening direct labor. The enterprise internalizes the capability of continual learning. People are expected to teach and learn from one another on an ongoing basis. There is more discipline in these organizations. Instead of bureaucracy, the enterprise is held together by an understanding of the core expectations of the organization—its vision.

The wealth-creating capacity of the enterprise is based on the knowledge and capabilities of its people. Much of this knowledge is only accessible through people, while other knowledge may be captured and embedded in application programs, databases, expert systems, neural networks, processes, and procedures. The creativity of the organization and its capacity to add value come through the intersection of its vision, its engagement in the present, and its knowledge.

If indeed the wealth-creating capacity of the enterprise is in its people, we should examine the practical considerations required for leveraging this capability.

## Ten Practical Considerations

The following ten considerations are not ordered by priority, but are interrelated. They should help us build human networking into enterprises. An enterprise must be able to:

1. Develop visioning capabilities so that the context is readily visible for the task-focusing teams

2. Develop functional centers of excellence

3. Develop a technical networking infrastructure that is easily reconfigurable

4. Develop a data integration strategy

5. Develop the ability to identify and track multiple-task teams

6. Develop learning, relearning, and unlearning capabilities

7. Develop norms, values, rewards, and measurements to support task-focusing teams

8. Develop the ability to support the teamwork of teams

9. Develop and grow the knowledge base

10. Extend virtual task-focusing teams to include suppliers, partners, distributors, and customers

These ten considerations are designed to support the conceptual principles of the early knowledge era: peer-to-peer networking, integrative process, work as dialogue, human time and timing, and virtual task-focusing teams (Figure 12.2).

## 1. Visioning Capabilities

Visioning provides the context which guides the multiple task teams. Enterprise visions are a composite of several elements: plans, goals, mission, philosophy, critical linkage factors (CLFs), and values, tempered with market realism. Planning helps set the overall direction of activities. Its value applies as much to the present as to the future, because, if it is done well, it can sort out many interrelated elements. It also helps in setting the strategic direction.

Well-chosen corporate goals can help to coordinate efforts in areas that cut across traditional functional boundaries. Stretch goals can be particularly effective in providing focus by measuring customer satisfaction, on-time delivery, problem-free installation, and cycle-time reduction. Goals may include internal measures such as inventory turns, process quality, reduced engineering change orders, or data quality.

The company's philosophy and values help define its spirit. Often these are simple, direct statements that can be captured on one or two pages. They usually include references to customer satisfaction, the importance of correct relationships, and the value of all employees. They may also include references to the importance of valuing differences and the necessity of honesty and integrity.

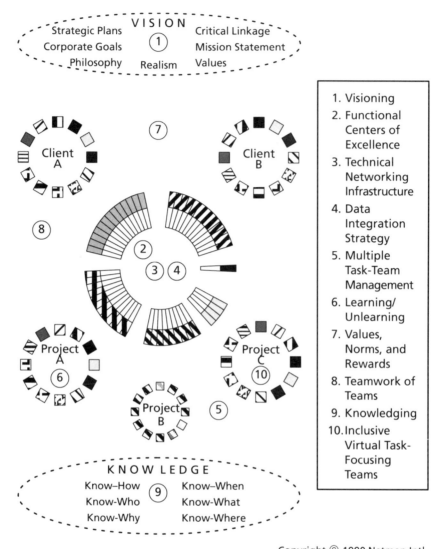

Figure 12.2 **Ten practical considerations**

Critical linkage factors, like critical success factors, are factors that bind the enterprise cross-functionally for success. For example, quality consciousness cannot be owned by one department. Others may refer to CLFs as mission-critical business processes. An order entry and management function cuts across many boundaries. In addition, many companies also develop architectures for materials, finance, and quality that must be linked together to be complementary and mutually reinforcing.

The often-overlooked element in a vision is its realism. It is easy to get carried away when "the rubber meets the sky." Realism works both ways. Timidity is as much of a trap as blind enthusiasm. This is where the enterprise's sense of timing and rhythm is so critical; it must be able to pace itself. It is too easy to become intoxicated on success, just as it is to become overly melancholy in defeat.

Good visioning comes from within the enterprise, not just from the top. If managers, professionals, and workers are not involved, the visions will seem irrelevant. In the best visioning, there is an active dialogue between the higher-level visions and specific capabilities. Often teams of engineers, marketers, service technicians, or manufacturing engineers will have ideas that can give generalized visions specific reality.

Virtual task-focusing teams should be expected periodically to challenge and enrich the enterprise visions, based on their specific work. This will help to keep the visions current and fresh. Real visions have meaning as they are realized in particular designs, products, processes, and services.

## 2. Functions: Centers of Excellence

As we shift from working sequentially to working in parallel with cross-functional teams, each person's knowledge and abilities will be even more significant. Therefore, the traditional functions must select the best people available and invest time and money to keep their knowledge on the cutting edge of their fields. It will be more critical than ever for professionals in functional departments to have both excellence in their own knowledge and a mastery of the procedures, standards, and operating norms of their group.

The functional department heads will need to work closely with the human resource department in hiring, promotion, and career development, as well as in training, education, and learning support programs to keep their people current in their areas of discipline. These department heads should get to know their people and their aspirations, dreams, capabilities, and uncertainties. Instead of being seen as bosses, they should build mentoring and coaching relationships with their people. One way to do this is to invite individuals to keep a reference description of their backgrounds, interests, and capabilities in an accessible database. These references can then be easily searched when putting together task teams. This approach allows us to see people in a new way. Instead of beginning with narrowly defined job descriptions, we can begin with richer and more varied self-definitions of personal interests and capabilities. It is through close personal contact that department heads will be able to help nurture and develop our professional resources.

These functional centers of excellence—marketing, sales, engineering, manufacturing, finance, personnel, and human resources—are resource centers. There will no longer be high walls encircling a functional department's turf; instead, managers, professionals, and workers in the centers will be available to participate in a variety of individual and team efforts. This enhances the networking process, encouraging these professionals to compose well-balanced teams.

## 3. The Technical Networking Infrastructure

We need to create virtual teams regardless of the location of individual persons. Physical and temporal proximity is of less importance when the enterprise has a well-designed and flexible technical networking capability. Electronic mail, computer note files, voice mail, distributed databases, integrated services digital network (ISDN), the seven-layer OSI model, and a host of proprietary communication systems are adding richness to the world of networking. As these networks grow and evolve, nodes will be added, moved, and removed.

Enterprise networking will link both internal and external resources. Closer internal linkages are being forged between marketing, engineering, manufacturing, finance, and service. Working digitally, products and processes can be designed concurrently and simulated even without a physical prototype. Bills of materials can be stripped out and sent to the manufacturing resource planning (MRP II) system, while information on the product's physical characteristics is sent to numeric control (NC) equipment and other information is sent to technical publications.

Externally, enterprises are expanding their electronic data interchange (EDI) networking capabilities to include technical data interchange (TDI). The aerospace and automotive companies are leading in these efforts, but many other industries, from banks to service companies, will become involved over time.

Technical networking develops through several stages. First, connectivity and interoperability are established; then professionals and applications are interfaced. Gradually, common user interfaces and common reference architectures are developed to provide more integration. As the technical networking infrastructure is developed, new horizons open in the use and deployment of internal and external resources. We find ourselves working in a web of interrelationships, some of them complex and delicate. In order to communicate well both within the enterprise and between enterprises, we pay more attention to the way we define products, processes, and services.

## 4. Data Integration Strategy

In the discussion in Chapter 8, we explored the "shades of meaning" problem, the questions involving language ambiguity that face companies as they attempt to computerize their steep hierarchies. Simply put, our languages use terms that can be very ambiguous. When computers were first used, the challenge was to conserve memory and CPU cycles. Now that memory and CPUs are relatively inexpensive, the challenge has shifted to "meanings management."

We now recognize how important it is to define a limited core set of data elements that can be used by all the different functions. Hewlett-Packard, a recognized leader in this regard, has carefully defined twenty to thirty core elements that cut across the enterprise. Many different functions use these same elements.

The tools and techniques for data integration are available. Computer-aided software engineering (CASE), computer-aided data engineering (CADE), data dictionaries, relational databases, and object-oriented databases help focus efforts toward the development of core data architectures. Instead of locking the data within each application, more and more companies are developing a shareable and extensible data architecture. This makes it possible for different applications to use the same core data.

We can standardize our tools and procedures, and we can ask the task teams to identify core data elements that can be added to the enterprise data dictionary and merged into the core data architecture. Over time, we can then expand our data architectures, developing consistent and agreed-upon meanings for the key terms. How do we start this process?

We begin by listing all existing applications and grouping them by function. Then, using a Netmap-like technology, we identify existing patterns of interfacing between these applications, flagging the translators. We then develop a list of twenty key items our enterprise needs, such as "part," "assembly," "project," "tolerance," "location," and "vendor." We choose ten key applications and see how these terms are defined, not only in the official data dictionary, but more importantly, in the context of the application, including attributes. This effort usually reveals a wide variety of definitions for the same or similar terms. It is the shades of meaning in these applications that make nightmares of many translation projects. People can deal with ambiguity in language; computers cannot.

Once our enterprises understand our spaghetti-like interfacing of applications and the different flavors of the definitions, we can begin to simplify our data architectures. This can be a daunting undertaking, but well worth the price, as shown by Ingersoll Milling Machine's success. In the 1970s, Ingersoll developed a common and shareable data architecture for multiple applications. This is integration. Most of our companies are still lost in the jungle of interfacing applications.

## 5. Multiple Task Team Management

As we switch from steep hierarchies to the use of multiple task teams, we will need to give these teams visibility and support. Unfortunately, in steep hierarchies, task teams often remain invisible to those who are not involved. Professionals and managers feel torn between their involvement on these teams and the work for which they normally get rewarded. This process needs to be reversed.

By aligning the organization in a circle, it is possible to show the clustering of multiple teams, as in Figure 12.2. With the appropriate windowing software, it will be possible to see the organization with its teams in one window, a list of themes they are working on in another, a list of participants in a third, and the project status in a fourth.

The teams should be responsible for defining their goals, purpose, and mission in a shareable database, together with their project plan. Teams can then scan various other activities to ask for help or share insights. Task teams will need to be brought together periodically so that they can exchange progress notes, clarify themes, focus on critical issues, and struggle with knotty problems. The teams need a rhythm to their meeting schedules in order to keep their work focused and on track. As these teams share their work, they will be aligning their efforts with the enterprise's visions and knowledge base.

The vitality of our enterprises is becoming more people- and team-dependent. We must put more time and effort into building sound and flexible team organizations, using all we have learned from employee involvement, sociotechnical systems, participative management, organizational development, and team building to increase our team management capabilities. When people know they have visibility for their participation in these activities, it is likely that they will put more of themselves into the effort, especially if the reward and measurement systems are also adjusted appropriately.

The use of centers of excellence together with multiple task teams means that both technical and human resources can be used more effectively and efficiently. It becomes a manageable virtual environment, based on human knowledge and capabilities. This approach can also generate rapid learning.

## 6. Learning, Relearning, and Unlearning

Traditional steep hierarchies focus primarily on training and education. A third component must be added: learning, relearning, and unlearning. In order to maintain self-generation and knowledge growth, we will need to become much more effective learners. As we sort out experiences, impressions, and past learning, we relearn the the key lessons. In the unlearning process, some old ideas are discarded.

Typically, when people participate in teamwork, they want to prove how much more clever they are than the others. For this competitive attitude we can thank our schools, where students are pitted against one another, vying for the teacher's accolades. Rarely are students taught how to learn from one another.

We are good at tearing down each other's ideas, not building them up. Moreover, learning is often impeded because we are afraid that if we give away our good ideas, someone else may get credit for them. Simply put, we have a lot of cultural baggage to overcome, or unlearn, if we hope to nurture a learning capability within our organizations.

If we hope to be successful in rapidly changing markets, our teams must spot the right patterns early by listening and learning, then respond quickly. We are dependent on one another's knowledge, insights, and experience to cut through the fuzzy and ambiguous clouds shrouding possible market opportunities. Sustained responsiveness requires that group learning be captured and applied to other efforts.

Unfortunately, many project teams fail to retain their knowledge as they proceed through the project. At the end of the effort, when they have disbanded, much of what they have learned evaporates into the ether. As we become more sophisticated in our expectations of task teams, we periodically will ask them to share their learning with other teams, thus contributing to the knowledge resources and visioning of the enterprise.

Some may object that this approach is too idealistic, that it will not work in the real world. People have learned to be very careful in sharing ideas. Their emotional scars are a reminder of how brutal some experiences can be. Certainly these experiences cannot be discounted.

As long as we are preoccupied with the idea of possession, we will limp along. On the other hand, if we can begin to understand the nature of human time and the importance of envisioning and remembering, we will gain a new perspective. Instead of seeing group participation as a power struggle, we will come to appreciate the human growth aspects of work.

A simple change of norms can open new possibilities. For example, if each time I participate in a group I actively try to learn two or three new things from the others in the room, I put myself into a learning mode. I gain—as do the others, because they feel listened to. One of the greatest rewards in life is to feel listened to. This is the basis of recognition, something we all seek. As we learn to listen carefully to one another, we are doing two things—learning, and affirming others as people. Unlike the Greeks' idea of work, our work is as rich as our leisure. As we grasp the nature of work dialogue and of human time, active learning will become an essential part of everyday life.

## 7. Values, Norms, Rewards, and Measurement Systems

It is easy to install a technical networking infrastructure within an enterprise. It is harder to shape new values and norms, and to support them with the proper reward and measurement systems. How do we manage the shift?

- The industrial era used the dexterity of the hand to grow. We need to build upon the dexterity of the mind.

- In the industrial era the past was a throwaway. In the knowledge era the past is a source of insight and knowledge.

- The industrial era assumed that the future was far ahead. The knowledge era finds the future contained in the present.

- Vision and knowledge were of minor importance to the industrial era. They are everything in the knowledge era.

- The mechanical model predominated in the industrial era. Today it is being replaced by a biological and organic model. Instead of gears meshing together, we appreciate minds growing.

Having worked in a machine shop, Frederick Taylor knew how work groups set their own quotas. He realized that the only way to break this process was to set up a planning office that would define a fair day's workload. This led to his idea of separating thinking from doing, which resulted in his scientific management theory.

However, if visibility and accountability are built into the system, Taylor's concerns are no longer problems. Instead, top management can stimulate, inspire, and challenge the teams, releasing much of the pent-up energy that is wasted in so many of our enterprises. Instead of beginning with a machine-like organizational model, we need a free-form approach that supports human networking, using our vision and knowledge.

Values are a particularly important component of the vision. They are not gained through a training course or through wall posters, but are nurtured and grown over time through personal interaction. Trust and openness reflect the attitude of top management as well as those of everyone else in the enterprise. These values grow slowly, yet they can disappear almost overnight. The fact that Digital employees are expected to "do the right thing" is a sign of trust in the employees—and a measure of management's integrity, honesty, and wisdom.

General Georges Doriot, whose venture capital firm invested the initial $70,000 in Ken Olsen's idea for Digital's interactive computer, was fond of stressing the importance of "generosity." By this General Doriot meant the willingness to give other people their due, to give them space to express themselves, and to listen carefully for the seed of an idea in what they are saying. Attitudes like these build trust, openness, and integrity.

Each enterprise determines the constellation of values that it deems important; there is no prescribed list. But as new norms emerge, we are able to see who has integrity and who misuses information. We know who listens and who strangles thought. We know who shares knowledge and who hides behind a position of authority. We know who is able to share leadership and who holds on to it.

Now we need to redefine our rewards and measurements to catch up with the times. When we think of rewards, we usually think first of monetary rewards. In doing so, we accept the Greek notion of work as punishment: if we give up our time to do something we do not like, then we should be rewarded handsomely.

Although these rewards will continue to be important, they will be complemented with another dimension of reward, that of quality human interaction. It can be very exhilarating to participate on a dynamic team that encourages human growth. There is reward in being listened to and challenged by our peers and reward in the sheer joy of accomplishment. This helps to bring out the best in us.

As we align ourselves in clustered work teams, we will be interacting peer to peer rather than superior to subordinate. The former supports growth; the latter kills inspiration. Perhaps the heads of centers of excellence will have the final say on rewards, but peer reviews will probably play a growing role in the reward process. This process will remain quite subjective, but its success will depend on the integrity of one's peers and on the heads of the centers of excellence, rather than on one's "boss." Since more rewards will be given for contributions to the team success and fewer for isolated individual firefighting, incentive systems will need to be adjusted accordingly. Cost accounting will tailor its systems around programs and projects rather than burdening direct labor. Much work remains to be done in this area.[1]

## 8. Teamwork of Teams

In the rhythm of the enterprise's work, some products or services are being born, others maturing, and still others being phased out. As different teams pursue their objectives, they will naturally overlap with one another; this is natural and wholesome. Instead of envisioning the organization as mutually exclusive boxes, we should think of overlapping teams, like Venn diagrams.

Once the enterprise installs its network, it can pull teams together across geography and time zones. We do not have to share the same office space; in fact, using extended networks, teams can include key people from supplier or client companies. Ingersoll Milling Machine has mastered this capability in a large project with an automobile maker.[2] Its project team includes engineers from the car company who work side by side with its team in design and build efforts.

Some companies use "management by event" as a powerful focusing technique. Professionals like to rise to the occasion; given an opportunity to show their worth, they often surprise even themselves. The enterprise can periodically stage events in which the task-focusing teams are asked to help grow the enterprise vision based on work that has been done.

Our challenge is to facilitate the teamwork of teams. Just as each task team has a rhythm of its own, so too there is a rhythm in the work between teams. A team developing a new iron reduction process may be dependent upon the developments of another team working on plasma arcs. (This idea is not new; the success of the Industrial Revolution was made possible by concurrent developments in many interrelated disciplines from fluid dynamics to metallurgy.) A technical networking infrastructure and shareable core data will help facilitate the interchange of themes between work teams.

Earlier we suggested that virtual task-focusing teams are like jazz combos. Each combo is capable of taking a theme and adding value to it in unique and individual ways. It can toss a theme to another combo to see how the other combo works with it. Its unique tempo, rhythm, and articulation can challenge and inspire the other combos or task teams.

## 9. Knowledging Capabilities

Networking enterprises are much freer in form than steep hierarchies. They are held together not by rigid bureaucracy but by shared visions and common knowledge resources, the most valuable of which are in people's heads. We humans have a wonderful knack of recombining what we have learned to find new ways to solve problems—for example, we may combine an understanding of metallurgy, electrical flux, and test results to discover why a particular type of disk drive fails. We can look at a situation in the larger context. Unlike computers, we can work with vague clues, fuzzy patterns, and ambiguous data.

Relational and object-oriented database technology makes it easier to dynamically reconfigure computer-based memory, but this technology is limited. On the other hand, if an enterprise captures 30 percent of its core knowledge in a consistent and shareable manner and in an understandable data architecture, then a partnership between people and processors can be quite powerful. Group technology has been a wonderful teacher of how to classify and code drawings and processes. Just-in-Time has helped us sort out basic relationships both within our organizations and with our suppliers.

We need tremendous discipline in the care and nurturing of our enterprise knowledge bases. We must be ready for the costs of maintaining both our legacy systems and new ones. As individual and team learning is codified in engineering standards, classification and coding systems, operating techniques, applications, data dictionaries, and customer profiles, an invaluable resource is developed. What teams in one plant learn in mastering surface-mount technology can benefit other plants in the same company.

Even if accountants have difficulty valuing the know-how represented in the knowledge base, it is a key resource for the enterprise and the source of new business visions. Mastery of unique knowledging capabilities gives the enterprise market differentiation. Therefore, task teams should be expected not only to solve the tasks at hand, but also to contribute to the knowledge base and to augment the shared business vision. The measurement and reward systems should acknowledge this added contribution.

## 10. Inclusive Virtual Task-Focusing Teams

As we learn to think beyond the four walls of our own enterprise, we can configure our task teams to include representatives from suppliers, partners, distributors, and customers. Just like internal resources, these people are virtual resources. For example, a product development team may include two representatives from a customer organization whose presence adds to the team's understanding of real-world customer expectations.

This approach also helps the enterprise involve the customer in delivery of the product or service. When automatic teller machines involve the consumer directly in the operation of the bank, the bank wins in two ways: it makes money from this extension of its service, and it reduces its own clerical staffing needs.

# Concluding Thoughts

We can either remain prisoners in the boxes and lines of our organizational charts or experience the challenge of working together in virtual task-focusing teams as was experienced in Book 1. We can either live by clock time, as prisoners of the present, or be inspired and nurtured in human time as we network our visions and knowledge. We can either look up to our bosses and down on our subordinates or engage as peers in a dialogue about the significant themes challenging our enterprises.

We can flounder in the separation of thinking and doing or engage in the integrative process of continual improvement. We can remain isolated from one another or seek out one another as individuals or through teams to get on with the work. Look again at the historical eras and the changes they have brought. The transition to human networking enterprises is not inevitable; it is up to us to bring it about.

Our new source of wealth is more a *capability* than a *possession*. Knowledging, our human ability to see and interrelate patterns on an ongoing basis, gives us a new mastery over time and improves our timing. As we network with one another, we are able to act decisively and overcome the fragmentation of the industrial era. Through this shift, we gain a new sense of accountability toward one another.

Think back over the previous chapters and substitute the concepts of "visioning" and "knowledging" (capabilities) for the words "vision" and "knowledge" (something possessed). These changes should underscore the significance of "work as dialogue" and "human time and timing" as key factors in putting the functions in touch with one another. This process can never be automated or computerized, although it can be supported by computers and networking.

No system by itself can overcome the fragmentation in our steep hierarchies. Only as people start to reach out and network with one another will this fragmentation be overcome. It will not always be easy, because old attitudes live on in strange ways. In fact, it is natural to expect that we will encounter many "gotchas" along the way. People who have a hard time listening and learning from one another will have difficulty working in cross-functional teams. Top management may be slow in learning to accept ideas from below. Teams will go off in different directions in an uncoordinated manner because the rhythm of the organization is not well established. Without many rungs on the career ladder, some managers will not know how to gauge relative success. Companies will just plain miss market signals, get behind the technology curve, and misinterpret developments. We will still have to contend with people's darker sides. These are all elements we will encounter and will have to deal with in one way or another. Will these "gotchas" be fatal? Probably not if we are clear about where we are going and what needs to be done; otherwise, there will be those who want to retreat to the comfort of the steep hierarchy where the stovepipes are warm and cozy.

Other management challenges deal with accountability, focusing and coordinating, and learning. It should be clear by now that accountability comes through visioning. Visions and knowledge also help the multiple virtual task-focusing teams to focus and coordinate their efforts. And as we break out of the web of industrial-era conceptual principles, we will be able to build into the daily life of our enterprises the practice of continual learning.

Dan Infante, vice-president of Digital Information Systems, has captured the spirit of fifth generation management when he writes: "A good place to work is one which engages the whole person—his or her thoughts, feelings, and, yes, even aspirations. It is a place which values diversity, and sees peoples' uniqueness as the seed of new ideas and possibilities." In addition, he believes "A good place to work is where people feel at ease collaborating cross-functionally and feel empowered to make decisions that are right for the organization."[3]

Ken Olsen's vision of this elegantly simple organization is realizable, especially as we work more in parallel. We can learn to use our education and knowledge to motivate and inspire one another as the business curve shifts from a "frown" to a "smile," as it did for Custom Products and Services, Inc., in Book 1. Fifth generation management is not only a possibility; it is a necessity in order to deal with the increasing complexity of our world markets.

Good luck on your journey toward the wholeness of human networking in elegantly simple enterprises. Please keep a log that you can share; learning is an ongoing process for us all. I hope the visions expressed in this book will speed you on your way, and I would like to learn from your experiences.

# CHAPTER NOTES

## Chapter 3. Wednesday

1. Art Hamill, Jr., of Digital Equipment Corporation developed the inverted curve in 1986 to illustrate the shifting nature of Digital's business.

## Chapter 5. Friday

1. This approach is based upon the work of Netmap International, which was started by an Australian, John Galloway, some fifteen years ago. It comes out of the efforts inspired by people like George C. Homans, who wrote *The Human Group* (New York: Harcourt, Brace & World, 1950). Like Homans, Galloway wanted to develop a way of identifying what some have called the informal group within an organization. He was aware that there usually is an official organization, as defined by the organizational chart, but that there also is a nonformal organization, the group that gets the work done. Over the years, Galloway has developed an approach, using a nonthreatening questionnaire, that makes it possible to identify who interacts with whom given a variety of topics and other variables. This process identifies what Galloway calls the *emergent organization*. He has developed software that allows the various

groupings of an organization to be seen on a computer screen in color or plotted on paper.

## Chapter 6. Introduction: The Past and Future

1. Stephen Grossberg, "Nonlinear Neural Networks: Principles, Mechanisms, and Architectures," *Neural Networks* 1, no. 1 (1988): 17–61.

2. Robert G. Eccles and Dwight B. Crane, *Doing Deals: Investment Banks at Work* (Boston: Harvard Business School Press, 1988).

3. Edward A. Feigenbaum and Pamela McCorduck, *The Fifth Generation: Artificial Intelligence and Japan's Computer Challenge to the World* (Reading, MA: Addison-Wesley, 1983).

4. Eric Teicholz and Joel N. Orr, *Computer Integrated Manufacturing Handbook* (New York: McGraw-Hill, 1987), pp. 1.4–1.5.

5. Peter Drucker, "The Coming of the New Organization," *Harvard Business Review* 66:5 (January–February 1988), p. 47. For an expansion on this article see Peter Drucker, *The New Realities* (New York: Harper & Row, 1989), pp. 173–252.

6. Ken Olsen, "Presentation at the Annual Meeting of Digital Equipment Corporation, Boston, November 6, 1986," in *Digital Equipment Corporation Second Quarter Report 1987* (Maynard, MA: Digital Equipment Corp., 1987), p. 4.

7. Paul Kidd, "Technology and Engineering Design: Shaping a Better Future or Repeating the Mistakes of the Past?" *IEE Proceedings*, vol. 135, pt. A, no. 5, May 1988.

8. Kazuto Togino, "A Global Programming Language and Orchestration of the Execution of Jobs and Tasks," National Research Council Canada, Symposium on Manufacturing Application Languages, June 20–21, 1988, Winnipeg, Manitoba.

## Chapter 7. Five Generations of Computers and Management

1. Gerhard Friedrich of Digital Equipment Corporation, together with the Industrial Liaison Program of MIT, organized a conference in May 1985 called "Managing the Transition to the Fifth Generation." Following the conference a videotape was produced entitled "Fifth-Generation Management."

2. Edward A. Feigenbaum and Pamela McCorduck, *The Fifth Generation: Artificial Intelligence and Japan's Computer Challenge to the World* (Reading, MA: Addison-Wesley, 1983), p. 17.

3. See reference to John von Neumann in *Computer Basics: Understanding Computers*, ed. by Russell B. Adams and Donald D. Cantley (Alexandria, VA: Time-Life Books, 1985), pp. 62–63.

4. Charles M. Savage, *Fifth Generation Management for Fifth Generation Technology* (Dearborn, MI: Society of Manufacturing Engineers, 1987), p. 3.

5. Adam Smith, *The Wealth of Nations* (London: Penguin Classics, 1987).

6. Frederick Winslow Taylor, *Scientific Management* (Westport, CT: Greenwood Press, 1947), p. 24.

7. Henri Fayol, *General and Industrial Management* (London: Pitman and Sons, 1949), p. 24. His fourteen points are as follows:
   1. Division of work (specialization belongs to the natural order).
   2. Authority and responsibility (responsibility is a corollary of authority).
   3. Discipline (discipline is what leaders make it).
   4. Unity of command (men cannot bear dual command).
   5. Unity of direction (one head and one plan for a group of activities having the same objectives).
   6. Subordination of individual interest to the general interest.
   7. Remuneration (fair, rewarding of effort, reasonable).
   8. Centralization (centralization belongs to the natural order).
   9. Scalar chain (line of authority, gangplank principle).
   10. Order (a place for everyone and everyone in his place).
   11. Equity (results from a combination of kindliness and justice).
   12. Stability of tenure of personnel (prosperous firms are stable).
   13. Initiative (great source of strength for business).
   14. Esprit de corps (union is strength).

8. Ibid.

9. According to Leslie Berkes, Netmap International has completed over 250 studies undertaken to discover the real structure of organizations—that is, the structure created by individuals in carrying out their vital tasks. These studies have been conducted in major international Fortune 500 corporations across a variety of industries, large privately held companies, government agencies, nonprofit groups, and service firms. Across all these studies fewer than 20 percent of formally designated managers proved to be key to the vital task networks. See also John J. Galloway, "Revealing Organizational Networks," Annual Conference of Australian Communication Association, Sydney, July 1987; John J. Galloway and Anne Gorman, *Going Places: How to Network Your Way to Personal Success* (Sydney: Allen and Unwin, 1987); and Donald

G. Livingston and Leslie J. Berkes, "Netmap: An Innovative Diagnostic Tool," *Journal of Managerial Psychology* 4, No. 4 (1989), pp. 7–14.

10. Stanley M. Davis and Paul Lawrence, *Matrix* (Reading, MA: Addison-Wesley, 1977).

11. Stanley M. Davis, *Future Perfect* (Reading, MA: Addison-Wesley, 1988), p. 86. See also Fred V. Guterl, "Goodbye, Old Matrix," *Business Month* (February 1989): 32–38.

12. Davis, *Future Perfect*, p. 87.

13. Digital Equipment Corporation, in recognizing the growing gap between technology and the organization, has done pioneering work in developing ways to intertwine the development of a company's *business, technology,* and *human resources.* See Dennis O'Connor and Wendy Wilkerson, *Guide to Expert Systems Program Management* (Maynard, MA: Digital Equipment Corp., 1985).

14. Shoshana Zuboff, *In the Age of the Smart Machine: The Future of Work and Power* (New York: Basic Books, 1988). Zuboff has raised the discussion of computer-based technology to a higher level of understanding. She has provided an insightful look at the impact of computers in the factory, bank, and office. According to Zuboff, "informating" is qualitatively different from automating. Automation removes the human element; informating, on the other hand, involves the individual in new and exciting ways. Although it suggests a process, "informating" connotes information, something that is already known in the past. "Knowledging," on the other hand, draws both on what is known and on our ability to envision what has not yet come into being.

15. Joseph Harrington, Jr., *Computer Integrated Manufacturing* (New York: Industrial Press, 1973); Jay Galbraith, *Designing Complex Organizations* (Reading, MA: Addison-Wesley, 1973); Daniel Bell, *The Coming Post-Industrial Society* (New York: Basic Books, 1973).

16. Peter Drucker, "The Coming of the New Organization," *Harvard Business Review* 66:5 (January–February 1988), p. 47; Davis, *Future Perfect*; Richard L. Nolan, Alex J. Pollock, and James P. Ware, "Creating the 21st Century Organization," *Stage by Stage* 8:4 (Lexington, MA: Nolan, Norton and Co., Fall 1988), pp. 1–11.

17. Drucker, "The Coming of the New Organization," p. 45.

18. Ibid., p. 50.

19. Ibid., p. 53.

20. Davis, *Future Perfect*, p. 89.

21. Nolan, Pollock, and Ware, "Creating the 21st Century Organization."

22. Ibid., p. 1.

23. Ibid., p. 2.

## Chapter 8. Computerizing Steep Hierarchies: Will It Work?

1. George Hess, "Computer Integrated Manufacturing—How to Get Started." Presentation at AUTOFACT, Detroit, MI, November 14–17, 1983 [unpublished].

2. Adam Smith, *The Wealth of Nations* (London: Penguin Classics, 1987).

3. Alfred D. Chandler, Jr., and Herman Daems, eds., *Managerial Hierarchies: Comparative Perspectives on the Rise of the Modern Industrial Enterprise* (Cambridge, MA: Harvard University Press, 1980), p. 16.

4. Ibid., p. 3.

5. Ibid., p. 9.

6. Paul R. Lawrence and Jay W. Lorsch, *Organization and Environment: Managing Differentiation and Integration* (Boston: Graduate School of Business Administration, Harvard University, 1967).

7. John T. Ward, *The Factory System* (New York: Barnes & Noble, 1970).

8. These include Dan Ciampa, *Manufacturing's New Mandate, The Tools for Leadership* (New York: John Wiley & Sons, 1988); Thomas G. Gunn, *Manufacturing for Competitive Advantage: Becoming a World Class Manufacturer* (Cambridge, MA: Ballinger, 1987); Robert W. Hall, *Attaining Manufacturing Excellence* (Homewood, IL: Dow Jones–Irwin, 1987); Robert H. Hayes and Steven C. Wheelwright, *Restoring Our Competitive Edge: Competing through Manufacturing* (New York: John Wiley & Sons, 1984); Rosabeth Moss Kanter, *The Change Masters: Innovation and Entrepreneurship in the American Corporation* (New York: Simon & Schuster, 1983); Paul R. Lawrence and Davis Dyer, *Renewing American Industry: Organizing for Efficiency and Innovation* (New York: The Free Press, 1983); Raymond E. Miles and Charles C. Snow, "Organizations: New Concepts for New Forms," *California Management Review* 28, No. 3 (Spring 1986), pp. 62–73; Tom Peters, *Thriving on Chaos: Handbook for a Management Revolution* (New York: Alfred A. Knopf, 1988); Robert B. Reich, *The Next American Frontier* (New York: Times Books, 1983); Robert H. Waterman, Jr., *The Renewal Factor, How the Best Get and*

*Keep the Competitive Edge* (New York: Bantam Books, 1987); and Shoshana Zuboff, *In the Age of the Smart Machine: The Future of Work and Power* (New York: Basic Books, 1988).

9. Eric Teicholz and Joel N. Orr, *Computer Integrated Manufacturing Handbook* (New York: McGraw-Hill, 1987), pp. 1.4–1.5.

10. Reich, *The Next American Frontier*, p. 96.

11. James Lardner, "Integration and Information in an Automated Factory," Presentation at AUTOFACT Conference, Anaheim, CA, October 1, 1984 (Dearborn, MI: Society of Manufacturing Engineers, 1984).

12. George Homans, *The Human Group* (New York: Harcourt, Brace & World, 1950).

13. Terry Winograd and Fernando Flores, *Understanding Computers and Cognition: A New Foundation for Design* (Reading, MA: Addison-Wesley, 1987).

14. Zuboff, *In the Age of the Smart Machine*.

15. George J. Hess, "1982 Industry LEAD Award Winner—Revisited in 1986," presentation at AUTOFACT Conference, Detroit, MI, November 12–14, 1986 (Dearborn, MI: Society of Manufacturing Engineers, 1986), p. 11-3.

16. See remarks by Warren Shrensker in *Fifth Generation Management, 1986 Round Table Summary Document*, ed. by Charles M. Savage (Dearborn, MI: Society of Manufacturing Engineers, 1987), p. 13.

17. David Stroll. Private correspondence, October 27, 1989.

## Chapter 9. Steep Hierarchies: Breaking Free

1. Adam Smith, *The Wealth of Nations* (London: Penguin Classics, 1987), p. 1.

2. Bernard Mandeville, *The Fable of the Bees*, ed. by Phillip Harth (London: Penguin Books, 1970).

3. Smith, *Wealth of Nations*, p. 234.

4. Ibid., p. 112.

5. Charles Babbage, *On the Economy of Machinery and Manufacturers* (London: Charles Knight, 1832).

6. Ibid., p. 173.

7. Edward S. Mason, *The Corporation in Modern Society* (New York: Atheneum, 1970); Adolf A. Berle and Gardiner C. Means, *The Modern Corporation and Private Property* (New York: Harcourt, Brace & World, 1932).

8. Alfred Chandler, *The Visible Hand: The Managerial Revolution in American Business* (Cambridge, MA: Harvard University Press, 1977).

9. Stanley M. Davis, *Future Perfect* (Reading, MA: Addison-Wesley, 1988), p. 140.

10. Jack Welsh, "The Mind of Jack Welch," *Fortune*, March 27, 1989.

11. Frederick Winslow Taylor, *Scientific Management* (Westport, CT: Greenwood Press, 1972).

12. Ibid., p. 38.

13. Ibid., p. 31.

14. Robert B. Reich, *The Next American Frontier* (New York: Times Books, 1983).

15. Claude S. George, *The History of Management Thought* (Englewood Cliffs, NJ: Prentice-Hall, 1972).

16. Lyndall F. Urwick, "Organization as a Technical Problem," in *Papers on the Science of Administration*, ed. by Luther Gulick and Lyndall F. Urwick (New York: Columbia University, Institute of Public Administration, 1937), p. 51.

17. James D. Mooney and Allan C. Reiley, *Onward Industry!* (New York: Harper and Brothers, 1931), p. 37.

18. Paul R. Lawrence and Jay W. Lorsch, *Organization and Environment: Managing Differentiation and Integration* (Boston: Graduate School of Business Administration, Harvard University, 1967), p. 167.

19. Jay Galbraith, *Organization Design* (Reading, MA: Addison-Wesley, 1977).

20. Chester I. Barnard, *The Functions of the Executive* (Cambridge, MA: Harvard University Press, 1938).

21. Ibid., p. 128.

22. Herbert A. Simon, *Administrative Behavior* (New York: The Free Press, 1946).

23. Reich, *The Next American Frontier*, p. 134.

24. Peter F. Drucker, *The Frontiers of Management* (New York: Dutton, 1986), pp. 220–221.

25. George J. Hess, "Computer Integrated Manufacturing—How to Get Started," presentation at AUTOFACT, Detroit, MI, November, 1983 (Dearborn, MI: Society of Manufacturing Engineers, 1983).

26. Douglas McGregor, *The Human Side of Enterprise* (New York: McGraw-Hill, 1960).

27. Aristotle, *The Politics of Aristotle,* Bk. I, Ch. IV, § 3, ed. and trans. by Ernest Barker (New York: Oxford University Press, 1958).

28. Eric Teicholz and Joel N. Orr, *Computer Integrated Manufacturing Handbook* (New York: McGraw-Hill, 1987).

29. Adriano Tilgher, *Homo Faber, Work through the Ages,* trans. by D. Fisher (Chicago: Regency, 1965).

30. Bill Lawrence addressing the Automation Forum, a group sponsored by the National Electrical Manufacturers Association during a visit to the Texas Instruments plant in Sherman, Texas, on March 23, 1988.

31. Joseph Harrington, Jr., *Computer Integrated Manufacturing* (New York: Industrial Press, 1973), p. 6.

32. Ibid., p. 7.

33. Joseph Harrington, Jr., *Understanding the Manufacturing Process: Key to Successful CAD/CAM Implementation* (New York: Marcel Dekker, 1984).

34. U.S. Air Force, Integrated Computer Aided Manufacturing, *ICAM Program Prospectus* (Dayton, OH: Air Force Materials Laboratory, Wright-Patterson Air Force Base, 1979).

35. David A. Marca and Clement L. McGowan, *SADT: Structured Analysis and Design Technique,* forward by Douglas T. Ross (New York: McGraw-Hill, 1988).

36. Dan Appleton, *Introducing the New CIM Enterprise Wheel* (Dearborn, MI: CASA/SME, 1986).

37. Ibid.

38. Phone conversation with John Hall, President, Marshall Aluminum Products, Cerna, CA, and former Chairperson of the CASA/SME Technical Council, September 14, 1989.

39. ESPRIT, Project No. 688, CIM/OSA, *A Primer on Key Concepts and Purpose* (Brussels, Belgium, 1987), p. 4.

40. Harrington, *Integrated Manufacturing,* p. 6.

41. Tom Peters, *Thriving on Chaos: Handbook for a Management Revolution* (New York: Alfred A. Knopf, 1988).

42. Radovan Richta, *Civilization at the Crossroads: Social and Human Implications of the Scientific and Technological Revolution,* trans. by Marian Slingova (Prague: International Arts and Sciences Press, 1968).

43. Nolan, Norton and Co., "Computer Integrated Manufacturing Payoff Working Group," March 25–26, 1987. [An unpublished working group report.]

44. Shoshana Zuboff, *In the Age of the Smart Machine: The Future of Work and Power* (New York: Basic Books, 1988), p. 310.

# Chapter 10. Human Networking: Self-Empowering

1. "Cords of Change," *World* (Chicago: Peat Marwick, Summer 1988). Interview discussion with Alvin Toffler, Leslie Berkes, and others.

2. Ibid.

3. H. Chandler Stevens, *The Network Notebook* (Washington, DC: National Science Foundation, 1978).

4. Peter B. Vaill, *Managing as a Performing Art: New Ideas for a World of Chaotic Change* (San Francisco: Jossey-Bass, 1989); and Marvin R. Weisbord, *Productive Workplaces: Organizing and Managing for Dignity, Meaning, and Community* (San Francisco: Jossey-Bass, 1987).

5. Charles M. Savage, *Work and Meaning: A Phenomenological Inquiry* (Unpublished Ph.D. Thesis, Boston College, 1973).

6. See Stafford Beer, *The Heart of the Enterprise* (New York: John Wiley & Sons, 1979); Tom Peters, *Thriving on Chaos: Handbook for a Management Revolution* (New York: Alfred A. Knopf, 1987); Peter Drucker, "The Coming of the New Organization," *Harvard Business Review* 66:5 (January–February 1988), pp. 45–53; Eric Trist, "The Evolution of Sociotechnical Systems: A Conceptual Framework and an Action Research Program" (Toronto: Ontario Quality of Working Life Center, Occasional Paper No. 2, June 1981); and John Briggs and F. David Peat, *Turbulent Mirror: An Illustrated Guide to Chaos Theory and the Science of Wholeness* (New York: Harper & Row, 1989).

7. See Robert H. Waterman, *The Renewal Factor: How the Best Get and Keep the Competitive Edge* (New York: Bantam Books, 1987); and Rosabeth Moss Kanter, *The Change Masters: Innovation and Entrepreneurship in the American Corporation* (New York: Simon & Schuster, 1983).

8. Savage, *Work and Meaning.*

9. The section on human time has been inspired by Edmund Husserl, *The Phenomenology of Internal Time-Consciousness,* ed. by Martin Heidegger and translated by James Churchill (Bloomington: Indiana University Press, 1964). I am using "human time" to refer to Husserl's idea of "internal time-con-

sciousness." See also William James, *The Principles of Psychology*, vol. 1 (New York: Dover Publications, 1950).

10. St. Augustine, *Confessions*, trans. with an introduction by R. S. Pine-Coffin (Baltimore: Penguin Books, 1961).

11. Ibid., p. 157.

12. Aristotle, *Physics*, 218b9 (Aristotle, *Selections*, ed. by W. D. Ross, New York: Charles Scribner's Sons, 1955), p. 122.

13. William James, *The Principles of Psychology*, vol. 1 (New York: Dover Publications, 1950), pp. 613 and 643.

14. Ronald M. Fortuna, "A Primer on Quality Function Deployment," *CIM Review* 5:1 (Fall 1988): 49–54. See also William E. Eureka and Nancy E. Ryan, *The Customer-Driven Company, Management Perspectives on QFD* (Dearborn, MI: ASI Press, 1988).

15. Charles F. Kiefer and Peter Stroh, "A New Paradigm for Developing Organizations," in John D. Adams, ed. *Transforming Work* (Alexandria, VA: Miles River Press, 1984).

16. Paul R. Lawrence and Davis Dyer, *Renewing American Industry, Organizing for Efficiency and Innovation* (New York: The Free Press, 1983).

17. See series of articles on simultaneous engineering in *Manufacturing Engineer*, 101:3 (September 1988).

18. Drucker, "The Coming of the New Organization."

19. Jan Hopland of Digital Equipment Corporation first suggested to me that the concept of virtual memory has an analogy: the virtual enterprise. See also: Jan Hopland and Charles Savage, "Virtual Teams and Flexible Enterprises," *Digital Technical Management Education Program News* 3 (July 1989); and "Digital Equipment Corporation: The Endpoint Model," Harvard Business School case study, 1988. [This case includes reference to "virtual integration."]

20. Jessica Lipnack and Jeffrey Stamps, *The Networking Book: People Connecting with People* (New York: Routledge and Kegan Paul, 1986); Jeffrey Stamps, *Holonomy: A Human System Theory* (Seaside, CA: Intersystem Publications, 1980); and Jessica Lipnack and Jeffrey Stamps, *How Groups Think* (Waltham, MA: Networking Institute, 1988, unpublished).

21. Stephen Grossberg, "Nonlinear Neural Networks: Principles, Mechanisms, and Architectures," *Neural Networks* 1:1 (1988), pp. 17–61; and Briggs and Peat, *Turbulent Mirror*.

22. Lipnack and Stamps, *How Groups Think.*

23. Robert Johansen, *Groupware: Computer Support for Business Teams* (New York: The Free Press, 1988).

24. Hayward Thomas, personal correspondence with the author dated January 26, 1989.

## Chapter 11. Confusingly Complex to Elegantly Simple Enterprises

1. Terry Winograd and Fernando Flores, *Understanding Computers and Cognition: A New Foundation for Design* (Reading, MA: Addison-Wesley, 1987).

2. Douglas McGregor, *The Human Side of Enterprise* (New York: McGraw-Hill, 1960); and Abraham Maslow, *Toward a Psychology of Being* (Princeton, NJ: D. van Nostrand, 1968).

3. T. S. Eliot, *The Complete Poems and Plays: 1909–1950* (New York: Harcourt, Brace & Co., 1952), p. 136.

4. Ken Olsen, "Presentation at the Annual Meeting of Digital Equipment Corporation, Boston, November 6, 1986," in *Digital Equipment Corporation Second Quarter Report 1987* (Maynard, MA: Digital Equipment Corp., 1987), p. 4.

5. James Gleick, *Chaos: Making a New Science* (New York: Viking, 1987).

6. Tom Peters, *Thriving on Chaos: Handbook for a Management Revolution* (New York: Alfred A. Knopf, 1988).

7. One of the pioneers in helping to change the fragmentation of our academic institutions has been Nathan Chiantella, who for several years administered an IBM grant program designed to encourage more effective interdisciplinary programs at our technical colleges and universities. He was also instrumental in initiating the Society of Manufacturing Engineers' Industry and University Leadership and Excellence in the Application and Development of CIM (LEAD) award programs. We owe a lot to people like Mr. Chiantella for their vision and accomplishments. They are helping to put people in touch at the universities and in industry.

8. Thomas Kuhn, *The Structure of Scientific Revolutions* (Chicago: University of Chicago Press, 1962).

9. Peter Drucker, "The Coming of the New Organization," *Harvard Business Review* 66:5 (January–February 1988), p. 50.

10. Henri Fayol, *General and Industrial Management* (London: Pitman and Sons, 1949).

11. Karl Weick, *The Social Psychology of Organizing*, 2nd ed. (Reading, MA: Addison-Wesley, 1979).

12. Winograd and Flores, *Understanding Computers and Cognition.*

13. Robert W. Hall and the AME Study Group on Functional Organization, "Organizational Renewal—Tearing Down the Functional Silos," *Target* [Association for Manufacturing Excellence's periodical news service] 4:2 (Summer 1988).

14. James Lardner, "Integration and Information in an Automated Factory," presentation at AUTOFACT Conference, Anaheim, CA, October 1, 1986 [unpublished].

15. Jens Rasmussen, "Models for Design of Computer Integrated Manufacturing Systems," paper presented at First International Conference on Ergonomics of Advanced Manufacturing and Hybrid Automated Systems, Louisville, KY, August 17, 1988.

16. Jack Welch, Jr., "Managing for the Nineties," presentation at the General Electric annual meeting of share owners, Waukeska, Wisconsin, April 27, 1988. See also Stratford P. Sherman, "The Mind of Jack Welch," *Fortune* (March 27, 1989), pp. 38–50.

## Chapter 12. Managing Human Networking

1. Tom Pryor, "Updating Cost Management: The CAM-I Cost Management System (CMS) Approach" (Arlington, TX: CAM-I, 1988) [unpublished].

2. Robert N. Stauffer, "Converting Customers to Partners at Ingersoll," *Manufacturing Engineering* (September 1988), pp. 41–44.

3. Donato Infante, "The Last Word: A Good Place to Work . . . Works for Everyone," *Manufacturing Engineering* (July 1989), p. 104.

# REFERENCES

Abernathy, William J., Clark, Kim B., and Kantrow, Alan M. *Industrial Renaissance: Producing a Competitive Future for America.* New York: Basic Books, 1983.

Abraham, Richard G. *Computer-Integrated Manufacturing,* ed. by Warren Shrensker. Dearborn, MI: Computer and Automated Systems Association, Society of Manufacturing Engineers, 1986.

Ackoff, R. *Creating the Corporate Future.* New York: John Wiley & Sons, 1981.

Adams, Russell B., and Cantley, Donald, eds. *Computer Basics: Understanding Computers.* Alexandria, VA: Time-Life Books, 1985.

Appleton, Dan. *Introducing the New CIM Enterprise Wheel.* Dearborn, MI: CASA/SME, 1986.

Argyris, Chris. "How Learning and Reasoning Processes Affect Organizational Change," in Paul S. Goodman and Associates, *Change in Organizations.* San Francisco: Jossey-Bass, 1982, pp. 47–86.

Argyris, Chris. *Integrating the Individual and the Organization.* New York: John Wiley & Sons, 1964.

Argyris, Chris. "Single-Loop and Double-Loop Models in Research on Decision Making," *Administrative Science Quarterly* 21 (September 1976): 363–377.

Aristotle. *The Basic Works of Aristotle,* ed. by Richard McKeon. New York: Random House, 1941.

Aristotle. *The Politics of Aristotle,* ed. and trans. by Ernest Barker. New York: Oxford University Press, 1958.

Arthur Young, *The Landmark MIT Study: Management in the 1990s.* New York: Arthur Young, 1989.

Ashton, T. S. *The Industrial Revolution, 1760–1830.* New York: Oxford University Press, 1964.

Augustine, St. *Confessions,* trans. with an introduction by R. S. Pine-Coffin. Baltimore: Penguin Books, 1961.

Babbage, Charles. *On the Economy of Machinery and Manufacturers.* New York: Augustus M. Kelley, 1963. [First published by Charles Knight, London, in 1832.]

Bacon, Francis. *Selected Writings.* New York: The Modern Library, 1955.

Barnard, Chester. *Functions of the Executive.* Cambridge, MA: Harvard University Press, 1938.

Beer, Stafford. *The Brain of the Firm.* New York: Herder & Herder, 1972.

Beer, Stafford. *The Heart of the Enterprise.* New York: John Wiley & Sons, 1979.

Bell, Daniel. *The Coming of Post-Industrial Society: A Venture in Social Forecasting.* New York: Basic Books, 1973.

Bellah, Robert N., et al. *Habits of the Heart: Individualism and Commitment in American Life.* New York: Harper & Row, 1985.

Bergson, Henri. *Duration and Simultaneity,* trans. by Leon Jacobson. New York: Library of Liberal Arts, 1965.

Berle, Adolf A., and Means, Gardiner C. *The Modern Corporation and Private Property.* New York: Harcourt, Brace & World, 1932.

Bikson, Tora, Strasz, Cathleen, and Mankin, Donald. *Computer Mediated Work.* Santa Monica, CA: Rand Corp., 1985.

Blache, Klaus M. *Success Factors for Implementing Change: A Manufacturing Viewpoint.* Dearborn, MI: Society of Manufacturing Engineers Press, 1988.

Bradford, D. L., and Cohen, A. R. *Managing for Excellence: The Guide to Developing High Performance in Contemporary Organizations.* New York: John Wiley & Sons, 1984.

Bray, Olin H. *CIM: Computer Integrated Manufacturing, The Data Management Strategy.* Burlington, MA: Digital Press, 1988.

Briggs, John, and Peat, F. David. *Turbulent Mirror: An Illustrated Guide to Chaos Theory and the Science of Wholeness.* New York: Harper & Row, 1989.

Bucher, Karl. *Arbeit und Rhythmus* (Work and Rhythm). Leipzig, 1924.

Buffa, Elwood S. *Modern Production Management.* New York: John Wiley & Sons, 1969.

Burbridge, John L. *The introduction of Group Technology.* New York: Wiley/Halstead, 1975.

Carlson, Howard. "The Parallel Organization Structure at General Motors," *Personnel* (September-October 1978), pp. 64–69.

Carlzon, Jan. *Moments of Truth.* Cambridge, MA: Ballinger, 1987.

Chandler, Alfred D. *Strategy and Structure.* Cambridge, MA: MIT Press, 1962.

Chandler, Alfred D. *The Visible Hand: The Managerial Revolution in American Business.* Cambridge, MA: Harvard University Press, 1977.

Chandler, Alfred D., and Daems, Herman. *Managerial Hierarchies: Comparative Perspectives on the Rise of the Modern Industrial Enterprise.* Cambridge, MA: Harvard University Press, 1980.

Chiantella, Nathan A., ed. *Management Guide for CIM.* Dearborn, MI: Society of Manufacturing Engineers, 1986.

Ciampa, Dan. *Manufacturing's New Mandate: The Tools for Leadership.* New York: John Wiley & Sons, 1988.

"Cords of Change," *World*, a publication of Peat Marwick (Summer, 1988).

Cousins, Steven A. *Integrating the Automated Factory.* Dearborn, MI: Society of Manufacturing Engineers, 1988.

Crosby, Philip B. *Quality Is Free: The Art of Making Quality Certain.* New York: New American Library, 1979.

Davis, Stanley M. *Future Perfect.* Reading, MA: Addison-Wesley, 1987.

Davis, Stanley, and Lawrence, Paul R. *Matrix.* Reading, MA: Addison-Wesley, 1977.

Deal, Terrence E., and Kennedy, Allan A. *Corporate Cultures: The Rites and Rituals of Corporate Life.* Reading, MA: Addison-Wesley, 1982.

Dearden, John. "Computers: No Impact on Divisional Control," *Harvard Business Review* (January–February 1967).

Dhalla, Nariman J., and Yuspeh, Sonia. "Forget the Product Life Cycle Concept," *Harvard Business Review* (January–February 1976), pp. 102–112.

Deming, W. Edward. *Out of the Crisis.* Cambridge, MA: MIT Center for Advanced Engineering Study, 1986.

Dertouzos, Michael L., et al. *Made in America: Regaining the Productive Edge.* Cambridge, MA: MIT Press, 1988.

Drucker, Peter. "The Coming of the New Organization," *Harvard Business Review* 66:1 (January–February 1988).

Drucker, Peter. "Management and the World's Work," *Harvard Business Review* 66:5 (September–October 1988), pp. 65–76.

Drucker, Peter F. *The Frontiers of Management.* New York: Dutton, 1986.

Drucker, Peter F. *Managing in Turbulent Times.* New York: Harper & Row, 1980.

Drucker, Peter F. *The New Realities: In Government and Politics/In Economics and Business/In Society and World View.* New York: Harper & Row, 1989.

Durkheim, Emile. *The Division of Labor in Society,* trans. by G. Simpson. New York: The Free Press, 1969.

Eason, Ken. *Information Technology and Organizational Change.* London: Tayler and Francis, 1988.

Eccles, Robert G., and Crane, Dwight B. *Doing Deals: Investment Banks at Work.* Boston: Harvard Business School Press, 1988.

Eliot, T. S. *The Complete Poems and Plays, 1909–1950.* New York: Harcourt, Brace & Co., 1952.

Emery, Fred, ed. *Systems Thinking.* New York: Penguin Books, 1969.

ESPRIT, Project Nr. 688, CIM/OSA. *A Primer on Key Concepts and Purpose.* Brussels, Belgium, 1987.

Etzioni, Amitai. *A Comparative Analysis of Complex Organizations.* New York: The Free Press of Glencoe, 1961.

Etzioni, Amitai. *A Sociological Reader on Complex Organizations,* 2nd ed. New York: Holt, Rinehart and Winston, 1969.

Eureka, William, and Ryan, Nancy. *The Customer-Driven Company: Managerial Perspectives on QFD* [Quality Function Deployment]. Dearborn, MI: ASI Press, 1988.

Fayol, Henri. *General and Industrial Management,* trans. by Constance Storrs. London: Pitman, 1949.

Feigenbaum, A. V. *Total Quality Control: Engineering and Management.* New York: McGraw-Hill, 1961.

Feigenbaum, Edward A., and McCorduck, Pamela. *The Fifth Generation: Artificial Intelligence and Japan's Computer Challenge to the World.* Reading, MA: Addison-Wesley, 1983.

Flaig, Scott. "Digital Equipment Corporation: The Endpoint Model," *Harvard Business School Case Study*, 1988.

Flatau, Ulrich. "Designing an Information System for Integrated Manufacturing Systems." In *Design and Analysis of Integrated Manufacturing Systems*, ed. by W. Dale Compton. Washington, DC: National Academy Press, 1988.

Fleischer, Mitchell, and Morell, Jonathan. "The Organizational and Managerial Consequences of Computer Technology," *Computers in Human Behavior* 1 (1985): 3–93.

Fortuna, Raymond M. "A Primer on Quality Function Deployment," *CIM Review* 5:1 (Fall 1988), pp. 49–54.

Friend, J. K., Power, J. J., and Yewlett, C. J. *Public Planning: The Intercorporate Dimension.* London: Tavistock Institute, 1974.

Fritz, R. *The Path of Least Resistance.* Salem, MA: DMA, Inc., 1984.

Fukuda, Ryuji. *Managerial Engineering: Techniques for Improving Quality and Productivity in the Workplace.* Stamford, CT: Productivity, Inc., 1983.

Galbraith, Jay. *Designing Complex Organizations.* Reading, MA: Addison-Wesley, 1979.

Gale, Richard M., ed. *The Philosophy of Time: A Collection of Essays.* New York: Anchor Books, 1967.

Galloway, John J. "Revealing Organizational Networks." Annual Conference of Australian Communications Association, Sydney (July 1987).

Galloway, John J., and Gorman, Anne. *Going Places: How to Network Your Way to Personal Success.* Sydney: Allen and Unwin, 1987.

George, Claude S., Jr. *The History of Management Thought*, 2nd ed. Englewood Cliffs, NJ: Prentice-Hall, 1972.

Gerelle, Eric G. R., and Stark, John. *Integrated Manufacturing: Strategy, Planning, and Implementation.* New York: McGraw-Hill, 1989.

Gide, Charles, and Rist, Charles. *A History of Economic Doctrines: From the Time of the Psyiocrates to the Present Day*, trans. by R. Richards. Boston: D. C. Heath, 1948.

Gilbreth, Frank B. *Motion Study: A Method for Increasing the Efficiency of the Workman.* New York: D. van Nostrand, 1910.

Gilbreth, Frank B. *Primer on Scientific Management.* New York: D. van Nostrand, 1912.

Gleick, James. *Chaos: Making a New Science.* New York: Viking Penguine, 1987.

Gouldner, Alvin. *Patterns of Industrial Bureaucracy.* Glencoe, IL: The Free Press, 1954.

Greene, Richard Tabor. *Implementing Japanese AI Techniques: Turning the Tables for a Winning Strategy.* New York: McGraw-Hill, 1990.

Grossberg, Stephen. "Nonlinear Neural Networks: Principles, Mechanisms, and Architectures," *Neural Networks* 1:1 (1988), p.17:61.

Grossberg, Stephen, ed. *Neural Networks and Natural Intelligence.* Cambridge, MA: MIT Press, 1988.

Gunn, Thomas G. *Computer Applications in Manufacturing.* New York: Industrial Press, 1981.

Gunn, Thomas G. *Manufacturing for Competitive Advantage: Becoming a World Class Manufacturer.* Cambridge, MA: Ballinger, 1987.

Guterl, Fred V. "Goodbye, Old Matrix," *Business Month* (February 1989), pp. 32–38.

Hall, Robert, and the AIM Study Group on Functional Organization. "Organizational Renewal—Tearing Down the Functional Silos," *Target* (Association for Manufacturing Excellence Periodical News Source) 4:2 (Summer 1988).

Hall, Robert W. *Attaining Manufacturing Excellence.* Homewood, IL: Dow Jones–Irwin, 1987.

Haney, Lewis H. *History of Economic Thought: A Critical Account of the Origin and Development of the Economic Theories of the Leading Thinkers in the Leading Nations,* 4th ed. New York: Macmillan Co., 1949.

Harbison, F., and Myers, C. *Management in the Industrial World.* New York: McGraw-Hill, 1959.

Harrington, Joseph, Jr. *Computer Integrated Manufacturing.* New York: Robert E. Krieger Publishing Co., 1979. [First published in 1973.]

Harrington, Joseph, Jr. *Understanding the Manufacturing Process.* New York: Marcel Dekker, 1984.

Hayes, Robert H., and Jaikumar, Ramchandran. "Manufacturing's Crisis: New Technologies, Obsolete Organizations," *Harvard Business Review* 66:5 (September–October 1988), pp. 77–85.

Hayes, Robert H., and Schumenner, Roger W. "How Should You Organize Manufacturing?" *Harvard Business Review* 57:1 (January–February 1979): 105–118.

Hayes, Robert H., and Wheelwright, Steven C. *Restoring Our Competitive Edge: Competing Through Manufacturing.* New York: John Wiley & Sons, 1984.

Hayes, Robert H., Wheelwright, Steven C., and Clark, Kim B. *Dynamic Manufacturing: Creating the Learning Organization.* New York: The Free Press, 1988.

Hegel, G. W. F. *The Phenomenology of Mind*, trans. by J. B. Baillie. New York: Harper Torchbooks, 1967.

Hess, George J. "Computer Integrated Manufacturing—How to Get Started." Presentation at AUTOFACT Conference, Detroit, MI (November 1983) [unpublished].

Hess, George J. "1982 Industrial LEAD Award Winner—Revisited in 1986." Presentation at AUTOFACT Conference, November 12, 1986. Dearborn, MI: Society of Manufacturing Engineers, 1986.

Hirschorn, Larry. *Beyond Mechanization.* Cambridge, MA: MIT Press, 1984.

Holland, John, ed. *Flexible Manufacturing Systems.* Dearborn, MI: Society of Manufacturing Engineers, 1984.

Homans, George C. *The Human Group.* New York: Harcourt Brace Jovanovich, 1950.

Hopland, Jan, and Savage, Charles M. "Charting New Directions," *Digital Enterprise* 3:1 (Spring 1989), pp. 8–12.

Hopland, Jan, and Savage, Charles M. "Virtual Teams and Flexible Enterprises," *Digital Technical Management Education Program News* 3 (July 1989): 3–6.

Husserl, Edmund. *The Phenomenology of Internal Time-Consciousness*, ed. by M. Heidegger and trans. by J. S. Churchill. Bloomington: Indiana University Press, 1969.

Imai, Masaaki. *Kaizen: The Key to Japan's Competitive Success.* New York: Random House, 1986.

Infante, Donato. "The Last Word: A Good Place to Work . . . Works for Everyone," *Manufacturing Engineering* (July 1989), p. 104.

Ishikawa, Akira. *Future Computer and Information Systems: The Uses of the Next Generation Computer and Information Systems.* New York: Praeger, 1986.

James, William. *Principles of Psychology*. 2 vols. New York: Dover Publications, 1950.

Jaques, Elliott. *Requisite Organization: The CEO's Guide to Creative Structure and Leadership*. New York: Cason Hall and Co., 1989.

Johansen, Robert. *Groupware: Computer Support for Business Teams*. New York: The Free Press, 1988.

Johnson, H. Thomas, and Kaplan, Robert S. *Relevance Lost: The Rise and Fall of Management Accounting*. Boston: Harvard Business School Press, 1987.

Johnston, Russell, and Lawrence, Paul R. "Beyond Vertical Integration—the Rise of the Value-Adding Partnership," *Harvard Business Review* 66:4 (July–August 1988), pp. 94–101.

Jurgen, Ronald K. *Computers and Manufacturing Productivity*. New York: IEEE Press, 1987.

"Kaiser Aluminum Flattens Its Layers of Brass," *Business Week* (February 24, 1973), pp. 8–14.

Kanter, Rosabeth M. *The Change Masters: Innovation and Entrepreneurship in the American Corporation*. New York: Simon & Schuster, 1983.

Kanter, Rosabeth Moss. "How Strategic Partnerships Are Reshaping American Businesses." In *Business in the Contemporary World*, ed. by Herbert Sawyer. Washington, DC: University Press of America, 1988.

Kanter, Rosabeth Moss, and Stein, Barry. "Building the Parallel Organization: Toward Mechanisms for Permanent Quality of Work Life," *Journal of Applied Behavioral Science* 16 (Summer 1980). Report on the "Chestnut Ridge" project.

Kaplan, Robert S. "Must CIM be Justified by Faith Alone?" *Harvard Business Review* (March–April, 1986).

Katz, Daniel, and Kahn, Robert. *The Social Psychology of Organizations*. New York: John Wiley & Sons, 1978.

Keen, Peter G. W., and Scott Morton, Michael S. *Decision Support Systems: An Organizational Perspective*. Reading, MA: Addison-Wesley, 1978.

Khandwalla, Pradip N. *The Design of Organizations*. New York: Harcourt Brace Jovanovich, 1977.

Kidd, Paul. "Technology and Engineering Design: Shaping a Better Future or Repeating the Mistakes of the Past?" *IEEE Proceedings* 135:5 (May 1988), pp. 297–302.

Kidd, Paul, and Corbett, J. M. "Towards the Joint Social and Technical Design of Advanced Manufacturing Systems," *International Journal of Industrial Ergonomics* 2 (Amsterdam: Elsevier Science Publishers, 1988), pp. 305–313.

Kiefer, Charles F., and Stroh, Peter. "A New Paradigm for Developing Organizations." In *Transforming Work*, ed. by John D. Adams. Alexandria, VA: Miles River Press, 1984.

Koestenbaum, Peter. *The Heart of Business: Ethics, Power and Philosophy*. New York: Saybrook Publishing Co., 1987.

Kuhn, Thomas S. *The Structure of Scientific Revolutions*, 2nd ed. Chicago: University of Chicago Press, 1970.

Lardner, James. "Integration and Information in an Automated Factory." *Proceedings of the AUTOFACT 1984*, Anaheim, CA. Dearborn, MI: Society of Manufacturing Engineers, 1984.

Lawler, Edward E., III. *High-Involvement Management: Participative Strategies for Improving Organizational Performance*. San Francisco: Jossey-Bass, 1986.

Lawrence, Paul R., and Dyer, Davis. *Renewing American Industry: Organizing for Efficiency and Innovation*. New York: The Free Press, 1983.

Lawrence, Paul, and Lorsch, Jay. *Organization and Its Environment*. Cambridge, MA: Harvard University Press, 1967.

Leavitt, Harold, ed. *Handbook of Organizations*. Chicago: Rand McNally, 1965.

Likert, Rensis. *New Patterns of Management*. New York: McGraw-Hill, 1961.

Lipnack, Jessica, and Stamps, Jeffrey. *How Groups Think.* Waltham, MA: Networking Institute, 1988. [Unpublished.]

Lipnack, Jessica, and Stamps, Jeffrey. "A Network Model," *The Futurist* 21:4 (July–August 1987).

Lipnack, Jessica, and Stamps, Jeffrey. *The Networking Book: People Connecting with People*. New York: Routledge & Kegan Paul, 1986.

Livingston, Donald G., and Berkes, Leslie J. "Netmap: An Innovative Diagnostic Tool," *Journal of Managerial Psychology* 4:4 (1989).

Loomis, Mary E. *The Database Book*. New York: Macmillan Co., 1987.

Majchrzak, Ann. *The Human Side of Factory Automation: Managerial and Human Resource Strategies for Making Automation Succeed*. San Francisco: Jossey-Bass, 1988.

Mandeville, Bernard. *The Fable of the Bees*, ed. by Phillip Harth. Baltimore, MD: Penguin Books, 1970.

Manufacturing Studies Board. *Human Resource Practices for Implementing Advanced Manufacturing Technology.* Washington, DC: National Academy Press, 1986.

Manufacturing Studies Board. *Toward a New Era in U.S. Manufacturing: The Need for a National Vision.* Washington, DC: National Academy Press, 1986.

Marca, David A., and McGowan, Clement L. *SADT: Structured Analysis and Design Technique,* forward by Douglas T. Ross. New York: McGraw-Hill, 1988.

Marsh, James, ed. *Handbook of Organizations.* Chicago: Rand McNally, 1965.

Martin, John M. "The Final Piece of the Puzzle," *Manufacturing Engineering* 101:3 (September 1988), pp. 46–51.

Maslow, Abraham. *Toward a Psychology of Being.* Princeton, NJ: D. van Nostrand, 1968.

Mason, Edward. *The Corporation in Modern Society.* New York: Atheneum, 1970.

Masuda, Yoneji. *The Information Society as Post-Industrial Society.* Tokyo: Institute for the Information Society, 1980. (Published in the U.S. by the World Future Society, Bethesda, MD, 1981).

McGregor, Douglas. *The Human Side of Enterprise.* New York: McGraw-Hill, 1960.

Miles, Raymond E., and Snow, Charles C. "Organizations: New Concepts for New Forms," *California Management Review* 28:3 (Spring 1986).

Minkowski, Eugene. *Lived Time: Phenomenological and Psychopathological Studies,* trans. by Nancy Metzel. Evanston, IL: Northwestern University Press, 1970.

Mintzberg, Henry. *The Nature of Managerial Work.* New York: Harper & Row, 1973.

Monden, Yasuhiro. "Adaptable Kanban Systems Help Toyota Maintain Just-in-Time Production," *Industrial Engineering* (May 1981), pp. 29–46.

Mooney, James D., and Reiley, Allen C. *Onward Industry!* New York: Harper and Brothers, 1931.

Moto-oka, Tohru., ed. *Fifth Generation Computer Systems: Proceedings of the International Conference on Fifth Generation Computer Systems.* Amsterdam: North-Holland, 1982.

Moto-oka, Tohru, and Kitsuregawa, Masaru. *The Fifth Generation Computer: The Japanese Challenge.* New York: John Wiley & Sons, 1985.

Mumford, Enid. *Designing Human Systems*. Manchester, England: Manchester Business School, 1983.

Mumford, Enid, and MacDonald, W. Bruce. *XSEL'S PROGRESS: The Continuing Journey of an Expert System*. New York: John Wiley & Sons, 1989.

Naisbett, John. *Megatrends*. New York: Warner Books, 1982.

Nolan, Norton and Co. "Computer Integrated Manufacturing Payoff Working Group," Lexington, MA: Nolan, Norton and Co., March 25–26, 1987 [unpublished].

Nolan, Richard, Pollock, Alex J., and Ware, James P. "Creating the 21st Century Organization," *Stage by Stage* 8:4 (Lexington, MA: Nolan, Norton and Co., Fall 1988): 1–11.

Nolan, Richard, Pollock, Alex J., and Ware, James P. "Toward the Design of Network Organizations," *Stage by Stage* 9:1 (Lexington, MA: Nolan, Norton and Co., Fall 1988):1–12.

O'Connor, Dennis, and Wilkerson, Wendy. *Guide to Expert Systems Program Management, Artificial Intelligence Guide Series, Intelligent Systems Technologies Group*. Maynard, MA: Digital Equipment Corp., 1985.

Ohmae, Kenichi. *The Mind of the Strategist*. New York: McGraw-Hill, 1982.

Olsen, Ken. "Presentation at the Annual Meeting of Digital Equipment Corporation, Boston, November 6, 1986." In *Digital Equipment Corporation Second Quarter Report 1987*. Maynard, MA: Digital Equipment Corp., 1987.

Ouchi, William G. *Theory Z: How American Business Can Meet the Japanese Challenge*. Reading, MA: Addison-Wesley, 1981.

Palgrave, R. H. I. *Dictionary of Political Economy*, 3 vols. London: Macmillan and Co., 1894.

Pascale, Richard T., and Athos, Anthony G. *The Art of Japanese Management: Applications for American Executives*. New York: Simon & Schuster, 1981.

Pava, Calvin. *Managing New Office Technology: An Organizational Strategy*. New York: The Free Press, 1983.

Perry, Barbara. *Enfield: A High-Performance System*. Maynard, MA: Digital Equipment Corp., 1982.

Peters, Tom. *Thriving on Chaos: Handbook for a Management Revolution*. New York: Alfred A. Knopf, 1987.

Peters, Tom, and Austin, Nancy. *A Passion for Excellence*. New York: Random House, 1985.

Peters, Tom, and Waterman, R. H. *In Search of Excellence.* New York: Harper & Row, 1982.

Pfeffer, Jeffrey. *Power in Organizations.* Boston: Pitman, 1981.

Porter, Michael E. *Competitive Advantage: Techniques for Analyzing Industries and Competitors.* New York: The Free Press, 1985.

Pryor, Tom. "Updating Cost Management: The CAM-I Cost Management System (CMS) Approach." Arlington, TX: CAM-I, 1988 [unpublished].

Ranky, Paul G. *Computer Integrated Manufacturing: An Introduction with Case Studies.* Englewood Cliffs, NJ: Prentice-Hall International, 1986.

Rasmussen, Jens. "Models for Design of Computer Integrated Manufacturing Systems." Paper presented at First International Conference on Ergonomics of Advanced Manufacturing and Hybrid Automated Systems, Louisville, Kentucky, August 17, 1988.

Reich, Robert B. *The Next American Frontier.* New York: Times Books, 1983.

Richta, Radovan. *Civilization at the Crossroads: Social and Human Implications of the Scientific and Technological Revolution,* trans. by Marian Slingova. Prague: International Arts and Sciences Press, 1968.

Rockart, John F., and Bullen, Christine V. *The Rise of Managerial Computing: The Best of the Center for Information Systems Research.* Homewood, IL: Dow Jones–Irwin, 1986.

Roitman, David B., and Sinha, Manoj K. "CIM as a Process of Organizational Change." Presentation at AUTOFACT Conference, November 9, 1987. Dearborn, MI: Society of Manufacturing Engineers, 1987.

Rothlisberger, Fritz J., and Dickson, William J. *Management and the Worker: An Account of a Research Program Conducted by the Western Electric Company, Hawthorne Works, Chicago.* Cambridge, MA: Harvard University Press, 1967.

Savage, Charles M. "The Challenge of CIM: 80% Organizational?" *CIM Review* 4:2 (Spring 1988).

Savage, Charles M. "CIM and Fifth Generation Management." In *Tool & Manufacturing Engineer Handbook,* vol. 5. Dearborn, MI: SME Press, 1988.

Savage, Charles M. "Fifth Generation Management." Workshop at AUTOFACT 86, Detroit, MI, November 1986.

Savage, Charles M. *Fifth Generation Management: 1986 Round Table Summary Document.* Dearborn, MI: Society of Manufacturing Engineers, 1987.

Savage, Charles M. *Fifth Generation Management for Fifth Generation Technology.* Dearborn, MI: Society of Manufacturing Engineers, 1987.

Savage, Charles M. "The Generation Gap: Between the Fifth Generation Technology and Second Generation Organizations." Yankee Group's Factory Systems Summit Conference, Chicago, May 16, 1984.

Savage, Charles M. "Organizational Integration: Open Windows of Opportunity," *CIM Review* (The Journal of Computer-Integrated Manufacturing Management) 1:1 (Fall 1984).

Savage, Charles M. "Organizational Integration: Renovating the Organizational Architecture," *CIM Review* 1:3 (Spring 1985).

Savage, Charles M. "Preparing for the Factory of the Future," *Modern Machine Shop* (January 1983).

Savage, Charles M. *Work and Meaning: A Phenomenological Inquiry.* Unpublished Ph.D. Thesis, Boston College, 1973.

Savage, Charles M., ed. *A Program Guide for CIM Implementation.* Dearborn, MI: Society of Manufacturing Engineers, 1987.

Schein, Edgar. *Organizational Psychology.* Englewood Cliffs, NJ: Prentice-Hall, 1961.

Schien, Edgar. *Process Consultation.* Reading, MA: Addison-Wesley, 1969.

Shaiken, Harley. *Work Transformed: Automation and Labor in the Computer Age.* New York: Holt, Rinehart and Winston, 1984.

Sherman, Stratford P. "The Mind of Jack Welch," *Fortune* (March 27, 1989), pp. 38–50.

Shonberger, Richard J. *Japanese Manufacturing Techniques: Nine Hidden Lessons in Simplicity.* New York: The Free Press, 1982.

Shrensker, Warren. "Fifth Generation Management: Round Table Straw-Person Organization," in *Fifth Generation Management for Fifth Generation Technology,* ed. by Charles M. Savage. Dearborn, MI: Society of Manufacturing Engineers, 1987.

Simon, Herbert. *Administrative Behavior,* 3rd ed. New York: The Free Press, 1976.

Simon, Herbert. *The New Science of Management Decision.* New York: Harper & Row, 1960.

Skinner, Wickham. "The Focused Factory," *Harvard Business Review* (May–June 1974), pp. 113-121.

Skinner, Wickham. "Manufacturing—Missing Link in Corporate Strategy," *Harvard Business Review* (May–June 1969), pp. 136–145.

Skinner, Wickham. *Manufacturing in the Corporate Strategy.* New York: John Wiley & Sons, 1978.

Slem, C., Levi, D., and Young, A. "The Effects of Technological Change on the Psycho-social Characteristics of Organizations." In *Human Factors in Organizational Design and Management,* ed. by O. Brown and H. W. Henrick. Amsterdam: Elsevier Science Publishing, 1986.

Smith, Adam. *The Wealth of Nations.* London: Penguin Classics, 1987.

Snyder, Richard. "To improve innovation, manage corporate culture." In Bennis, Warren, Benne, Kenneth, and Chin, Robert, eds. *The Planning of Change.* New York: Holt, Rinehart and Winston, 1985.

Sobczak, Thomas V. *A Glossary of Terms for Computer Integrated Manufacturing.* Dearborn, MI: Society of Manufacturing Engineers, 1984.

Stamps, Jeffrey. *Holonomy: A Human System Theory.* Seaside, CA: Intersystem Publications, 1980.

Stauffer, Robert N. "Converting Customers to Partners at Ingersoll," *Manufacturing Engineering* (September 1988), pp. 41–44.

Stevens, H. Chandler. *The Network Notebook.* Washington, DC: National Science Foundation, 1978.

Strassmann, Paul. *Information Payoff: The Transformation of Work in the Electronic Age.* New York: The Free Press, 1985.

Suzaki, Kiyoshi. *The New Manufacturing Challenge: Techniques for Continuous Improvement.* New York: The Free Press, 1987.

Taguchi, Genichi. *On-Line Quality Control During Production.* Tokyo: Japanese Standards Association, 1981.

Taguchi, Genichi, and Wu, Yu-in. *Introduction to Off-Line Quality Control.* Nagaya: Central Japan Quality Control Association, 1983.

Taylor, Frederick Winslow. *Scientific Management* (comprising "Shop Management," "Principles of Scientific Management," and "Testimony Before the Special House Committee"). New York: Harper and Brothers, 1947.

Teicholz, Eric, and Orr, Joel N. *Computer Integrated Manufacturing Handbook.* New York: McGraw-Hill, 1987.

Thacker, Robert M. *A New CIM Model: A Blueprint for the Computer-Integrated Manufacturing Enterprise.* Dearborn, MI: Society of Manufacturing Engineers, 1989.

Thompson, J. *Organizations in Action.* New York: McGraw-Hill, 1967.

Tilgher, Adriano. *Homo Faber: Work through the Ages,* trans. by D. Fisher. Chicago: Regency, 1965.

Toffler, Alan. *The Adaptive Corporation.* New York: McGraw-Hill, 1985.

Togino, Kazuto. "A Global Programming Language and Orchestration of the Execution of Jobs and Tasks." National Research Council Canada, Symposium on Manufacturing Application Languages, June 20–21, 1988, Winnipeg, Manitoba.

Trevor, Malcolm. *The Japanese Management Development System.* Wolfeboro, NH: Frances Printer Ltd., 1986.

Trist, Eric. "The Evolution of Sociotechnical Systems: A Conceptual Framework and an Action Research Program." Toronto: Ontario Quality of Working Life Center, Occasional Paper No. 2, June 1981.

Turner, Victor. *The Ritual Process.* Chicago: Aldine, 1969. (Concept of *Communitas*).

Urwick, Lyndall. *The Elements of Administration.* New York: Harper, 1943.

U.S. Air Force, Integrated Computer Aided Manufacturing. *ICAM Program Prospectus.* Dayton, OH: Air Force Materials Laboratory, Wright-Patterson Air Force Base, 1979.

Vaill, Peter B. *Managing as a Performing Art: New Ideas for a World of Chaotic Change.* San Francisco: Jossey-Bass, 1989.

Vogel, Ezra F. *Japan as Number One; Lessons for America.* New York: Harper & Row, 1979.

von Neumann, John, and Morganstern, Oskar. *The Theory of Games and Economic Behavior.* Princeton: Princeton University Press, 1944.

Walton, Richard E. *Innovating to Compete.* San Francisco: Jossey-Bass, 1988.

Walton, Richard E. *Up and Running: Integrative Information Technology and the Organization.* Boston: Harvard Business School Press, 1989.

Ward, John T. *The Factory System,* 2 vols. New York: Barnes & Noble, 1970.

Waterman, Robert H. *The Renewal Factor: How the Best Get and Keep the Competitive Edge.* New York: Bantam Books, 1987.

Weber, Max. *The Theory of Social and Economic Organization,* trans. by A. M. Henderson. New York: The Free Press, 1969.

Weick, Karl E. "Organization Design: Organizations as Self-Designing Systems." *Organizational Dynamics* (Autumn 1977), pp. 31–32.

Weick, Karl E. *The Psychology of Organizing,* 2nd ed. Reading, MA: Addison-Wesley, 1979.

Weisbord, Marvin R. *Organizational Diagnosis: A Workbook of Theory and Practice.* Reading, MA: Addison-Wesley, 1978.

Weisbord, Marvin R. *Productive Workplaces: Organizing and Managing for Dignity, Meaning, and Community.* San Francisco: Jossey-Bass, 1987.

Welch, Jack, Jr., "Managing for the Nineties," presentation at the General Electric annual meeting of share owners, Waukeska, Wisconsin, April 27, 1988.

Wiener, Norbert. *God and Golem, Inc.: A Comment on Certain Points where Cybernetics Impinges on Religion.* Cambridge, MA: MIT Press, 1964.

Wiener, Norbert. *The Human Use of Human Beings: Cybernetics and Society.* Garden City: Doubleday Anchor, 1954.

Winograd, Terry, and Flores, Fernando. *Understanding Computers and Cognition: A New Foundation for Design.* Reading, MA: Addison-Wesley, 1987.

Young, Andrew, Levi, D., and Slem, C. "CIM Success Requires that Human Resource Needs Be Met," *Information Week* (April 13, 1987).

Young, Andrew, Levi, D., and Slem, C. "Common Fallacies about the Introduction of Manufacturing Technology and People," *Industrial Engineering* 19:11 (1987).

Zuboff, Shoshana. "Automate/Informate: The Two Faces of Intelligent Technology," *Organizational Dynamics* 14:2 (Autumn 1985), pp. 5–18.

Zuboff, Shoshana. *In the Age of the Smart Machine: The Future of Work and Power.* New York: Basic Books, 1988.

# INDEX

Numbers in italics refer to figures.